JOURNALS, OBJECTS & EPHEMERA

JEFF BUCKLEY
HIS OWN VOICE

EDITED BY

MARY GUIBERT & DAVID BROWNE
photography by GEOFF MOORE

DA CAPO PRESS

About the Photographer: Los Angeles–based photographer/director Geoff Moore came up in the early 1990s Hollywood music and arts scene. He has worked with artists ranging from The Red Hot Chili Peppers to Jewel, and he shot the images for the book *Cobain Unseen*. A self-taught visual artist, Moore regularly shoots many of the top faces in pop culture and global advertisements, as well as his award-winning fine art. Visit him online at www.geoffmoorestudio.com.

This book is dedicated to Jeff's fans:
the old ones and the new ones, the ones who
blast his music with the windows open,
who sing at the top of their lungs no matter who's
listening, whose eyes have welled up with
tears, and whose hearts have leaped with love.
His voice, these words, are for you.

MG & DB

THE MAN THAT GOT AWAY

THE NIGHT IS BITTER
THE STARS HAVE LOST THEIR GLITTER
THE WINDS GROW COLDER
SUDDENLY YOUR OLDER
AND ALL BECAUSE OF THE MAN THAT GOT AWAY

NO MORE HIS EAGER CALL
THE WRITING'S ON THE WALL
THE DREAMS YOU'VE DREAMED HAVE ALL GONE ASTRAY.

THE MAN THAT WON YOU
HAS RUN OFF AND UNDONE YOU
THAT GREAT BEGINNING
HAS SEEN A FINAL INNING
I DONT KNOW WHAT HAPPENED, ITS ALL A CRAZY GAME

NO MORE THAT ALL TIME THRILL
FOR YOU'VE BEEN THROUGH THE MILL
AND NEVER A NEW LOVE WILL BE THE SAME

GOOD RIDDANCE, GOODBYE
EVERY TRICK OF HIS YOUR ONTO
BUT FOOLS WILL BE FOOLS
AND WHERE'S HE GONE TO?

THE ROAD GETS ROUGHER
ITS LONLIER AND TOUGHER
WITH HOPE HELL BURN UP, TOMORROW HE MIGHT TURN UP
THERES JUST NO LET-UP THE LIVE LONG NIGHT AND DAY

EVER SINCE THIS WORLD BEGAN, THERE IS NOTHING SADDER THAN
A ONE-MAN WOMAN LOOKING FOR THE MAN THAT GOT AWAY ~~

INTRODUCTION

In these accelerated days of video blogs, tweeting, and other social media communiqués, the image is impossibly quaint. Hunkered down in a café or on a bus or plane, a young man pulls a spiral-bound notebook from his bag and begins scribbling whatever thoughts come to mind. Out pour lists of chores, ideas for poems or love letters, silly doodles, or keen observations of his surroundings. When it's time to move on, he stuffs the pad back into his bag, where it will be retrieved another day for further jottings.

Befitting someone who unfortunately didn't live to see the twenty-first century, Jeff Buckley was one of those diarists. During the last decade of his life, he would routinely grab whatever was available—usually one of those wire-bound notebooks we all had in high school, although stray pieces of paper would sometimes suffice—to hash out his thoughts and buttress his memories. Jeff's journals were his forum for debating with himself on which ways to turn, musically and emotionally, and they reflected whatever mood he was in: calm and meditative (precise, legible calligraphy) or stressed (oversize, caffeinated lettering). In ways that felt private yet with one eye cast on his own history, he continually documented his life, albeit in a more discreet way than subsequent generations, who would have no qualms posting their musings on YouTube.

In some regards, Jeff's life could be seen as fairly straightforward: talented child fulfills his dream of becoming a musician before passing away at a tragically young age. Of course, his story was far more complex than that. Born in 1966, the son of musician Mary Guibert and singer-songwriter Tim Buckley, Jeff came of age in and around Orange County, California. His bond with music was apparent practically from birth (he could sing songs in key at the age of two). By high school he was already a proficient guitarist. After graduating, he moved to Los Angeles, attending a music school; afterward, in search of his musical identity, he played reggae, jazz fusion, and other genres. (To eschew comparisons with his musician father, he initially avoided singing and focused on his guitar.) After appearing at a tribute concert to Tim Buckley in New York in 1991, he was "discovered" by the music business and began weekly performances at Sin-é, a storefront coffeehouse in the East Village. Word of mouth spread so fast that it became difficult to see him: the first night I tried, in the summer of 1993, Sin-é was so crowded I had to listen from the sidewalk. Only on a second visit, when I arrived early and found a seat, did I glimpse the waiflike kid in a T-shirt and baggy pants singing a mind-bendingly eclectic range of songs (Elton John! Nina Simone! Bad Brains!) and tossing off jokes and impersonations like a seasoned comic.

Jeff was a singer, guitarist, and writer of uncommon range, sensitivity, and power—part rock and roller, part chanteur, entirely arresting. Columbia, which signed him to a contract and beat out several other labels in the process, rightly saw him as a vital part of the label's legacy of enduring talents like Bob Dylan, Bruce Springsteen, and Miles Davis—an artist for the ages. The label released an EP, *Live at Sin-é*, in 1993 that included a few of Jeff's originals alongside interpretations of other artists' material. That introduction was followed by his first full album, 1994's *Grace*.

All these years later, it's easy to forget how jarring *Grace* was, even to those who knew Jeff at the time. It swam against the current of everything in vogue in the music business in the '90s: it was not grunge, ironic, caustic, or hostile. It did not incorporate samples. It was unabashedly passionate and earnest, reflecting the life of someone who grew up with nearly every possible genre of music, from classic to alternative rock, prog to cabaret. With its array of styles held together by Jeff's multi-octave voice and air of impassioned, often melodramatic romanticism, *Grace* made immediate fans of Bono, Jimmy Page, Robert Plant, and Paul McCartney, among others. In 1995, *Grace* was awarded the International Record Grand Prix of the prestigious French organization Charles Cros Academy.

Three short years later, Jeff's story was over: at the age of thirty, he accidentally drowned in the Wolf River, a tributary of the mighty Mississippi, as he waited for his band to fly into Memphis to start recording his long-delayed follow-up to *Grace*. By then, Jeff had established himself as an artist in his own right, which only made his passing all the more heartbreaking. Here was someone who worried that people would only care about him because he was the son of a semi-famous rock star—and who, after finally coming into his own, had it taken away far too soon. It is both the most human and most mythic of tales, set against the backdrop of the music business.

Grace sold just under two hundred thousand copies by the time Jeff died, but in the years since, his stature has grown immeasurably. His haunted, penetrating rendition of Leonard Cohen's "Hallelujah" has become a cultural touchstone—covered on *American Idol* and its British counterpart, *The X Factor*, and utilized in many a dramatic or poignant scene in movies and television, including an Emmy-winning episode of *The West Wing*. In the last decade, the song was downloaded over one million times, and a copy currently resides in the Library of Congress's National Recording Registry. "Everybody Here Wants You," from the posthumous release *Sketches for My Sweetheart the Drunk*, was nominated for a Grammy for best male rock vocal performance in 1998. His praises continue to be sung, most recently by Adele (who called *Grace* one of her favorite albums of all time), Coldplay (whose "Shiver" was a blatant Jeff tribute), Radiohead, Sia, and Lana Del Rey. *Rolling Stone* named *Grace* one of the "500 Greatest Albums of All Time." Mary Guibert, Jeff's mother and executor of his estate, has presided over a series of compilations of unreleased and live material (and expanded reissues of his catalog) that have painted a deeper picture of his music and possible future.

And to further enhance his legacy, we now have his journals as well.

Mary isn't sure precisely when her son began committing his interior thoughts and feelings to paper. But it seems likely that the process began after he graduated from high school in 1984 and moved to Hollywood. He continued writing in his notebooks right up until his death. In the chaos and confusion that followed, some of those journals were lost, stolen, or possibly destroyed, but a batch of them—along with several file cabinets full of his correspondence, fan mail, even phone bills—was returned to his estate and stored at the Jeff Buckley archives in Los Angeles. During my research for *Dream Brother: The Lives and Music of Jeff and Tim Buckley* (2001), Mary generously allowed me to peek at this material and use a small but significant amount of it in the book. I found Jeff's writing to be astonishing—detailed, passionate, funny, and self-effacing, like mood swings committed to paper. In the years since, more of his writing—a few more notebooks as well as other documents and mementos—have surfaced, fleshing out other periods in his life.

When Da Capo Executive Editor Ben Schafer inquired about the journals and the possibility of publishing them in book form, Mary asked if I could assist in compiling and editing them. We all knew the material was special, but we also knew that sensitivity was paramount. We took our time—eight years since the idea was presented—to mull it over and then ensure we selected the most appropriate and least intrusive entries. It was neither an overnight nor ill-considered decision on anyone's part, and we pored over the three-hundred-plus pages of journals, personal effects, and notepads with care.

One of the foremost reasons we felt this project was worth pursuing was as a way for Jeff to explain himself. During my research and reporting of *Dream Brother*, I often wondered why Jeff made a particular decision or wandered down a particular path: What made him sing certain songs, be so innately skeptical of the business, pick that specific photo for the cover of *Grace*, rerecord "Eternal Life" as a metal rave-up, or move to Memphis? Since he was not around to ask, I relied on those in his life—family, friends, band members, business associates—to help answer those questions. Given that Jeff led a fairly compartmentalized life, it wasn't surprising when different people gave different answers to the same questions.

With *His Own Voice*, Jeff finally has his say. In these pages, arranged to create what we hope amounts to the memoir he was never able to write, we follow Jeff through his life and read, for the first time, what was in his mind at many crucial moments. We see his early, scattered musical brain at work and the way it sharpened once he arrived in New York. We read his thoughts on his musical and ancestral heritage; vivid and sometimes painful childhood memories of growing up in Southern California; recollections of his first move to New York and his backstage meeting with Bob Dylan. We encounter his combination of wonder and wariness about signing with Sony Music (Columbia's parent company) and entering the corporate music business, along with the personal and creative turmoil that engulfed him after the release of *Grace* and expectations for his career mounted. The manic highs and lows of the period, when he was trying to write and record that never-completed second album, are often chillingly captured in his later entries.

Throughout, we encounter Jeff's sense of both humor and melodrama, his love of visceral imagery, and his compassion for underdogs. We read moments of focus and confusion, moments of delight and desperation. We observe as Jeff grapples with issues of self-worth and his artistic voice. Little was more important to Jeff than being true to himself, but as these writings demonstrate, that vision was wildly in flux during the last year or two of his life, resulting in further consternation and the sometimes overbaked lyrics on *Sketches for My Sweetheart the Drunk*.

In particular, the journals shed many beams of light on Jeff's songwriting process and its development over the years. In these pages we are witness to how "Dream Brother" and "Lover, You Should've Come Over," among others, gradually coalesced by way of multiple drafts and correspondence. We see his music-school training at work when he begins adapting structure and chord changes to those words. We can peruse lyrics for songs that were never recorded but captured his state of mind at any given point. Here and there we have augmented those writings with carefully chosen items from his archives—his gear, music collections, clothing—to further bring his world to life.

Jeff never lived to see an era in which rock stars began publishing their often ghostwritten memoirs. He probably would have both scoffed at them *and*, at the same time, immersed himself in them. (During an interview I conducted with him in 1993 for the *New York Times*, he smiled when the topic of a Led Zeppelin tell-all book came up, admitting he'd happily devoured it.) We'll never know if he himself would have ever written such a volume, just as we will never know the many musical paths he would most likely have taken. It's easy to imagine Jeff following in the footsteps of heroes like Dylan, Elvis Costello, and Van Morrison, restless creative souls who were unafraid to follow their muses and unworried about the commercial consequences. But with *His Own Voice*, we now have a more profound, more intimate sense of where Jeff came from, where he was heading, and the struggles he endured along the way. To paraphrase Jeff, he fell into the light with his voice, his love of music—and his writings.

—DAVID BROWNE
NEW YORK, FALL 2018

MARTIN LUTHER HOSPITAL

Certificate of Birth

ANAHEIM, CALIFORNIA

<table>
<tr><td colspan="2">

COUNTY OF ORANGE

HEALTH DEPARTMENT

Santa Ana, California

☑ FEE: $2.00

☐ NO FEE GOVERNMENT PURPOSES

This is to certify, if impressed with the seal of the Orange County Health Officer, that this is a true copy of the permanent record filed in this office.

Edw. Lee Russell

EDW. LEE RUSSELL, M.D.
Health Officer and Local Registrar of Vital Statistics of Orange County

MAR 17 1967

DATE:

</td></tr>
</table>

STATE FILE NUMBER	**CERTIFICATE OF LIVE BIRTH** STATE OF CALIFORNIA—DEPARTMENT OF PUBLIC HEALTH	LOCAL REGISTRATION DISTRICT AND CERTIFICATE NUMBER **3000 16306**

1A. NAME OF CHILD—FIRST NAME JEFFREY	1B. MIDDLE NAME SCOTT	1C. LAST NAME BUCKLEY

2. SEX Male	3A. THIS BIRTH, SINGLE, TWIN, OR TRIPLET? Single	3B. IF TWIN OR TRIPLET, THIS CHILD BORN 1ST, 2ND, 3RD?	4A. DATE OF BIRTH—MONTH, DAY, YEAR November 17, 1966	4B. HOUR 10:49 P.M.

5A. PLACE OF BIRTH—NAME OF HOSPITAL Martin Luther	5B. STREET ADDRESS 1825 West Romneya Drive ☑ INSIDE CITY LIMITS ☐ OUTSIDE CITY LIMITS

5C. CITY OR TOWN Anaheim	5D. COUNTY Orange

6A. MAIDEN NAME OF MOTHER—FIRST NAME MARY	6B. MIDDLE NAME IVETTE	6C. LAST NAME GUIBERT	7. COLOR OR RACE OF MOTHER Caucasian

8. AGE OF MOTHER (AT TIME OF THIS BIRTH) 18 YEARS	9. BIRTHPLACE (STATE OR FOREIGN COUNTRY) Panama Canal Zone	10. MAILING ADDRESS OF MOTHER

11A. USUAL RESIDENCE OF MOTHER—STREET ADDRESS 241 Garnet Street	11B. IF INSIDE CORPORATE LIMITS ☑ CHECK HERE	IF OUTSIDE CITY CORPORATE LIMITS ☐ ON A FARM ☐ NOT ON A FARM

11C. CITY OR TOWN Anaheim	11D. COUNTY Orange	11E. STATE California

12A. NAME OF FATHER—FIRST NAME TIMOTHY	12B. MIDDLE NAME CHARLES	12C. LAST NAME BUCKLEY III	13. COLOR OR RACE OF FATHER Caucasian

14. AGE OF FATHER (AT TIME OF THIS BIRTH) 19 YEARS	15. BIRTHPLACE (STATE OR FOREIGN COUNTRY) Maryland	16A. PRESENT OR LAST OCCUPATION Vocal Artist	16B. KIND OF INDUSTRY OR BUSINESS Recording Company

I HAVE REVIEWED THE ABOVE STATED INFORMATION AND HEREBY CERTIFY THAT IT IS TRUE AND CORRECT TO THE BEST OF MY KNOWLEDGE	17A. PARENT OR OTHER INFORMANT—SIGNATURE *Mary Ivette Buckley*	17B. DATE SIGNED BY INFORMANT November 18, 1966

I HEREBY CERTIFY THAT I ATTENDED THIS BIRTH AND THAT THE CHILD WAS BORN ALIVE AT THE HOUR, DATE AND PLACE STATED ABOVE	18A. PHYSICIAN—SIGNATURE *William Anderson M.D.*	18B. ADDRESS W. Anderson, M.D. 1655 W. Broadway, Anaheim

19. DATE ON WHICH NAME ADDED BY SUPPLEMENTAL NAME REPORT	20. LOCAL REGISTRAR—SIGNATURE *Edw. Lee Russell M.D.*	21. DATE RECEIVED BY LOCAL REGISTRAR NOV 23 1966

Birth
of
Certificate

MARTIN LUTHER HOSPITAL

ANAHEIM, CALIFORNIA

MARTIN LUTHER HOSPITAL

This Certifies that JEFFREY SCOTT

was born to MARY AND TIMOTHY BUCKLEY III

in this Hospital at 10:49 *o'clock* P .m, on THURSDAY

the SEVENTEENTH *day of* NOVEMBER 19 66

In Witness Whereof *the said Hospital has caused this Certificate to be signed by its duly authorized officer and its Official Seal to be hereunto affixed.*

_____
ATTENDING PHYSICIAN

_____
ADMINISTRATOR

He was born in evening blue. Under the moon.
Witnessed by the glowing eyes of the sky,
Into the splintered song of coyotes.
Each one's voice rising, like glowing embers from a fire,
Were his lullaby.
Her cool breath and the warm desert wind
Were the blankets for his fragile skin.
But the whole world lived within
His mother's singing voice.
Such tiny, tiny hands.
And tiny eyes. Black stones his eyes,
More piercing than any man's,
More precious than any glittering prize.
The entire earth revolved ~~cold~~ ~~the whole within his the skin~~.
Within the warmth upon his father's skin.
The baby's body swathed in his protective, beaming face.
Look upon you, the ~~thing~~ that no man's treasure
Can replace.

I REMEMBER

FACING PAGE: Jeff called several towns in Southern California his home. Between 1969 and 1981, he lived in Anaheim, Fullerton, Riverside, Sunnymead, and Garden Grove, before he and Mary returned to Anaheim for Jeff's high school years. In this undated journal entry from the spring of 1996, Jeff may have been inspired by writer, author, and artist Joe Brainard's influential *I Remember* collection of reflections on childhood. Here, Jeff combs through his memories, good and mixed, of life as a child of the '70s and early '80s.

I REMEMBER SYDNEY FINK
I REMEMBER AWFUL BROWN CARPETING
I REMEMBER THE 100 YARD DASH
I REMEMBER BRIAN'S BROKEN HAND
I REMEMBER HIS FEET
I REMEMBER DESERT ALL AROUND
I REMEMBER ROACHES AT NIGHT
I REMEMBER WASHING DISHES
I REMEMBER THE GARDEN
I REMEMBER MY RECORDS THROWN IN THE STREET
I REMEMBER I HAD A SILVER COIN
I REMEMBER GRANDPA HOLDING ME OVER THE WATER
I REMEMBER STARR
I REMEMBER TED NUGENT BLASTING FROM CHUCK'S CAR IN NOWHERE CA.
I REMEMBER NIXON ON TELEVISION
I REMEMBER K-TELS 52 PARTY-HITS
I REMEMBER FALLING ASLEEP AT 13, AT 25
I REMEMBER MOM BUYING ME WHISKEY AT 14
AND I FELL ASLEEP THEN, TOO.
I REMEMBER THE LAUNDRY PILED UP TO HERE
I REMEMBER A LADY'S BLACK EYE UNDER A GREEN
SEE-THROUGH SCARF
I REMEMBER SHOOTING AT CLAY PIGEONS AND
FEELING SO PUZZLED, SO FAR FROM HOME
I REMEMBER MY GRANDMOTHER'S FALSE TEETH
ONLY ONCE EVER IN A GLASS

FACING PAGE: Whimsical memories of a 1975 boyhood "crime spree" with his stepbrother Keith. Undated journal entry, spring 1996.

AS A CHILD I WOULD ALWAYS LOVE TO HAVE LOTS OF
CANDY. SOMETIMES WE NEEDED IT SO BAD THAT WE STOLE IT
FROM LIQUOR STORES. WE WERE LITTLE BLOND BOYS. SEVEN OR
EIGHT YEARS OLD (BEFORE I MET THAT MAN OF MINE.
THE YEAR I MET MY FATHER) ME AND MY STEP STEP BROTHER,
KIETH, WOULD WALK TO THE LIQUOR STORES JUST OFF OF
PRITCHARD STREET. WE'D GO IN TO TRY TO STEAL CANDY AND
"WEREWOLF-BY-NIGHT" COMICS BOOKS, "MASTER OF KUNG-FU"
COMICS. MAYBE I SUCCEEDED ONCE OR TWICE WITH BOTH. I WAS
CAUGHT BY HIS WIFE* ONE DAY....STEALING MY FAVORITE
WINTERGREEN LIFE SAVERS. THEY WERE SO FUCKING GOOD

MY
STEPFATHER'S
WIFE

FACING PAGE: Thoughts on Mary's father, George Guibert. Undated journal entry, spring 1996. (Notice the bits of developing lyrics from "The Sky Is a Landfill" and "Haven't You Heard" upside down on top.)

TELEPHONE WIRES
AWAY FROM THE SCREEN
IT'S GOT YOU LOOKING
3 DIMENSIONAL
E.T.E CONTROL IS
GOING TO BE THE
DOWNFALL
... SECURITY CITY

I REMEMBER TWO THINGS ABOUT MY
GRANDFATHER, THE BAD CHAPTER OF MY
FAMILY HISTORY
~~MY CHILDHOOD~~. ONE, HE HELD ME IN HIS ARMS
WHILE SLOWLY MAKING HIS WAY FROM THE BEACH
TO A PLACE WHERE THE WAVES WOULD SOAK HIS BELLY
HIT IT, IN FACT, CAUSE I REMEMBER THE SOUND
THE SIZZLE AND SUDDEN RUMBLE ALL AROUND US ~~AS A SND~~
THEN THE IMPACT AGAINST HIS BODY AS I CURLED
UP DRY AND WARM IN A BLUE BLANKET FROM THE CAR
I DON'T KNOW WHY ALL THESE RINKY-DINK MEMORIES
ARE COMING TO ME NOW, I NEED NUMBER TWO
THE OTHER MEMORY IS HIS

I COULD BE YOU
COULD
LIKE YOU ROB A BANK DRESSED AS A SCHOOLTEACHER.
I'LL THE TIME IT TAKES TO FANTASIZE YOUR DEATH
YOU'LL WATCH THEM WIN ALL YOUR CHIPS
AND FEEL LIKE THE INSECT THEY MARKED YOU FOR

Fullerton Road Trick

Jeff Buckley ✓

I'VE FELT THIS SEASON BEFORE
AS A CHILD PLAYING DEAD NEAR THE ROAD
ONE CURIOUS BLANKFACED SUMMER — *Nice line*
UNAWARE THAT THE FLESH WILL ERODE

I'm not so sure about this comparison.

MY CHILD-HEART RACED WITHOUT RECORD
OF JUDGEMENT TOWARD SELF, SIGHT OR SMELL
THAT WOULD HINDER MY NAKED DIVE INTO THE DEEP
OF DISASTER, ~~THAT~~ HALLOWEEN SPELL

Nice enjambement

MY BROTHER AND I, WE THE CRAZY
WE THE STUPID YOUNG BLIND, WE THE COARSE
WE THE JAGGED DISHONEST MUSIC PRODUCED
BY DESPERATE TRYST AND DIVORCE

This repetition is great.

WE THE SOILED, WE THE TWIN BASTARD KIN
OBLIVIOUS TO LOCKS AND SAFETY ~~CAPS~~ CAPS FOR PILLS
OR MOTIVES FOR MOTORISTS' RESCUES OR SINS
OR THE BASEMENTS THEY KEEP IN THE HILLS

In a way, I want to see this developed

~~THE~~ ~~STURT~~ ~~COLOR~~ ~~OUR~~ ~~FEET~~ ~~THROUGH~~ ~~DIRT~~

WITH OUR EYEBALLS IN PAIN FROM NOT LAUGHING
SOME STRANGER STEPS OUT FROM HIS CAR
AND FOR SOME REASON OPENS THE TRUNK WITH HIS KEYS
NEVER ASKING HOW BOTH OF US ARE

re-structure

Too understated. How can someone "not asking how both of us are" inspire the hurling of dirt clods?

WE JUMP TO OUR FEET HURLING DIRT CLODS
a little clichéd.
LIKE THE RAPID FIRE KISS OF AFFECTION
WE BURST BACK TO HOME THROUGH THE NOWHERE

I don't know what this is. Use a more concrete simile.

Indent → TO SLEEP

~~THE~~ ~~IN~~ ~~THE~~ ~~SEASON~~ ~~RIGHT~~ ~~OF~~ ~~SUMMER~~ ~~DESTRUCTION~~

~~IN~~ THE SEASON OF SUMMER DESTRUCTION

FACING PAGE: In the spring of 1996, Jeff enrolled in a poetry class in New York. One of his surviving assignments, "Fullerton Road Trick," was named after the blue-collar Orange County town where Jeff lived from 1970 to 1975 with Mary, his half brother Corey, and, for a time, Mary's second husband, Ron Moorhead. Here, Jeff describes the time he and Corey engaged in dark-humor pranks—like lying by the side of a road, pretending to be dead, and running off as soon as a car stopped to check on their supposed remains. The comments in the margins are courtesy of Jeff's teacher, who instructs him to "use a more concrete simile," among other tips.

PAGES 14–15: Of the possibly dozens of journals Jeff kept, many are missing. Some were burned by Jeff in a ceremonial purging of his past, and others were water-damaged thanks to a burst pipe in the apartment above his in the East Village. Others were stolen. Only these six—the source of *His Own Voice*—survive in the Buckley archives. As seen on the bottom right, Jeff used an iconic Daniel Kramer photo of Bob Dylan (playing chess in 1964 in Woodstock, New York, where Jeff recorded *Grace*) for the cover of one notebook, augmenting it with his own doodles.

The notebook on the right reads:

I'm postin

NEXT WEEK, WE

~~BEFORE~~ I

THE PAGE BEFORE I

I'VE BEEN SAVING FOR

I HAVE AL

ABOUT MY FATHER

LAST THREE YEARS.

GOOD WRITERS OR B

TO THE PUBLIC. I

INTIMATE FOR YOU.

As I HAVE SAID

DEAF EARS, IT'S NOT

I DESPISE AND AVOID.

MASS OF PEOPLE IN

EDITORS AND WRITERS

WHOM I HAVE ALWAY

CONTRAST, COMPARE AN

OF MY FATHER, SOMET

THEY HAVE THE KNOWLE

I'VE KNOWN SINCE I

IN WAS A FACTOR I K

~~○○○○~~ . HE WOULD BE T

TRIVIALIZED ALONG WITH

RABID EXPECTATION FOR

A DAUNTING ~~THREAT~~ fo

EXCEPT FOR A GNAWIN

A LOAD OF BULLSHIT. "G

HOW COULD I CARE

REVERENT HIPPIES

WHEN THEY WOULD

ISTE MS. CONF-BY. FLOATING

The notebook at the bottom reads:

NOW 2.

(INVERTED) MANNAZ
THE SELF

THE STARTING POINT IS THE SELF. ITS ESSENCE IS W
ONLY CLARITY, WILLINGNESS TO CHANGE, IS EFFECTIVE NO
CORRECT RELATIONSHIP TO YOUR SELF IS PRIMARY, FO
IT FLOW ALL POSSIBLE CORRECT RELATIONSHIPS WITH O
AND WITH THE DIVINE.

REMAIN MODEST — THAT IS THE OR
COUNSEL. REGARDLESS OF HOW GREAT YOUR MERIT, BE
DEVOTED AND MODERATE, FOR THEN YOU HAVE A TRUE D
FOR YOUR WAY OF LIFE.

BE IN THE WORLD BUT NOT OF IT, THAT IS
HERE. AND YET DO NOT BE CLOSED, NARROW, OR JUD
BUT REMAIN RECEPTIVE TO IMPULSES FLOWING FROM
DIVINE WITHIN AND WITHOUT. STRIVE TO LIVE THE ORDINARY
A NON-ORDINARY WAY. REMEMBER AT ALL TIMES WHAT IS
~~TO~~ BE AND PASSING AWAY, AND FOCUS ON THAT WICH AB
NOTHING LESS IS CALLED FOR FROM YOU NOW.

THIS IS A TIME OF GROW
RECTIFICATION AND, AS A RULE, RECTIFICATION MUST C
PROGRESS. THE FIELD IS TILLED BEFORE THE SEED IS PLAN
GARDEN IS WEEDED BEFORE THE FLOWER BLOOMS, AN
MUST KNOW STILLNESS BEFORE IT CAN DISCOVER ITS TRUE

THIS IS NOT A TIME TO SEEK CREDIT FOR ACCOMPLI
OR TO FOCUS ON RESULTS. RATHER, BE CONTENT TO DO YO
FOR THE TASK'S SAKE. THIS IS MORE A PROBLEM FOR THOSE
EYES ARE ALWAYS ON THE GOAL ~~AND~~ THAN FOR THOSE WHO H
FORGOTTEN HOW TO PLAY AND CAN MORE EASILY FIND TH
IN DOING THE WORK FOR ITS OWN SAKE. HEREIN LIES
OF EXPERIENCING A TRUE PRESENT.

IF YOU TAKE THE RUNE OF THE SELF AND CUT IT D

The black notebook cover reads:

mead

70 sheets/wide ruled
10½ x 8in/26.7 x 20.3cm

1 subject notebook

MADE IN USA

05510   The Mead Corporation, Dayton, Ohio 45463

The gray notebook cover reads:

mead

3 subject notebook
75 sheets/college ruled
11 x 8½ in/27.9 x 21.5 cm

© 1987 The Mead Corporation, Dayton, Ohio 45463 U.S.A.

THE WOODSTOCK
ORANGE COUNTY'S HOTTEST NIGHT CLUB PROUDLY PRESENTS

THE BIT
FIRST CAUSE
MAHRE BUKHAM
KNIGHTS

9:00

SAT. OCT. 9
$1.00 OFF WITH FLYER

BREW W/I.D

AT THE
WOODSTOCK
CONCERT THEATER
951 SOUTH KNOTT AVENUE
ANAHEIM CALIF.
714-761-9840

NO AGE LIMIT

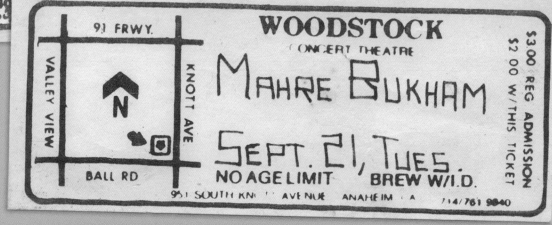

WOODSTOCK
CONCERT THEATRE

Mahre Bukham

Sept. 21, Tues.

NO AGE LIMIT   BREW W/I.D.

$3.00 REG ADMISSION
$2.00 W/THIS TICKET

951 SOUTH KNOTT AVENUE ANAHEIM CA   714/761 9840

FACING PAGE: Jeff's first band was dubbed Mahre Bukham in honor of different parts of each member's name: drummer Tim Marse, guitarist Robin Horry, Jeff, and bassist Jason Hamel. Formed in the spring of 1982, during Jeff's sophomore year at Loara High, the group specialized in covers of songs by the Police and prog bands like Rush, Genesis, and Yes. Mahre Bukham made its debut on September 21, 1982, at the Woodstock Concert Theatre, a strip-mall metal club in Anaheim. The group would only perform in public four times, yet its impact on Jeff—who hadn't yet turned sixteen during their earliest shows—would be immeasurable. The September 21 ticket here is, in essence, the first memento of a Jeff Buckley live performance.

PAGES 18–19: Jeff's first published interview appeared in the *Saxon Shield*, Loara High's school newspaper, during the Mahre Bukham days of the fall of 1982. Although he would later downplay his time learning prog, his love of that genre emerges here in his reference to it as "the thinking man's music." Given he was only about two weeks shy of turning sixteen when this was published, Jeff's comments about a career in music—surely the result of his knowledge of Tim Buckley's rocky road—reveal an almost innate caution toward the music business. He wants his group to "get more of our own repertoire" before they go in search of a record deal, and then start a "good slow climb to the top" to avoid overnight fame.

Mahre Bukham 'plays ar

By Adrian Imonti & Gabriel deLeon

Many a teenager has dreamed of becoming a rock 'n' roll musician. Ever since the days of Elvis Presley and Chuck Berry and The Beatles, teenagers have stood in front of bedroom mirrors jamming on imaginary guitars and drum kits and mouthing the words of songs coming out of their stereos. Most of these dreamers, however, soon give up their dreams of stardom for other pursuits, and turn their attention away from their rock 'n' roll fantasies.

There are, of course, those few who pursue their dreams, those who strive to become as good and as well-renowned as the musicians they idolized in their youth. Four of these striving musicians have formed a band which they call Mahre Bukham.

Mahre Bukham is a four-piece rock band with lead guitarist/vocalist, Jeff Buckley; bass guitarist/vocalist, Jason Hamel; drummer, Tim Marse; and rhythm guitarist, Robin Horry. Jeff Buckley, junior, and Jason Hamel, senior, are both students at Loara.

The quartet formed in April of this year. Jason Hamel, Tim Marse, and Robin Horry had a band together called Powerage. Powerage, however, was in need of a lead guitarist. Jeff then joined the band, and the group changed its name to Mahre Bukham. (They created the name "Mahre Bukham" by combining their last names together).

Mahre Buckham is what is commonly referred to as a "progressive rock" band, playing what guitarist, Jeff Buckley, refers to as "the thinking man's music." Not only do they perform cover versions of songs from other bands, but they also play their own original material.

Among the songs they play are "Roxanne" from The Police, "Woman From Tokyo" from Deep Purple, "Long Distance Runaround" from Yes, and two songs from Rush, "Free Will" and "The Spirit of Radio." They also have four original compositions: "Atmosphere," "Correct Use of Imagery," "Megabroad," and "Murder in Ojai."

Lead guitarist/vocalist, Jeff Buckley, and bass guitarist/vocalist, Jason Hamel, are both members of

Loara's Jazz Band. His main influences are Steve Howe (formerly of Yes and now of Asia) and Al Dimeola. Jason, who is a senior, has played bass for the past three years, as well as guitar, banjo, piano, and drums. His main influences are Chris Squier (one of the founding members of Yes) and Cleveland Edie, who works with jazz great, Count Basie.

At this time, Mahre Bukham has been performing around Orange County. For the most part, they have been playing at parties, but they also have played at The Woodstock, a night club here in Anaheim.

What do they get out of performing? Jason Hamel said, "You don't

ROCKIN' AWAY — Bassist, Jason Hamel (left) displays his skill along with other Mahre Bukham members: Robin Horry, Jeff Buckley, and Tim Marse.

(Photo courtesy of Mahre Buckham)

The Who tours goodbye

By Joe Lazaer

On October 29, almost 100,000 people waited shoulder to shoulder in a five block long line when, an hour earlier than scheduled, gates of the Los Angeles Memorial Coliseum opened for perhaps the best rock concert put on by The Who.

While being shoved to the entrance, one can be reminded of the Cincinnati tragedy when eleven people were trampled to death. At the Coliseum, after breaking into a run, people were halted by firm security

A group called T-Bone received a cold welcome with hot dogs, frisbees, and cokes thrown at them.

By the time the Clash came on, the rather large crowd had settled down, the main portion of the people on the field. Just before the Clash, a streaker was apprehended and dragged out on his stomach out of the Coliseum.

The Clash put on an excellent show. Although a deep ditch set the stage apart from the crowd, people

Finally, after waiting several hours, The Who came on for their farewell concert. The crowd was roaring and on its feet.

A video screen enlarged the groups actions. Tunes included: "Baba O'Riley," "Don't Get Fooled Again," "Pinball Wizard," "Summertime Blues," and "My Generation."

A jump in the air or a twirl of the microphone brought roars from the audience. A spectacular light show

ound' with style

et a big thrill or excitement out of aying — it's just kind of fun. All e stuff that goes with being in a and is the most fun part." Jeff uckley, however, feels differently. I get a good rush out of it," he says, ut I have to get off with the au- ience or I don't get off at all."

The members of Mahre Bukham, f course, want to succeed in the orld of rock 'n' roll, but unlike any other musicians, they do not ant instant success. Says Jeff uckley, "We'd like to get more of ur own repertoire and not get a ecording right away. We want a ood slow climb to the top...when ou start at the top, you can't go nywhere but down."

And Mahre Bukham is steadily vorking their way to the top. Right ow, they are working on their ongwriting and establishing their wn style of music. The material hey have written thus far, which eems to have been influenced by ands such as Yes, Genesis, Rush, nd to a lesser extent, The Police nd Pink Floyd, is fresh and shows hat Mahre Bukham possesses a lot f talent and a lot of potential.

Unlike many other bands emerg- g on the local scene, they are play-

ing varying styles of music, not just the normal blase hard-rock or new wave which today has become com- monplace and dull. Mahre Bukham is truly doing something pro- gressive, and we can be sure to hear from them for years to come.

MOVING UP: Junior, Jeff Buckley, is lead guitarist/vocalist of Mahre Bukham (photo courtesy of Mahre Bukham)

Drum major 'fishes' for the band

By Joe Lazaer

Roaring rapids crash against sharp, jagged rocks in the longest river of the Himalayas. A salmon jumps, a bass jumps, and a trout jumps. Suddenly, there is a sharp tug on you fishing rod. Your four leader hookup has caught a 65 pound tarpon, 35 pound salmon, 26 pound bass, and a small 12 pound trout. You leap into the water, the power- ful white water current tries to pull you under. Your two pound test line pulls taut, and after seven days, while listening to Styx play live 100 feet from the bank, you land the

help newcomers with marching. Twirling a baton and performing are customary jobs.

After practicing and trying out last year, Andy was chosen for this responsible job. "Thanks to my per- sonal teacher, Tom Inman, (last year's drum major) I'm where I am now," remarked Andy.

His message to the band, aimed mainly at freshmen is this: "Never stop the hard work, because no mat- ter how good our group gets there will always be room for improve-

WELCOME TO MUSICIANS INSTITUTE GRADUATION

September 15, 1985

Opening remarks.........................by Pat Hicks

We are proud to present the following entertainment and special awards....

1. "Samba De Confusion" - written by Keith Silverman - Keith Silverman, Rick Nash, Cheryl Bullock, Michael Martin, Enzo Todesco, Rob Catalano and Morris Beeks

2. "Hey Jerk" - Phil Burno, Guy Evangelista, Nick Evangelista, Tim Miller and Mike Morobitto

3. "Angel Eyes" - Joseph Field, Rob Alberts, Tony Marryatt and Enzo Todesco

OUTSTANDING HUMAN RELATIONS AWARD - PIT

Courtesy of ZILDJIAN

4. "Trooper" - Ken Daniel, Jim Phelps, James Birkenshaw and Paul Scali

5. "The Ill-Mannered Flailing Barrage" - Dale Shimizu, Leonard Stevens and Scott Duncan

OUTSTANDING HUMAN RELATIONS AWARD - BIT

Courtesy of FENDER

6. "Mexicali" - Marie-Ange Martin, Jean-Victor DeBoer, Patrick Berrogain and Peter Hastings

7. "Once Again" - Per Hovensjo, Eiji Yamaguchi, Rick Nash, Enzo Todesco and Melanie Vasquez

OUTSTANDING HUMAN RELATIONS AWARD - GIT

Courtesy of OVATION

8. "Squawkin' In The Henhouse" - Todd Barth, Jimmy Herring, Rick Nash and Steve Gallagher

9. "Shakin All Over" - Paul Gilbert, Bruce Eisenbeil, Mike O'Brien and Peter Sharpe

OUTSTANDING STUDENT AWARD - PIT

Courtesy of YAMAHA

10. "Straight No Chaser" - Jean-Marc Belhadi, Peter Hastings and Jean-Victor DeBoer

11. "Crank That Puppy" - Barrett Tagliarino, Grant Melcher, Lucio Costa and Dean Brown

OUTSTANDING STUDENT AWARD - BIT

Courtesy of YAMAHA

12. "The Rent" - Barrett Tagliarino, Leesa Poole, Rob Alberts, Lucio Costa and Chris Sternal

13. "Pearl On The Half-Shell" - Jeff Buckley, Tony Marryatt and Randall Stoll

OUTSTANDING STUDENT AWARD - GIT

Courtesy of GIBSON

Solo Performances by...
    Marie-Ange Martin
    Justin Deneau

Presenting the MI Graduates, Class of 85'

GOOD LUCK GRADUATES!

We wish you the very best in your careers.

From the MI Staff...

PAGES 20–21: After graduating from Loara High in 1984, Jeff moved to Hollywood and enrolled in Musicians Institute, a vocational school for budding virtuosos that allowed him to spend hours playing and practicing on his Ovation guitar. At this point, Jeff was focusing entirely on his guitar chops, rarely if ever singing, and pursuing a future in prog or fusion. Fittingly, he and two classmates, bassist Tony Marryatt and drummer Randall Stoll, performed Weather Report's "Pearl on the Half-Shell" at the class of 1985 graduation ceremony. Jazz guitarist Joe Pass, the commencement speaker, congratulated Jeff on his performance afterward.

FACING PAGE: Letter to Mary Guibert, undated from late '80s. Living in various apartments in Hollywood and working the graveyard shift at the front desk at the Magic Hotel, a way station for actors, musicians, and societal refugees, Jeff took his first steps toward adulthood. As this letter reveals, those duties included tending to his family members. Notice the signature—to his mother and others on the Guibert side, he remained "Scottie."

Mom,

Guess what I found.
One of those "finds" that makes you say,
"Hm? Why it's, uh OH MY LAAAAWWWD!"

It was sitting with a bunch of other papers in
one of my notebooks ...... nice.
O.K., so this is IT! No Mo' Tax-Schism.

I hate taxes, man.

You Job Hunter, you! I called you
the Monday after Mother's Day and the
machine wasn't on — you was hunting.
Things are fine and still the same.
What else is new? O.K. My final requests:

1) Keep the turntable (it's really good) get a new needle for it, build
yourself a real stereo system and TRASH THE OLD ONE !!!
2) Sell the Roland! Sell! Sell! Sell! As soon as you get
the money, tell Vandergrift to rev up that truck and haul all
my stuff over here. Give the rest of the money to
Grandma, no ifs ands or buts, cause I know she'll probably say
"No." Give it to her to pay off the Marshall a little. There'll
be more coming to her, wich is trez-cool. I don't want
to go lower than $375.00 on that little beast. OK.?
Take care and I love you!   Aotio   P.S. Got my passport,
                                                   got a bank account!

JEFF BUCKLEY BIO

SINGER, GUITARIST, SONGMAKER, STYLE: [scribbled out] PARA-

POST MODERN

ULTRA VIOLENT ROMANTIC

FACING PAGE: Although it's difficult to determine precisely when Jeff began jotting in notebooks and journals, by 1989 he'd begun chronicling his thoughts and feelings. This entry from August 5, 1989, is his earliest journal entry in the possession of his estate. His reference to the "best fucking band in the world" likely remains one that hasn't come together yet for the twenty-two-year-old. But from his dismissal of "Oscar-award mugging" to his disdain for "faking anything in life," his determination to succeed while being true to his sense of self is already established.

24

FACE IT. YOU ARE HEADING FOR THE TOP, FOR THE VERY TOP, TO THE TIP TOP OF THE TOP AND YOU'RE GOING TO EARN EVERY INCH OF THE WAY. THIS WILL BE THE BEST FUCKING BAND IN THE WORLD. FACE THIS, ACCEPT THIS FACT AND YOU'LL BE BETTER OFF FOR IT. THE DEEPER YOU GO, THE HIGHER YOU FLY, THE HIGHER YOU FLY THE DEEPER YOU GO, SO COME ON, COME ON!!

THE MUSIC IS THE THING, THE KEY. BUT, YOU MUST BE STRAIGHT UP, NO PRETENTION AND NO OSCAR-AWARD MUGGING, NO BULLSHIT, BECAUSE THAT SHIT IS JUST TOO TOO SHALLOW TO GET YOUR FEET WET, KNOW WHAT I'M SAYING? AND THAT'S THE KIND OF GARBAGE THAT SO EXPERTLY FUCKS EVERYTHING UP, THE MUSIC, YOUR MIND, YOUR WHOLE LIFE.... FAKING ANYTHING IN LIFE HAS A SUBTLE, FRIENDLY, COMFORTING WAY OF KILLING YOUR SOUL. SO DOES CYNICISM, PESSEMISM, PASSIVITY, FEAR, WORST OF ALL I THINK, ALL OF THAT STUFF CAN ROT YOUR HEART INTO A BLACK SPONGE THAT DESPERATELY TRIES TO SUCK AND ABSORB LIFE FROM EVERY SOURCE, BUT IT'S OWN. THEN YOU HAVE LOST; THEN YOU ARE DEAD FROM THE INSIDE OUT. YOU ARE NOTHING BUT YOU KNOW HOW MUCH IS INSIDE YOU AND YOU HAVE IDEAS OF HOW TO GET IT OUT INTO THE OPEN TAP THE SOURCE AND LET IT FLOW AND DON'T WASTE A DROP BY TAKING IT FOR GRANTED. THE MORE YOU THINK, THE MORE YOU UNDERSTAND AND THE DEEPER YOU MAY FALL INTO LOVE WITH LIFE... OR GOD... WHATEVER IT IS

8/10/89

I MUST QUIT THE HOTEL BUT HOW AND WHEN ARE
THE QUESTIONS. HOW? MOVE TO NEW YORK TO LIVE. WHEN
8/12/89 - 2/10 89 GET ABOUT $1800.00 VIA HOTEL, ODD GIGS,
TOURS, BUDGETING STRICTLY, LETTERS, SONGS, GUITAR,
SINGING, WORK 7:45 TO 4:00+, GET TO GIGS AHEAD
OF TIME, AMATUER CONTESTS WITH PRIZE $, 8121 CLUB,
SHAMROCK, CENTRAL, BE THE COLD JEFF OF DOOM,
BUS INSTEAD OF DRIVE, SAVE SAVE SAVE, MONEY GIGS ONLY
MAKE MONEY

RENT $475.00 ← GOT TO WORK ON THIS, MOVE IN W/ SOMEONE
INSURANCE $90.17 ← THIS TOO, CHANGE ADDRESS (TO MOM'S
PHONE $30.00
MARSHALL $50.00
FOOD $40.00
        $685.17
GAS $20.00
        $705.17
JEFF MAKES $1000.00
AND SAVES $300.00 IN 7 MONTHS I'D HAVE $2100.00

32 MONTHS OF $50/MTH WOULD PAY FOR MARSHALL
THATS 2 YEARS AND 8 MTHS, INSANE

I STILL HAVE TO KNOCK OFF CAR EXPENSES:
TIRES, ALIGNMENT, SPARKS, RADIATOR,
LIGHTS, TAILPIPE, BREAKS, IGNITION, UPHOLSTERY
HATCHLOCK, OIL SWITCH, THERMOSTAT, A/C,
WINDOWS, BELTS, U-JOINT, OIL CHANGE, FINISH,
CARPETS, DOORS, FLUIDS, TUNE UP, LEAKS.
EQUIPMENT HANDCART, A/B SWITCH, CORDS, TICKET ONE-WAY

8/15/84 RALIEGH STUDIOS
WAITING FOR BROOKE AND SLOANE

SITTING IN THIS VACANT LOBBY
THINKING ABOUT HOLLYWOOD
AND HOW ~~LITTLE~~ OF IT IS ANY DAMN GOOD
DRIVING DOWN THE CONGESTED AVENUES
  BECOMING HOT UNDER MY COLLAR
THE GREATEST COMMON DESIRE OF THESE
PEOPLE IS TO SEE AND BE SEEN BY
EACH OTHER. NOT MUCH ELSE CAN MATTER.
NOBODY IS GOING TO WALK JUST FOR MOVING
OR TO THINK FOR THE SAKE OF THINKING
FOR THE ECSTACY OF WITNESS BRINGS ON
A WHOLE NEW MEANING.

PAGES 26–27: As the '80s began to wind down, Jeff's so-called career in Los Angeles mostly amounted to playing on demos for other singers and working with a variety of bands, from reggae (the AKB Band) to hard rock (Group Therapy, fronted by his friend, singer Kathryn Grimm). By the summer of 1989, he was already dreaming of leaving the frustrating Hollywood scene behind and relocating to New York. As this note reveals, his financial planning for such a trip was beginning in earnest, and he began keeping tabs on his savings. Raleigh Studios, where he wrote about meeting up with two friends, was an in-demand location for TV, movie, and video production; around the time Jeff wrote this note, Madonna filmed her "Like a Prayer" video there.

FACING PAGE: By the dawn of the '90s, after he'd spent time with producer Michael Clouse and musician friends like Fishbone's Chris Dowd and drummer Carla Azar, Jeff's musical tastes began expanding beyond the prog and jazz of his teen years and into grittier, funkier, and dirtier rock and roll. This playful riff on Prince, complete with oh-so-naughty fantasies about his bandmates Wendy and Lisa, is both a parody of, and tribute to, a performer whose multiple-threat skills as a musician, singer, producer, and songwriter clearly had an impact on Jeff.

O' PRINCEMAS TREE

MY CONCERTS GLOW WIT MY IRRESISTABLE CHARM
RAISE YOUR HAND UP, SMELL YOUR UNDERARM
I MAKE YOUR LIFE A VIRUS BEFORE I ADMIT DEFEAT
CUZ IF IT WEREN'T FOR ME, YOUR ASS BE ON THE STREET
MY VICTORY IS THEIR WORSHIP
ADULATION IS MY FOOD
~~YOU MUST PLAY IT~~ THEY'VE GOT TO CALL YOU A GENIUS
~~BECAUSE~~ BEFORE YOU COP AN ATTITUDE
WHILE ALL THE OTHERS PLAY IT SAFE
TO AVOID THE FINANCIAL RISK
~~I~~ I'M WAITING FOR ANOTHER INCURABLE DISEASE
SO I CAN PUT IT ON MY COMPACT DISC
WICH IS CALLED ~~"HATERPHONY"~~ ~~"SMELLFONKY"~~

~~"FUNKGYNA"~~   ~~"LUSTPOXY."~~
   "BRAINSQUIRMY"

I   OUGHTA BE IN PIKCHERZ
DUN, DAT'S JUST WUT AHMA GUNNA DOooooooooo
MAH NAME IS PRINCE AND AHM @ 102 TIMES BETTER THAN
     ALL OF U, AWW GOOD LAWD

OH LITTLE COFFEE COLORED LOVER
PROVE TO ME THAT YOU'RE MY SLUT
I'M GONNA PLAY MY GUITAR SOLO
WHILE YOU FRENCH-KISS MY NASTY BUTT.

                    WANT
DON'T U ~~LOVE~~ MY LOVIN
DON'T YOU LOVE MY BOD,
          TWIST
GONNA ~~XXXX~~ YOUR SENSE OF REALITY
AS A SACRIFICE TO MY GOD. WATCH OUT! (FAKE SOLO)

DON'T U LUV WENDY? LISA?
ADORE THE REST O' MY BAND
I LOVED TO STROKE THEIR
PRETTY WHITE CHEEKS
AND THEN WACK 'EM WITH
THE BACK O' MY HAND
NEVER LET THEM HAVE ANY FUN
I NEVER LET 'EM HAVE NO FRIENDS
I TOLD 'EM ALL SIMULTANEOUSLY
THAT THEY WERE THE BEST
AND THE WORST THAT HAD EVER BEEN

AND NOW THAT I'VE ASKED YOU TO BE MINE

THERE'S NO WAY ANYONE CAN TELL ME

THAT LOVE ~~IS JUST ANOTHER~~ IS JUST ANOTHER WEAKNESS

JAZZ VOCAL NOTES

A CAPELLA PIECE E-
SWING - SHUFFLE - JAZZ

CONCEPT: MAN IN DIRE STRAITS

CONVINCING HIS LOVER THAT IF HE

HAS ANYTHING TO DO WITH IT, HE'LL

BRING THEIR LIVES INTO THE

PROSPERITY HE'S ALWAYS DREAMED OF.

"LORD KNOWS I'VE TRIED"

~~KNOWING~~ ~~THOROUGHLY SOLD~~

~~THAT LOVE~~

KNOWING YOU, I CAN'T BELIEVE THAT

TRUE FRIENDSHIP IS JUST A DREAM

AND NOBODY CAN TELL ME THAT

LOVING YOU IS JUST MY WEAKNESS.

F♯   A CAPELLA PIECE

LIKE THE MUSIC IN MY DREAM.

NO PULSE -

ONE LEAD VOICE SINGING THE PHRASES

(REMEMBER THE LINE: "JUST DON'T SEEM TO

BRING ME SATISFACTIONNNN") AND ALL OTHER VOICES INTERACTING w/ HARMONY ACCOMPANIED

LIKE A CHURCH CHOIR CUT DOWN TO

FOUR VOICES

ALSO THE TWO BASS VOICES SINGING IN 4TH'S

"I TR—Y, I TR—Y, I TR—Y, I TR—Y"

CONCEPT: PERSON SPEAKING OUT ON HOW

THERE MAY BE MANY ENTITIES IN LIFE THAT

ARE DISTRACTING, EVIL, SENSELESS, IRRESISTABLE

BUT HE ONLY WISHES TO LOVE AND SEE THAT WICH IS GOOD.

FACING PAGE AND BELOW: Jeff's ambition and workaday life—as well as his overly eclectic musical tastes at this phase of his career—emerge in these notes, especially the one about an early, perhaps unfinished, a cappella piece in "swing-shuffle-jazz" style.

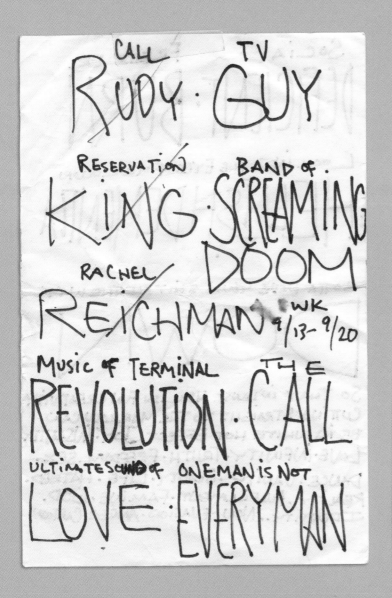

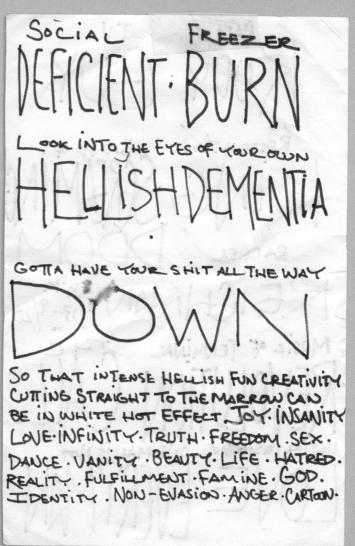

PAGES 32–33: Little reflects Jeff's eclectic taste in music more than his LP collection, which included pop classics (Joni Mitchell's *Court and Spark*, Elvis Costello's *Armed Forces*), jazz (John Coltrane's *Impressions*, Duke Ellington's Central American–influenced *Latin American Suite*), international pop (French orchestral pop bandleader Paul Mauriat's *From Paris With Love*), and prog (his treasured picture disc of Rush's *Hemispheres*, prominently featured on his bedroom wall during his high school years), along with albums by heroes like Nina Simone and poet Allen Ginsberg.

ALWAYS REMEMBER:

① THE VOODOO CREW ARE NOT STUPID, DEADWEIGHT, THEY EACH DESERVE RESPECT AND OPENNESS, AND PROBABLY TRUST, MOST OF ALL.

② I HAD BETTER DO A GREAT JOB WHILE THE SUPERVISOR IS GONE, BECAUSE MY ASS IS UNDER CLOSE SCRUTINIZATION BY DIANA AND T.O. GLOVER (DC: IS DIANA EVIL?) AND THE HOTEL HAS GOT TO BE SLAMMIN FULL SPEED, OR ELSE I WILL BE SO DISAPPOINTED AND PROBABLY FIRED. WE CAN DO IT!!

③ BE STRONG IN YOUR WILL AND HONEST IN YOUR SOUL, WHAT BETTER WAY TO BE WHEN YOU'RE SITTING IN THE SUPERVISOR'S CHAIR, DEALING WITH HER PAPERWORK, REDIRECTING THE BLOOD OF THE HOTEL; THE MONEY, AND BEING THE LAST STOP OF THAT BUCK PEOPLE PASS WHEN THINGS GET TOUGH? BE STRONG AND HONEST AND DIRECT — IT'S THE RIGHT THING.

④ CHECK ALL THE WORK YOU DO VERY CAREFULLY — BECAUSE GETTING THINGS RIGHT THE FIRST TIME IS THE ONLY THING.

---

26. COMPOSE NOTE OF INSTRUCTION FOR CREW ON HOW TO READ NHCA CHARGE TABLE. AND MAKE COPIES OF TABLES.

27. ALL OF THIS, EVERY SINGLE TASK ON THIS PAGE, EXECUTED SUPERBLY, WILL BRING YOU CLOSER TO NEW YORK. THE ENERGY, THE CONCENTRATION, THE HANDLING OF RESPONSIBILITY, THE EXPERIENCE, THE CONFIDENCE BUILDING, THE GROWTH, THE MONEY, ALL OF THESE THINGS ARE MINE IF I DO THESE THINGS RIGHT; AND EACH ARE STEPS ON THE STAIRWAY TO WHAT AWAITS ME IN THE BIG APPLE. NEW YORK AND MUSIC — THAT'S WHERE I BELONG.

FACING PAGE: Jeff's determination to do the best job possible at the Magic Hotel, and earn enough money at it to propel him out of California, again emerges in this summer 1989 passage. More and more, New York had begun taking on a mystical, life-saving aura to him. He writes as if he is destined to not only move there but also see his musical and career dreams be fulfilled in Manhattan. At this point, even he couldn't have imagined how true, and complicated, that wish would become.

PAGES 36–39: Clearly fired up by the idea of heading east and realizing his dreams, Jeff devoted several pages in August 1989 to contemplating imagined relationships, new, over-the-top approaches to music ("it isn't that prog shit," he notes, tellingly), and live performances. "Don't repress!! Express!!" he writes. At this point, Jeff wants to smash any and every rule—from making an album with only one song to bypassing the traditional music video. Not every one of those ideas would reach fruition (he would eventually succumb to making videos), but one declaration—"tours are like religious crusades"—will embody the mesmerizing, immersive performances on his *Grace* tour five momentous years later.

LIGHT INTO DARKNESS INTO THE UNKNOWN.
(POINT 4) I WANT EACH HOUR TO SEEM AS LONG
AS A DAY, EACH MINUTE TO BE AS A LIFETIME,
AND IN TURN TO BE CHARGED BY EACH DAY I LIVE
WITH ... HAPPINESS, FUN, EVERYTHING, SADNESS, POWER
MUSIC, LIFE. TIME
9/18

TODAY I WAS THINKING ABOUT LOVERS. WHAT KIND OF GIRL DO I
DREAM ABOUT? EASY! THE GORGEOUS BEAUTY QUEEN STRANGER
THAN FICTION, STRONGER THAN STEEL SUPERHUMPYGIRL WITH
GREAT BIG HOOTERS! NO, NO, NO. SHE IS INVENTIVE,
INDEPENDENT, AND A NON-CONFORMIST LIKE ME. NO WEAKNESS
FOR HEADGAMES OR MANIPULATION. BEAUTIFUL. HER FEATURES ARE
VERY DEFINED, AS IF HER SPIRIT IS PUSHING OUTWARD FROM INSIDE OF
HER BODY IN ORDER TO MAKE ROOM FOR ITSELF. FLAMING RED HAIR. SHE LIVES
APART FROM "PUBLIC SENSIBILITY", TRENDS, MUSIC, PHSYCO-BABBLE,
CLICHÉ. SHE'S VERY OPEN AND CHILDLIKE, KNOWING AT THE SAME
TIME THAT SHE LIKES LIVING WITH MATURITY AND WISDOM, THINGS SHE
KNOWS ARE INEVITABLE BECAUSE THEY'RE BROUGHT TO HER BY TIME, ITSELF.
NO PETTY SCRAMBLING AROUND TRYING TO FORCE HERSELF BACKWARDS,
TO STRAIN THE FACT OF HER AGE LIKE A FAT WOMAN STUBBORNLY
PUSHING HER LEGS INTO JEANS MEANT FOR A MORE SLENDER BUILD.
BUT SHE IS SO VERY BEAUTIFUL, SHE IS LIKE A DANCE ... A DANCE
THAT IS MEANT TO REVEL IN THE PLEASURE OF GRACE AND OSTENTATIOUS
IMAGINATION. IT'S A DANCE WITH MOVEMENTS SO PURE THAT ● TO
WITNESS IT, TO BE IN THE PRESENCE OF THE DANCER IS TO HAVE
YOUR BLOOD RESIGN AND THE ADRENALIN TAKE OVER YOUR BODY.
THIS IS THE KIND OF LOVER I WILL HAVE IN MY LIFE, NO LESS. (JEFF HASA)
WHAT ABOUT THE IDEAL ME? ALWAYS ON TOP OF MY ABILITY, SUPERIOR
FREAK MIND, DOES THE IMPOSSIBLE, CREATES THE OTHERWORLDLY, SERIOUS HARD
SLAMMIN MUSIC MAKER, SINGING GUITAR PLAYER, HEROIC, LIVING ALWAYS ON
THE EDGE AN NEVER PLAYING IT SAFE WHERE VALUE IS CONCERNED, ...

HAS A VAST AND POWERFUL INTELLECT WITH A SUBCONCIOUS HELLISH HEAVENLY DEMENTIA TO MATCH, BUT NEVER, ~~EVER~~ TALKS ABOUT STUFF HE DOESN'T KNOW ABOUT ~~BUT~~ WHILE PRETENDING TO. I.E. IS ALWAYS COMING FROM A BASIC, HONEST FRAME OF MIND, CAN NEVER BE FOOLED EASILY BY ANYONE, HE'S SO FUCKING BRILLIANT, ALWAYS SPEAKS HIS MIND OPENLY AND FORTHRIGHTLY — NEVER HOLDS BACK — HAS HIS OPINIONS THOROUGHLY CONCRETE, NO LOOPHOLES, BASED ON FACT AND PERSONAL REFLECTION, NOT ASSUMPTIONS AND CONJECTURE OUTSPOKEN, OUTGOING, TRAILBLAZING, BEAUTY WORSHIPPING, HUMAN LOVING, EVER REACHING, EVER GROWING, MAYBE THE FIRST HUMAN BRAIN TO HAVE ALL 100% PUT TO USE, FINDS THE ANSWER TO THE ANSWER CALLED MUSIC, HE IS NOT MERELY AN AVERAGE PASSIVE BIPED BUT IS A POSITIVE FORCE OF NATURE, EVER UPWARD, EVER DEEPER, EVER STRONGER, EVER LOVING, FOREVER. HE BECOMES STRONGER EVEN IN OLD AGE, HIS CAPACITIES ARE CHARGED UP TO MAXIMUM INTENSITY IN HIS 60'S TO 100'S ON AND ON AND ON UNTIL HIS VERY LAST SECOND ON EARTH. HE LIVES LIFE TO OVERFLOWING DEATH DEFIANCE, UNTIL HE SAYS IT'S TIME TO GO. JEFF WILL BLOW HIS OWN WHISTLE TO END HIS OWN GAME; NEVER BETRAYS THE IDEALS OF HIS YOUTH, HE IN FACT IMPROVES THEM, CONFRONTS THEM, MAKES THEM WHOLE AND ACTUAL, TO LIVE HIS ENTIRE LIFE VIBRATING WITH THE BLOOD AND MIND AND DRIVE OF A YOUNG MAN ALONG WITH THE VISION, THE WISDOM AND AUTHORITY OF AN ELDER OF MEN. AMEN.

. HAD A GREAT IDEA TWO DAYS AGO. RADIO PLAY. I LOVE STORIES AND I LOVE SOUNDS — RADIO STORIES BY JEFF BUCKLEY ~~Also~~ I WOULD WRITE A SCRIPT AND LINE UP A CAST, DIRECT IT, WE COULD ALL GET GREAT MUSIC TOGETHER AS WELL AS SOUND EFFECTS AND IT WOULD BE SO FUCKED UP — HELLISH DEMENTIA.

. ALSO — CULTIVATED SOUNDS THAT ARE TOO SCARY BUT NOT SUPERNATURAL. NIGHTMARE NOISES — A QUALITY THAT IS PURE TERROR, WITH LIGHTER SHADES OF COURSE. HELICOPTER WITH SPEAKER GOING, APREHENDING SOMEONE, ARMIES SPRINGING TO ACTION IN THIS TOWN, INCONGRUITY AND VIOLENT SURPRISE

- ALSO - MUST RECORD MY NIGHTMARE MUSIC - COMMANDO MACHINE GUNNING HIS WIFE AND CHILD UPON RETURNING THROUGH GREY VACANT CITY STREETS UNDER A GREY DAY. BIG MARCHING BAND BASS DRUM, BACKWARD JACK IN THE BOX, SYNTHESIZER DRONE ON BASS NOTES, FOOTSTEPS, DOOR OPENING, MACHINE GUN - REAL SURREALISTIC SCARINESS.
- HAVE MANY STRENGTHS BUT ONE - IMPROVISING FUCKED UP SONGS ON SITE.
- MUST CONCENTRATE ON DREAMING MUSIC AS WELL - I LOVE IT - PLUNGING INTO NIGHTMARES AND WONDERFUL DREAMY VISIONS; STARK BIZARRE STRANGENESS
- KEEP WORKING, KEEP WORKING 9/18 - 10/18 UNTIL SONGS ARE DONE AND TAKE THEM OUT, INVENT TUNES ON GIGS RIGHT ON THE SPOT. 2 FUCKEDUP.
- IMPROVISE - LET IT COME OUT / GOD DAMMIT! LET IT COME AND SHOUT IT OUT RISK IT ALL ~~FORCE~~ TO MAKE IT LIVE! DON'T TALK, DO! DON'T IMITATE! ORIGINATE! DON'T REPRESS!! EXPRESS!!
- BAND - WOULD LOVE A TRIO (BIGGER THAN THE BEATLES, MAN THEY WERE SO FUCKING POP BUT I LOVE THEM). ALL WRITE ALL SING ALL MONSTEROUS ALL MALE. NO VIDEOS TILL LATER, LIVE SONGS ARE KING - WE ~~XXXX~~ HAVE A LIVE THING HAPPENING THAT IS AS FOCUSED AND PRESENT AS AN EVENING. BESIDE THE CD PLAYER WHERE OF COURSE THE SONG GETS OVER EASILY YOU ARE CAPTIVE AND IT'S A CONTROLLED ENVIRONMENT COMFORTABLE, DRINK IN ONE HAND - LIVE YOU GOT NONE O' THAT !! THE BAND YOU HAVE GOT TO SEE LIVE IN ORDER TO SEE WHAT GREATNESS MEANS - IT MEANS BURNING BRIGHTER, GOING OUT OF YOUR MIND BECAUSE THE PERCEPTION IS SO HIGH, COLORS ARE TOO INTENSE TO BEAR - ORGASM - PICTURES FLOAT BY WAY OF SOUND AND VIBE AND WORDS AND ACTION, EXPERIENCE. LIKE NOTHING ELSE - THAT'S WHAT I WANT FOR US THE BAND AND SO WILL IT BE FOR THE FANS AND POTENTIAL FANS OUT IN THE AUDIENCE, EVEN IN BIGGER HALLS, WHERE WE ALTERNATE FROM THEATRICAL EXCESS TO ONLY WE THREE OR FOUR ONSTAGE WITH MINIMAL LIGHTING - NOT BIG BUDGET, NO WAY, BUT BIG VISION - EVEN THE AUDIENCES' SURROUNDINGS ARE PART OF THE ENVIRONMENT WITH SCENERY AND DIFFERENT KINDS OF SPEAKER PLACEMENT. SOUND EFFECTS HAPPENING SOMETIMES OTHER TIMES ONLY VOICES WITH BARE DRUMS BASS GUITARS AND AMPS.

BUT THE AUDIENCE - BAND / SEATS - STAGE RELATIONSHIP I MEAN
IS LIKE THIS - AT OUR GIGS NOBODY KNOWS WHAT'S GOING
TO HAPPEN NEXT. WHEN THEY WALK INTO THE FORUM
SUDDENLY ITS NOT THE FORUM ANYMORE, BUT A COLISEUM FROM
SOMEWHERE OUT OF THE BANDS' IMAGINATIONS, FREAKED.
OUR AUDIENCES COME UP WITH FUCKED UP SHIT AS WELL, YOU KNOW.
LIKE CHANTING SOMETHING TO US - NEVER TO SHOWBOAT BUT TO PARTICIPATE
TO EXPRESS THEMSELVES TO HAVE SOME FUN - LIKE WERE ALL
WIRELESS - DRUM MACHINE BASS, GUITAR AND WE ALL GET SO
OUT OF OUR SKULLS THAT WE FUCKING JUMP INTO THE AUDIENCE -
MASSIVE TRUST BEING EXCHANGED HERE, VERY EXCITING -
AND WE'RE PASSED AROUND THE WHOLE PLACE LAYING DOWN
THE GROOVE THE WHOLE TIME - MAGIC HAPPENING EVERYWHERE
AND NEVER THE SAME THING TWICE - TOURS ARE LIKE RELIGIOUS
CRUSADES - THE THING COMING FROM THE AUDIENCE IS NEVER
DESTRUCTIVE OR MOBBISH, BUT FRIGHTENINGLY POWERFUL
BECAUSE THEY KNOW ITS BECAUSE OF THEIR INDIVIDUALITY
THEY CELEBRATE, OR THEY'RE LEARNING ABOUT IT ANYWAY.
AND THE MASSIVE POWER IS POSITIVE, ITS **LED** BY
OUR MUSIC, THE MUSIC COMES FROM US THREE (OR FOUR).
IT ISN'T THAT PROG SHIT THAT HAS LOFTY INTENTIONS
AND ORNATE LITTLE TRICKS THAT STUMBLE AROUND IN ORDER TO
SIEZE ATTENTION LIKE SOME KIND OF VILLAGE IDIOT MUMBLING INCOHERENT MUCK.
NO ONE IS REALLY INTO HIS TRIP, THEY JUST GAWK ENDLESSLY WITH AMAZEMENT
AND DISGUST UNTIL THEY GET BORED AND BAIL OUT ONE BY ONE.

• AN ALBUM WITH ONE LONG SONG ALL THE WAY THROUGH • AN ALBUM WITH 25 SONGS • AN ALBUM
WITH 90 MEMBERS • AN ALBUM OF ACOUSTIC SONGS • MAYBE THREE KILLER DEBUT
A WHOLE BUNCH OF BARE BAND ALBUMS • B-SIDES GALORE • HITS UP
THE BACKBONE • DARKNESS ALBUMS WHIMSY ALBUMS • FUCKED UP
EP'S FOR OBSCURE ENJOYMENT • SERIOUS CONCENTRATED BUSINESS TACTICS •
FUN • FUN • FUN • JUST FUN!!!
KILLER DEBUT! • FOLLOW UP DEVESTATING • HAT TRICK GENIUS • ON INTO THE FUTURE

FACING PAGE: As the summer of 1989 wraps up, Jeff begins mapping out his New York expedition the following February. Again, his analytical mind reveals itself in his meticulous planning and financial calculations. He realizes he may encounter "some really bad people" in Manhattan, but it doesn't matter. As he cleverly notes, "I'm going to hit the ground playing."

8/31/89 Thursday

LINED UP TICKET FOR 2/20/90 6:00 AM ONE-WAY
BY THEN I'LL HAVE SAVED 1,800 or 16-1800, NOT
INCLUDING SELLING THE CAR OR MY TAX MONEY
FOR '89 AND '90 AND OTHER SUNDRY PROFITS.
I'LL HAVE BEEN COMPLETING A WHOLE
ROOMFUL OF SONGS AND GETTING MY TRIPLE-
JAM THANG TOGETHER (W, S, P.) AS WELL AS
MY READING AND CONTACTS. ALSO, I'LL HAVE A/AD A
LONG SET OF INTENSE JAMS BEHIND ME.
WHEN I GET THERE, I'M GOING TO HIT
THE GROUND PLAYING. WHAT JOHN SAID ABOUT
MUSIC BEING 1% INSPIRATION AND 99% PERSPIRATION
I'LL PUT MYSELF TO THAT ULTIMATE TEST FROM HERE TO
MANHATTAN, BECAUSE THAT PRINCIPLE MUST BE IN FULL EFFECT
THERE. BE COOL, BE OPEN AND PLUGGED INTO THE PRESENT
AND NEVER SETTLE FOR LESS. THERE ARE SOME REALLY BAD PEOPLE
THERE, BUT THERE ARE EVEN GREATER PEOPLE THERE AS WELL.
I WANT LIFE TO BE WHAT I KNOW IT MUST BE, IF
ONE LIVES IT RIGHT: BRILLIANT, INTENSE, UNCOMMON,
AGONIZING AND PAINFUL, WIERDER THAN WIERD, BEAUTIFUL,
AN EPIC ADVENTURE INTO EXISTENCE - THAT'S LIFE.

9/1/89 FRIDAY   3 6 9 12 15 18   S O N D J F

BANK BAL. $708.17
RENT $475.00 $233.17
HUMPHREY G'MAN $100.00 $133.17
INSURANCE $90.17 $43.17
FOOD $30.00 $13.17

SO, I SAVE THE 9/16 PAYCHECK IN TOTAL - PRETTY
CLOSE TO $350.00. NOT BAD AT ALL!! YEAAAY!

9/6 – 2/20

Non Evasion . Deep Opinion . Sure Efficacy
Insatiable Curiosity . Brilliant Execution .
Justice . Understanding . Simplicity (Austerity.)
Non - Contradiction . Ever Forward . Anti Convention .
Pro - Love . Anti - Violence . Pro - Reason . Anti - Death .
Pro - Life . Magic . Childbrain . Fun . Laughter .
Creation . Dreams . Future Vision . Energy . Invention .
Action .

FACING PAGE: Before he embarks for New York on February 20, 1990, Jeff ruminates on his goals for the trip.

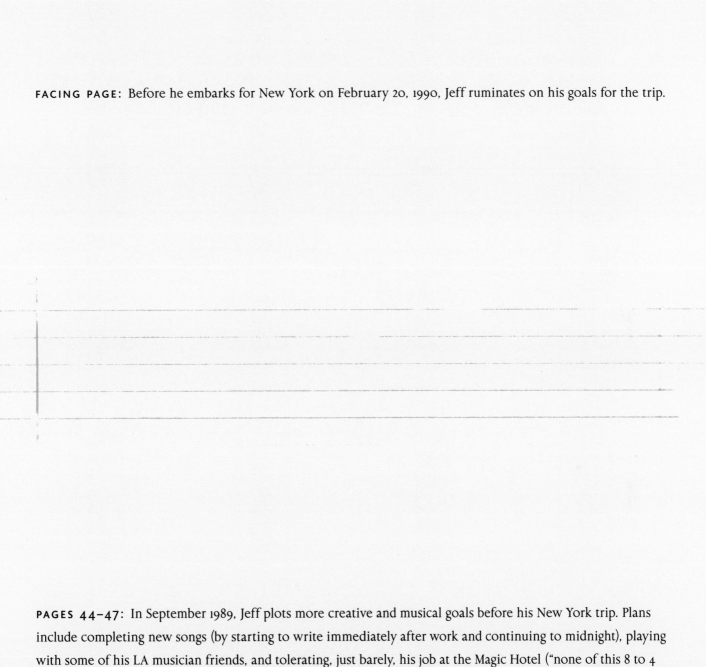

PAGES 44–47: In September 1989, Jeff plots more creative and musical goals before his New York trip. Plans include completing new songs (by starting to write immediately after work and continuing to midnight), playing with some of his LA musician friends, and tolerating, just barely, his job at the Magic Hotel ("none of this 8 to 4 bullshit"). "I will have done anything and everything necessary to train myself into making a name for myself," he writes. Interestingly, one such idea—"write words melody music for playing by myself, getting songs over in clubs with nothing to stand on"—will become a reality three years later when he starts an unofficial one-man-show residence at the East Village coffeehouse Sin-é.

9/16/89

SLAM. LAST NIGHT I KNEW WHAT I HAD TO DO IN
ORDER TO BE A GOOD FRONTDUDE, TO PLAY AND SING
AND WRITE MUSIC TO THE POINT WHERE I'D BE
THROWING DOWN THE SERIOUS TUNE-OUT JAM.
① WRITE WORDSMELODYMUSIC FOR PLAYING BY MYSELF,
GETTING SONGS OVER IN CLUBS WITH NOTHING TO STAND
ON. ② COMING UP WITH WORDMELODIES FOR CB'S MUSIC
AND BILL'N'ED'S JAMS — ~~XXXXXXXXXXXXXXXXXXXXXX~~
③ INFILTRATE ALIEN TERRITORY AND BE A SINGER
FRONTING A BAND .... LIKE YOU USED TO, JEFF. FUCK THE LEGACY,
YOU ARE YOU. ③ JUMP, PLUNGE INTO IMPROVISATION
IMPROVISING WORDMELODY. THE SUBJECT
OF ~~THE~~ EACH SONG SHOULD STAY THE SAME, THE EMOTION,
THE AURA, THE RAWNESS MUST BE FRESH AND
DIRECT TO THE SURFACE BY WAY OF THE MEANING
OF THE LYRICS ON ONE HAND — TO MAKE SOME SERIOUS
MAGIC HAPPEN BECAUSE OF THE PICTURES THAT MY LYRICS
ALONE CREATE, THE MUSIC (HARMONY AND LINE) ON THE
OTHER HAND — TO PAINT AND TO CONSTRUCT.... TO CREATE
ANOTHER ENVIRONMENT WICH IS APART FROM
EVEN THIS REALITY BUT STILL .... NOT ESCAPE BUT
BETTER. ④ MUSICONFRONTATION. FUCK IT, ITS ALSO
JUST MY EXPRESSION, SO SIMPLE!
(POINT 1) (GOOD IDEA TO ~~USE~~ PLAY COFFEEHOUSE SONGS (ACOUSTIC SOLO)
WITH TONY AND MIKE ON STAND UP BASS AND HAND PERC./SNARE.
AND PLAY COFFEEHOUSES AND JAM NIGHTS TOGETHER,
REHEARSE AT MY APT. SONGS FIRST 9/17–10/17
NO WORD UNTIL THEY EXIST. ACTIONS SPEAK LOUDER...
(POINT 2) STRONG PEOPLE KNOW THEIR MIND. THEY USE IT
ALL THE TIME AND HARD, TOO NOT JUST TO SURVIVE, BUT
TO CREATE THEIR LIFE. THEY INSTIGATE LIGHT & DARKNESS
(POINT 3) WORK. HARD. DIFFERENTLY. WITH RESULTS
WORK COMPLETELY AND PLUGGED INTO REALNESS. INTO

- We have our own unique merchandising twists — our own design of BAND-anas, different design of T-shirts w/ FUCKED UP ART, even fucked up trousers, 4 different kinds, with special band type designs having something to do with the newest album or tour theme. NEVER TOO EXPENSIVE!! Not one matches the other — don't want an audience militia uniform, just fan-oriented momentos.

9/20

~~DECIDE~~ Look up Jason — GREAT BASSIST — GET 10 songs — HARD SLAMMIN' SONGS = OVER-CAPACITY IDEAS — OVER THE FUCKING EDGE set of tunes to gig with. DO THIS BEFORE ANYTHING ELSE. GET SET TOGETHER BY Oct. 20th, REHEARSED BY THE 31st. DOWN/BOOK GIGS FROM NOV. ALL THE WAY TO FEB. 10th or so. ME, JAKE AND A DRUMMER. RAJI'S, SHAMROCK, COCONUT TEASER (TROUBADOR, GAZZARI'S, WHAT THE FUCK, JEFF, IT'S FUCKING PAY TO PLAY!) HIDEAWAY, ~~GASLIGHT~~ O.C. CLUBS, FM STATION, PALOMINO, AND YES, SASCH, ANTI-CLUB, EXPOSURE 54, PARTIES, CLUB LINGERIE, WHISKEY CHINA CLUB, COUNTRY CLUB — IS THAT PAY TO PLAY? — OPENING SPOTS FOR BIGGER VENUES FEATURING BIGGER BANDS. NOBODY IS GONNA FUCKING TELL ME THAT MY LIFE IS BORING, NO-ONE IS GONNA FUCKING OPEN MY DOORS OR HOOK ME UP AND GET ME OUT OF MY OWN "RUT" I'M NOT GONNA RIDE IN ON ANYONE'S FUCKING SHIRT-TAILS — FUCK THAT SHIT BABY!! I CAN DO IT AND WHAT'S MORE IS I'M FUCKING DOIN IT RIGHT NOW SO FUCK YOU!!

Nothing is gonna fucking stand in my way or in the way of my band's progress not even the band — we will slam in the six long ass months I've gotta rot in this crummy town. I'm going out with a BOOM and Jake that brilliant motherfucker is gonna get in there again —— he's too fucking rare to sit in his fucking apt. in that fucking rest home they call a city and waste that talent! I want us to live better than that and I'll stick it out til it comes together and blasts off.

9/21

I refuse to have any bullshit come down on me at the hotel — that piddly crummy fucking operation — I will not have people calling me up at home, I will not have guests complaining about me or suffering in any way if I have something to do with it. I will not stand for any superiors "doing" any bit of my job for me or bossing me around or pressuring me or threatening me or bending the fucking rules to suit their personal whim or any injustice to my mates at the front desk. I refuse to even fraternize or become familiar or warm up to anyone there. No alliances no cliques no clout by

ASSOCIATION. NO LITTLE JOKES. NO AFFECTION.
I DO NOT WANT TO ANSWER ANY QUESTIONS
BY BEGINNING "UM... LEMME SEE" NO!! I
MUST HAVE IT ALL TOGETHER AND IN CLEAN
OPERATION TO WHERE NOBODY CAN SAY SHIT
TO ME AND ANY QUESTIONS ARE ANSWERED
RIGHT AWAY WITH NO BREAKS IN BETWEEN!
EIGHT HOURS AND FIFTEEN MINUTES A
WEEKDAY, FIVE DAYS A WEEK. ONCE
I WALK IN THAT ROOM AND PUNCH IN
THE PLACE IS MINE AND IN MY CHARGE.
AND BY THE TIME I LEAVE I WILL HAVE KNOWN
WHAT REAL AUTHORITY IS AND WHERE IT LIES
IN THE SOUL. I REFUSE TO SUFFER IN ANY
WAY BECAUSE OF THAT PLACE, I SIMPLY
REFUSE. EVERYONE THERE WILL BE THERE
STILL IN 2 OR 3 YEARS DOING THE SAME FUCKING
THING NEVER GIGGING NEVER TOURING
NEVER DOING ANY SESSIONS, PARTIES, NO
MUSIC EXCEPT ME. I WILL HAVE DONE
ANYTHING AND EVERYTHING NECESSARY
TO TRAIN MYSELF INTO MAKING A NAME FOR
MYSELF OR A LIVELYHOOD FOR MYSELF PLAYING
MY OWN MUSIC AND TAKING IT OUT THERE AND
GROWING AND LEARNING AND LIVING THE REAL LIFE
NONE OF THIS 8 TO 4 BULLSHIT! MORE LIKE
SATURDAY TO WEDNESDAY, TUESDAY TO JULY
THAT KIND OF NON-ROUTINE. REALITY!!

P.S. OK. FROM NOW ON I WILL NEVER BE LATE TO FUCKIN' WORK.
UP WITH THE ALARM AND INTO THE SHOWER - EAT YUM, YUM -
PLAY GUITAR AND LEAVE AT 7:35 AM. ONCE I GET HOME
AT 4:30 I'VE GOT TO WORK ON TUNES UNTIL 12:00.

FACING PAGE: Jeff's fascination with the literary fringe permeated his book collection, which was peppered with outlaw authors and Beat writers. ("I carry Allen Ginsberg with me everywhere," he said in a 1994 interview.) As seen by the Ray Charles, Edith Piaf, and Chuck Berry autobiographies here, he was also taken with pop music memoirs.

Édith Piaf — L'Hymne à l'amour

RILKE — SONNETS TO ORPHEUS — MacINTYRE — CALIFORNIA

Arthur Rimbaud

HANK WILLIAMS — THE COMPLETE LYRICS — DON CUSIC EDITOR

ABSALOM, ABSALOM! — William Faulkner

T. S. ELIOT — SELECTED POEMS — HARCOURT BRACE JOVANOVICH

WILLIAM S. BURROUGHS — QUEER — ISBN 0 14 00.8389 8

Delmore Schwartz — SELECTED POEMS: Summer Knowledge — NDP241

JIM CARROLL — THE BASKETBALL DIARIES — ISBN 0 14 01.0018 0

SELECTED POEMS OF ANNE SEXTON — HOUGHTON MIFFLIN

Bob Dylan — A RETROSPECTIVE — Edited by Craig McGregor — MORROW PAPERBACK EDITIONS

JACK KEROUAC — THE SUBTERRANEANS — GROVE WEIDENFELD

DELMORE SCHWARTZ — IN DREAMS BEGIN RESPONSIBILITIES — NDP454

BAUDELAIRE — PARIS SPLEEN — NDP294

leonard cohen — VIKING COMPASS

Gospel Choirs — Derrick Bell — Basic Books

John Miller Chernoff — African Rhythm and African Sensibility — Chicago

SPOKEN URDU — ابتدائی اردو — VOL. I

Bukowski — Tales of Ordinary Madness — City Lights

BROTHER RAY — RAY CHARLES' OWN STORY — RAY CHARLES & DAVID RITZ — 0482 — DA CAPO

fear of dreaming — the selected poems of Jim Carroll — ISBN 0 14 058 695 4

McFeely — FREDERICK DOUGLASS — NORTON

THE LAND WHERE THE BLUES BEGAN — ALAN LOMAX — PANTHEON

RUMI — We Are Three — MAYPOP BOOKS

HUNTER: THE STRANGE AND SAVAGE LIFE OF HUNTER S. THOMPSON — E. JEAN CARROLL — PLUME

Chuck Berry THE AUTOBIOGRAPHY

FACING PAGE: In an undated entry from late 1989 or early 1990, Jeff takes stock of his songwriting catalog—real or imagined. Most, if not all, of these titles refer to songs that were incomplete or unrealized. Only "One Man Is Not Everyman" will eventually emerge in his notebooks.

SONGS

1. ONE MAN IS NOT EVERY MAN

2. SONG OF LOVE (ULTIMATE SONG OF LOVE)

3. PLUG IN TO NOW SONG & JAM

4. LOVE GOSPEL

5. WAR IN MY TOWN

6. SHE AIN'T KNO-NOTHIN BOUT THE BLUES

7. FLY LIKE IN DREAMS

8. BIG MAMA SONG

9. THAT PHENOMENON OF THINGS, NOISES, WEATHER, ANIMALS ANYTHING THAT IS SO GIGANTIC, SO HUGE BEYOND BELIEF, BUT MUST BE BELIEVED BECAUSE IT'S RIGHT THERE IN FRONT OF. YOU. NO WORDS TO DESCRIBE IT, NO WAY IN HELL TO MEASURE IT BECAUSE IT IS SO IMPOSSIBLY HUGE AND POWERFUL. IT CAN DESTROY YOU IN A SECOND BUT STILL YOU ARE DRAWN TO IT IF ONLY TO WITNESS ITS UNDULATING LARGENESS. YOU COULD DIE, BUT STILL YOU STAY.

10. HOW, OUT OF DESPERATION FOR LOVE, A MAN CAN SINGLEHANDEDLY ORCHESTRATE AND DESTROY A RELATIONSHIP WITH AN INNOCENT WOMAN.

I. ONE MAN

SAY WHAT YOU LIKE BUT ONE DAY
IT'S GONNA COMEBACK SO HARD ON YOU
ONE MAN IS NOT EVERY MAN
LAST NIGHT I WAS THINKING OF THE HUMAN ~~PART BRAIN~~
WHAT MAKES US ALL THE SAME   BEINGS
IS IT THE ~~████~~ DIMENSIONS OF THE BRAIN
THE MOUTHS THAT TALK OF THE ONE FINAL DAY
AND WHISPER SECRETLY AND DREAMS OF FLYING WINGS
AREN'T PEOPLE JUST LIKE YOU AND ME?
WE ALL HAVE HANDS WITH SKINS THAT SENSE PLEASURE
~~AND~~ WORR~~IES~~ OF PAIN, WOMEN CHECK THEIR MIRRORS AND THEIR MEN
WHO ARE EVERY BIT AS VAIN, IT'S ALL THE SAME,
LAST NIGHT I COULDN'T GET TO SLEEP
I WAS THINKING, I WAS CONSTANTLY THINKING
OF THE DIFFERENCES BETWEEN EVERYONE
AND HOW I WAS ALWAYS TOLD
TO THINK FOR THE GOOD OF ALL AND I THOUGHT IT WAS
SO BEAUTIFUL, FOR THE GOOD OF EVERYONE.
WHEN I SAW, I WAS SO AMAZED AT THE MEANING OF THE PHRASE
THE SHEER CRAZINESS FRIGHTENED ME FOR DAYS AND DAYS
THE BRIGHTEST YOUNG ~~BOYS~~ BOYS WERE NOT THE BROTHERS
OF THE HUMAN LITTER THAT BEGGED FOR THEIR QUARTERS
AND I THOUGHT THAT EVEN THEN THERE ARE ~~███~~ HONEST MEN
WHO ARE DREAMING IN THE GUTTERS BUT
~~BUT WHO ARE OUR BROTHERS?~~ ~~███████~~ WHO ARE YOU
TO SAY THAT THESE ARE MY ~~BROTHERS~~?
DON'T TRY, DON'T TRY, DON'T EVEN BEGIN TO TRY.
THOSE WORDS YOU USE TO MAKE US ONE BIG TRIBE WILL
~~██████████████~~ NET US IN LIKE CATTLE
CROWDED SO NONE CAN MOVE FREELY OR MAYBE JUST ESCAPE
BECAUSE OF COURSE BY THEN THE BEST YOU CAN HOPE FOR
IS THE ELECTRIC PROD TO STUN YOU AND SOON YOU'RE ON SOMEONE'S
DINNERPLATE ~~█████~~, ALL WILL BE LED TO SLAUGHTER. ONE MAN IS NOT
EVERY MAN.

FACING PAGE: "One Man," referred to as "One Man Is Not Everyman" in the previous list of developing material, stands as one of the earliest attempts at a lyric discovered in Jeff's archives. Given its loose-knit structure, it's hard to tell if he intended "One Man" as a lyric or merely a poem or rumination. But in lines about an "electric prod to stun you" lie the seeds of the visceral, image-heavy writing that would later emerge in his lyrics and journals. It's also a sign of the way Jeff was striving for higher ground: "I thought that even then there are honest men who are dreaming in the gutters" is downright Dylanesque. No recording of this lyric has yet to be found.

PAGES 54–55: In this entry from September 23, 1989, Jeff dwells on creativity, originality, and the importance of music in his life. During his childhood, he'd been a superb mimic, and he reflects here on the way he escaped the "reality of chores and parents and school" by way of playing air guitar to Kiss records. But now he chastises himself for too many years playing pretend music ("I have wasted valuable valuable time") and realizes he must move on "from doing impressions of things." With his flair for the melodramatic, he writes about leaving behind "the fiery death of living hell that is every-day life" but also, in more measured tones, sums up his goals: "I only want to be above the norm."

9/23 SATURDAY 3:53 PM 18 MINS OF DIARY
JUST GOT OFF THE PHONE WITH JAKE AND TALKED ABOUT
EVERYTHING. I HOPE HE'S STILL ROCK 'N' ROLL. IT'S
OKAY, THOUGH. I WILL BE THE TOTAL ROCKING EXAMPLE AND
THE NON-PRETENTIOUS NON-SUPERIORITY VALUE SYSTEM BULLSHIT INSTIGATOR
I ONLY WANT TO BE ABOVE THE NORM, MORE SPLENDID
THAN ANYTHING THE EXISTING "CONVENTIONS" COULD EVER
OFFER ME. TO ALWAYS PUSH FOR THE HIGHEST CONCEPTS
WITH FULL POWER AND TOTAL AWARENESS AND A INFINITELY
COLOURED AND INFINITELY POSITIVE SENSE OF LIFE
TOTALLY ANTI-DERIVATIVE, ALWAYS SOUL-GENERATED.
ANYTHING IS POSSIBLE IN THE NAME OF ● HEAVEN.
ALL THIS MUST BE SO HAPPENING, SO REBELLIOUS, SO
FUCKING ROCKING THE HOUSE, ALWAYS EXTREMELY UNCOMMON
APART FROM THE PAST, I FOLLOW NO-ONE, I COMMAND NO-ONE,
THIS HAS GOT TO BE HUGE, THE HUGEST, THE NEW
STANDARD. ALWAYS ON THE LIVING EDGE WHERE
ONLY DREAMS AND NIGHTMARES DWELL. WHILE I SAIL THE FURIOUS
SHIP OF REALITY THROUGH THE HEART OF THEIR DOMAIN. SPARKLING
DANGER, COLORS AS INTENSE AS SUNLIGHT, MORE INTENSE, SOUNDS
OF ETERNITY, WORDS OF INFINITY, FLYING ON BLUE-WHITE FIRE.
THESE ARE MY OBJECTIVES. THIS IS MY LIFE. LIKE NONE BEFORE
AND NONE AFTER. TO BREAK THROUGH THE FIERY DEATH OF LIVING
HELL THAT IS EVERY-DAY LIFE TO DESTROY THE WALLS OF FEAR IGNORANCE
DENIAL EVIL OPRESSION DISHONESTY CONFORMITY TO BREAK THROUGH THEM
ALL AND LIVE TO CLIMB HIGHER, LIVE TO REAP MY RICHES, TO GO ON TO
SEEK ALL ANSWERS. 4:30 PM ... 47 MINS. ... OUT.

P.S. UM I ESTIMATE THAT I'VE BEEN DOING THIS AIR-GUITAR
BEHIND CLOSED DOORS ROUTINE SINCE I WAS IN THIRD GRADE - THAT'S
14 FUCKING YEARS AGO OKAY? I SAY IT'S ABOUT TIME TO SAY
THAT I'VE GRADUATED FROM DOING IMPRESSIONS OF THINGS

BETTER LIVED THAN ACTED OUT, OK? I'M A GOOD MIMIC, FINE,
IT'S BEEN A LOT OF LAUGHS, LOTS OF ENERGY AND TIME BEING UTILIZED
THERE. IT'S A LEFTOVER GAME OF A LITTLE BOY WANTING
TO ESCAPE FROM THE GOOFY REALITY OF CHORES AND PARENTS
AND SCHOOL BY WAY OF A KISS RECORD AND A CARDBOARD
LES PAUL MADE FROM TWO BOXES AND A KITCHEN KNIFE.
I MEAN, DID I ACTUALLY GET A REAL ELECTRIC GUITAR
JUST SO I COULD AIR-GUITAR WITH A LITTLE MORE FLAIR?
THAT SHIT IS FOR PRE TEENAGED DORK-WEENIES, ~~XXXXX~~
I HAVE WASTED VALUABLE VALUABLE TIME WITH AN ACTIVITY
THAT IS TOTALLY USELESS, YOU KNOW? ESCAPE IS NO LONGER
CALLED FOR OR EVEN ESPECIALLY HEALTHY. ESCAPE FROM LIFE IS DEATH
AND THE DEATH IS SLOW AND DISGUSTING TO EXPERIENCE, I KNOW
BECAUSE I'M GETTING A LITTLE TASTE OF IT RIGHT NOW. MUSIC
IS MY LIFE AND IT ALWAYS HAS BEEN SINCE I WAS BORN.
MUSIC IS WHAT I'LL HAVE AS MY STRENGTH AND MY
FUEL TO GO ON AND MY REASON TO LIVE. NOTHING ELSE EXISTS.
IT'LL BE THE GREATEST THING TO USE THE GIFTS I HAVE TO MIMIC AND COPY
AND HEAR NOTE FOR NOTE AND QUIRK FOR QUIRK AND TRANSFORM THAT
TALENT INTO SOMETHING OF A MUSICAL STRENGTH ... SOMEHOW ... TO
INVENT MELODIES AND STORIES AND LYRICS TO USE FOR SONGS:
~~TO MAKE UP ... COMP~~ TO REEDEEM THE LAST FOURTEEN YEARS.
IN THE SPACE OF ONE. SEPT '89 TO SEPT '90 AND THEN ON TO HELLISH DEMENTIA.

Voodoo Notes

11/6
EXPECT UPS for #310 Fields —
C.O.'s 108 CLEANS 104, 208 210 301 302 304 309
406 408 C.I.'s 207 ② DAILY
MAIDS, PHONES,
RENTS, T.B.B.'s DUE,
DRAWER KILL, BOOK,
#109 TV REPAIR, LINES w/GRAY BAD SOUND, TOILET HINGE BROKEN on TOP LID,
#205 CHANGE SOFA LINEN, 108 TV REPAIR./CHECKUP.
MOSELEY PHONE.

WELL I'M LYING ON MY BED THE BLAN...
SAFE FROM HARM STILL SMELL YOUR HAIR...
SKIN TO KEEP ME WHOLE IF YOU COULD...
IF I COULD HOLD YOU FAST WOULDN'T...
THE PAST WIPE OUT THE MEMORIES K...
PORNOGRAPHIC DEATH RIPPED AND...
I DON'T WANT TO WISH FOR YOU DON...
I'M IN TORTURE THE HOT BRUISES...
GIVE ME MORE GIVE ME MORE SEN...
DOWN MY BACK GIVE ME MORE, Y...
I'VE SEARCHED SO HARD FOR , GIVE...
TO ME FOR AWHILE 'CAUSE MY LOVE...
MY LOVE IT'S COMING DOWN ON YOU...
GOLD AND ~~TURQUOISE~~ PEARLS IN OYSTER...
TO LOVE, BORN AGAIN FROM THE RHYTHM SCR...
AND YET I'M ONLY THERE IN YOUR ARMS...
GOING TO DIE TOMORROW MOST LIKELY, I...
IF YOU LAID AT MY SIDE , WOULDN'T...
~~XXXX~~ CURSE UPON ME FOR MAKING YOU G...
HORSES ~~BLOW~~ THE MEMORIES FIRE THE R...

11/22/89

©

is WARM THIS BODY is NEVER

ck RIBBONS OF COAL TOUCH MY

ly CALL ME RIGHT NOW

eed MY BOTTLES TO WIPE OUT

he MEMORIES WATCH THEM DIE ^

om SHREDDED STEAMING MESS.

ant TO KNOW I'M BLIND

w. THE WELTS OF YOUR SCORN, MY LOVE

e STINGING WHIPS OF OPINION ALL

I'VE WAITED ALL MY LIFE TO SEE IT'S YOU

for MY SMILE GIVE IT ALL UP

ming DOWN is LIKE THE DEVIL ON TRIAL

honey SMILE, PRECIOUS PRECIOUS SILVER AND

, DROP DOWN WE TWO TO SERVE AND PRAY

ing DOWN FROM HEAVEN AGELESS AGELESS

n ONLY NAKED AND ALONE AND SHIVERING LONELY,

ly YOU   WERE   HERE   WITH   ME,
                                    SATISFIED
d NO MOJO DREAM TO KEEP ME ~~Satisfied~~.

m BLIND I'm IN TORTURE THE WHITE

ms FALL SLOW BLACK BEAUTY I LOVE YOU SO .

Jeff
Buckley

any

ody

PAGES 58–59: Jeff first began singing and playing "Mojo Pin" during his tenure with Gods and Monsters, the New York band (founded by guitarist Gary Lucas) that Jeff briefly joined in 1991. But as this entry reveals, the origin of its lyrics dates back even earlier, to November 1989. In this untitled entry, the first line would survive as the first words we hear in the finished song, and other phrases, including "precious precious silver and gold" and "screaming down from heaven," would also appear in the final version heard on *Grace*. Jeff would later tell friends and interviewers that the phrase "mojo pin" referred to a needle (and how he had once dreamt of seeing an African American woman inject herself between her toes). But here the line is the far more ambiguous "mojo dream."

PAGES 61–63: This vintage saxophone case served various purposes for Jeff. At one time it held his CDs. Once that collection outgrew the case, he used it for journals, souvenirs, notes, jewelry, and a blue feather boa. The bird-decorated fan shown here was one of many handed out at his memorial services at St. Ann's Church in Brooklyn on two sweltering nights in 1997.

FACING PAGE: In February 1990, Jeff finally made his move east, flying to New York with a one-way ticket. He first lived in Harlem with a drummer, a former classmate at Musicians Institute, before moving into a shared Upper West Side apartment with another friend, actress Brooke Smith. Here is an early, unfinished snippet of his first evening in the city and a sense of the new discoveries he would make there.

THE FIRST EVENING THAT I EVER SLEPT IN N.Y. WAS THE NIGHT THAT I HAD FIRST ~~LAID~~ LAID EYES ON A QAWWALI. MANHATTAN CABLE T.V. HAD SEX AND VIOLENCE AND FOR

SOME REASON

I AM THE OUTSIDER
I MOVE FROM TOWN TO TOWN AND NEVER STAY,
I'M ON THE OUTSIDE STARING IN AND I LIKE IT THIS WAY,
DON'T HAVE NOODLE TO DEPEND ON NEVER KEEP A LOVE FOR LONG
DON'T KNOW WHAT A FRIEND IS, BUT I KNOW HOW DEEP THE END IS,
~~W~~ I WAS BORN, DRIFTING ON A SEA OF DESPERATION
GIPSY MOTHER GIVE ME STRENGTH
LONG LOST FATHER WISH ME HOPE ~~FROM THE GRAVE~~
AND GRAVESTONES GIVE ME MY EDUCATION, ~~I AM THE OUTSIDER~~.

I HAVE NO FEAR I $^{INSIDE ME}$ GOT EMOTION TO BURN
~~NO~~ ~~ONE~~ UNDERSTANDS ME **BUT** IT'S NONE OF MY CONCERN.
I DON'T NEED YOU, I DON'T NEED ANYONE.
~~I AM THE OUTSIDER~~ TO SHOW ME HOW TO GET THINGS DONE
I AM THE ~~BRIDGE DRIFTER~~ BRIDGE BURNER
FRIENDS I'VE LOVED HAVE LONG SINCE ~~PUT TOGETHER~~ $^{BEEN FORGOTTEN}$
~~AS SKINNY BOYS~~ WE WALKED THE STREETS AS BROTHERS
BUT NOW I'VE BEEN GONE, SO ~~SIXTEEN~~ HOMES SO ~~SEVENTEEN~~ YEARS ~~OLDER~~
THIS LIFE IS HARD BUT ONCE YOU LEARN IT STAYS WITH YOU FOREVER.
THIS LIFE IS HARD BUT I KEEP MY HEAD TOGETHER
IT AIN'T SO HARD ANYMORE, I AM THE OUTSIDER.
I LOVE THE MIDNIGHT HOUR WHEN THE TOWN GOES TO SLEEP
DREAMS OF CHRISTMAS DREAMS OF LOVE AND TOMORROW
REMINDS ME OF ~~SLEEPING~~ HUDDLED FLOCKS OF SHEEP
~~THE ROAR OF RANDOM CARS AND~~ HEELS
~~AND THE CLICK OF HIGH HEELED FEET.~~ DAD ~~RAINY NIGHT~~
~~BRIDGE BURNER PAGE TURNER~~ A VACANT STREET
I ONLY DREAM OF FACELESS VOICES ~~IF I'M RIGHT~~
THEY ASK ME IF I'VE MADE THE RIGHT CHOICES
THEY'VE BEEN INSIDE MY HEAD FOR AS LONG AS I CAN REMEMBER
THEY WON'T LET ME SLEEP UNTIL I GIVE THEM ALL THE ~~R~~
ANSWERS

FACING PAGE: Unrecorded song circa 1990, most likely inspired by his East Coast relocation. (In the scratched-out portion of the lyrics, "the click of high heeled feet" on "a vacant street" feels very Manhattan.) Jeff refers to friends and family members he no longer sees and implores, "Gypsy mother give me strength / Long lost father wish me hope."

PAGES 68–69: Jeff's obsession with the music of Pakistani singer Nusrat Fateh Ali Khan, the leading voice of Qawwali music, began when he arrived in New York and heard Khan's recordings by way of his first roommate. In these pages, he writes about that discovery and what the mesmerizing, chant-like devotional music means to him. Later, some of these thoughts would be used as the basis for his liner notes for Nusrat's 1997 anthology, *The Supreme Collection Volume 1.*

I WAS LIVING IN HARLEM NEAR THE AUTUMN OF 1990
WHEN I FIRST HEARD THE VOICE OF NUSRAT FATEH ALI
KHAN. FROM THEN ON I HAVE ALWAYS KEPT HIS MUSIC
CLOSE TO ME, NOT MERELY FOR THE BEAUTY AND POWER OF
QAWWALI MUSIC, BUT SIMPLY ~~POTENT~~ BECAUSE OF ITS
POTENT ABILITY TO SPEAK, DIRECTLY TO ~~THE~~ MY SOUL: BEYOND LANGUAGE
DIFFERENCE, ~~BEYOND~~ CULTURE, BEYOND THE NEEDLESS BOUNDARIES
OF STYLE AND DEMOGRAPHIC. SOME PEOPLE, LIKE ME, PLAY MUSIC
OR ARE CALLED MUSICIANS OR WORSE; THESE MEN, THE QAWWALS,
ARE MUSIC ITSELF. THIS MUSIC, LARGELY THROUGH THE RECORDINGS AND
PERFORMANCES OF NUSRAT FATEH ALI KHAN AND HIS PARTY,
~~■■■■■■~~ IS SPEAKING TO THE HEARTS OF HUNDREDS OF THOUSANDS OVER
THE WORLD. SOME OF YOU PEOPLE OUT THERE IN READERLAND
WERE LUCKY ENOUGH TO HAVE SEEN JIMI HENDRIX WAY BACK
IN THE DAY, OR JAMES BROWN, OR THE BAD BRAINS — BACK
IN THEIR PRIMES OF SHAMANISTIC GLORY. EVEN ELVIS? O.K. SURE,
I MISSED ALL OF THAT. BUT, NOW I UNDERSTAND YOUR EXPERIENCE ~~THE~~ ~~■■■■■■~~ BEYOND
A SHADOW OF A DOUBT. THIS IS THE MAN. RIGHT HERE AND NOW.
DON'T EVEN DARE TAKE MY WORD FOR IT. GO TO THE SHOW AND
PREPARE YOURSELF TO BE UPLIFTED, DESTROYED AND REASSEMBLED
MANY TIMES OVER BY SOMETHING AS SIMPLE AS A MELODY, A LYRIC,
A RELENTLESS BEAT, A VOICE COMING FROM THE THROAT OF A
MAN WHO IS SO DEEP INSIDE THE MUSIC THAT HE DOES NOT
EXIST ANY LONGER. SOUND IMPOSSIBLE? ~~ASK YOUR BOY EDDIE~~
~~■■■■. ■■■■■ ■■■ THE MAN IS~~ EVERYONE KNOWS BY NOW.
NUSRAT FATEH ALI KHAN IS THE MAN.

RELENTLESS ~~ENDLESS JOY~~
ENDLESS JOY PEAKING INTO
TEARS, RESTING INTO CALMNESS,
A SIMMERING BEAUTY. IF YOU
LET YOURSELF LISTEN WITH THE
WHOLE OF YOURSELF, YOU WILL
HAVE THE PURE FEELING OF
FLIGHT WHILE FIRMLY ROOTED TO
THE GROUND ... YOUR SOUL CAN
FLY ~~soaring~~ OUTWARD STRINGED
TO YOUR RIBCAGE LIKE A SHIMMERING
KITE IN THE SHAPE OF AN OPEN
HAND. BE STILL AND LISTEN TO
THE EVIDENCE OF YOUR OWN HOLINESS.
QAWWALI IS THE FIRST MUSIC I'VE
ENCOUNTERED THAT OFFERS THIS DYNAMIC
WHOLLY AND UNASHAMEDLY TO THE LISTENER.
THE ~~record~~ ONLY OTHER MUSIC
WITH THIS SAME OFFERING? EVERYTHING
BEFORE AND AFTER I HAD HEARD
THE VOICE OF NUSRAT FATEH ALI KHAN.

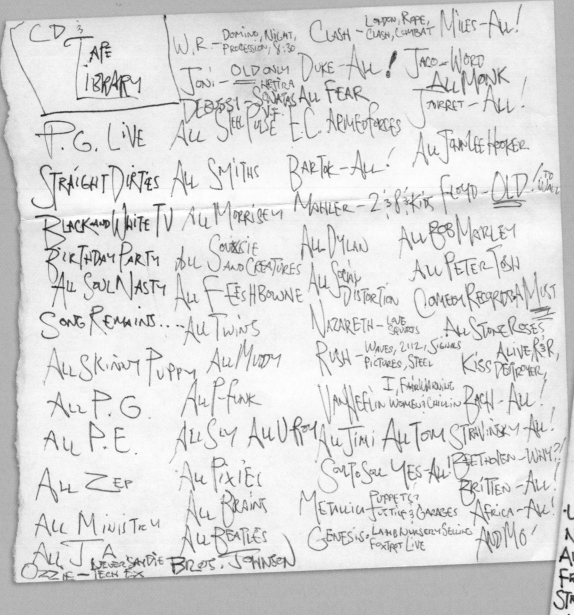
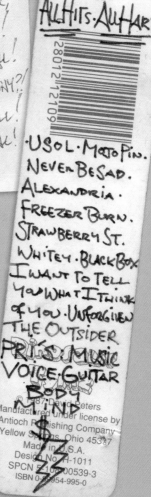

FACING PAGE: Jeff takes stock of his music library. Given the genres he had cycled through since high school, it's hardly surprising that this collection includes his teen favorites (Genesis, Kiss, Rush), the moody alternative rock he discovered later in the '80s (the Smiths, Siouxsie and the Banshees), the reggae he dove into in LA (Peter Tosh, Bob Marley), and classical music he had heard along the way (Gustav Mahler, Benjamin Britten). As seen on the back of the bookmark, the collection includes a demo tape of songs he had recorded by 1990. (This is not the famed *Babylon Dungeon Sessions* tape from that fall, as seen on page 223.) "Unforgiven" was the original title of "Last Goodbye." By this point, "Mojo Dream" had become "Mojo Pin."

PAGES 72–73: As with his record collection, Jeff's pile of cassette tapes attested to the way he devoured all styles of music. Tapes from the '80s sit alongside punk, country, indie rock, R&B, and classic rock. "I'll always be a slobbering idiot for people I love: the Grifters, Patti Smith, the new Ginsberg boxed set, MC5," he once said. "I listen to Sun Ra. Kiss. Led Zeppelin. Bad Brains. Shudder to Think. Tom Waits. Lou Reed."

JEFF BUCKLEY BIO

SINGER, GUITARIST, SONGMAKER; STYLE: VOCALIST -
POST MODERN. 25 YRS. OLD. ULTRA VIOLENT ROMANTIC

BEEN SINGING AND PLAYING SINCE CHILDHOOD.
HAS BEEN PLAYING AND SINGING IN PROFESSIONAL
SITUATIONS SINCE 1980.

No. CAL '80 FIRST ROCK N ROLL BAND: "AXIS"
So. CAL '81 SECOND R'N'ROLL BAND: "MAHRE BUCKHAM"
    MUCH LOCAL GIGGING AND BASIC PARTY-BAND
    TYPE ACTIVITY WITH THIS ONE. (IN ANAHEIM)
So. CAL '84 DID TIME AT A VOCATIONAL COLLEGE
IN L.A. — MUSICIANS INSTITUTE — FOR ONE YEAR.
'85 – '87
    GUITARIST FOR AN ELECTRIC-JAZZ OUTFIT "B#"
FOR PROFIT, MOSTLY.
    LOTS OF STUDIO WORK AS A HIRED GUN
    FOR VARIOUS DANCE-FUNK/BLACK-RADIO-DEMOS
THAT NEVER WENT ANYWHERE
'88 – REGGAE BAND "THE AKB" — THIS WAS A BACKUP
DID ROAD TRIPS WITH JUDY MOWATT (BAND OF BOB MARLEY I-THREES)
AND RASTA-RAPPER "SHINEHEAD"
PLAYED BOB MARLEY DAY AT LONG BEACH SPORTSAREM
? BACKED UP DANCE HALL LEGEND "DADDY U-ROY"
"AL CAMPBELL", "HAILE MASKEL" AND JUDY MOWATT.
'89 – JOINED ROCK OUTFIT NAMED "GROUP THERAPY"
SIMULTANEOUSLY W/ "AKB" MORE LOCAL GIGS IN L.A.
ALSO BEGAN LONG STRETCH OF PRODUCING, ARR.
AND PLAYING THE INSTRUMENTS ON OTHER PEOPLES
DEMOS AT A ████████ 16 TRACK IN N. HOLLYWOOD
'91 PLAYED AT ST. ANNE'S AT MY FATHER'S TRIBUTE.

FACING PAGE AND BELOW: By late 1990, Jeff had returned to Los Angeles, where he once again attempted to jump-start his music career, but New York would beckon anew. In April 1991, he was invited to participate in "Greetings from Tim Buckley," a tribute concert to his late father at St. Ann's Church in Brooklyn, organized by producer Hal Willner. There, he met Gary Lucas, as well as his future love, Rebecca Moore, and his performances at the concert made everyone at St. Ann's—and, quickly, the music scene in New York—take note. Jeff made return trips to New York during the summer and fall of 1991, in part to work up material with Lucas for Gods and Monsters. The group played a few clubs, and on March 13, 1992, Jeff found himself back at St. Ann's for Gods and Monsters' formal debut concert. Asked to write a bio of himself for the program, Jeff dashed off this two-page synopsis of his life to date. His reference to "a new project of mine sometime in '92" hints at his increasing dissatisfaction with Gods and Monsters and his longing for a career of his own. The program was never printed up, and Jeff's life overview is published here in its entirety for the first time.

ALSO COLLABORATING W/ GUITARIST GARY LUCAS
UNDER THE MONIKER "GODS & MONSTERS"
WILL BE PERFORMING AT ST. ANNE'S IN MARCH OF
'92.
    AND I'M NOW IN THE PROCESS OF RADICAL
DEVELOPMENT MUSICALLY WICH WILL CULMINATE
IN A NEW PROJECT OF MINE SOMETIME IN
'92.

THE END

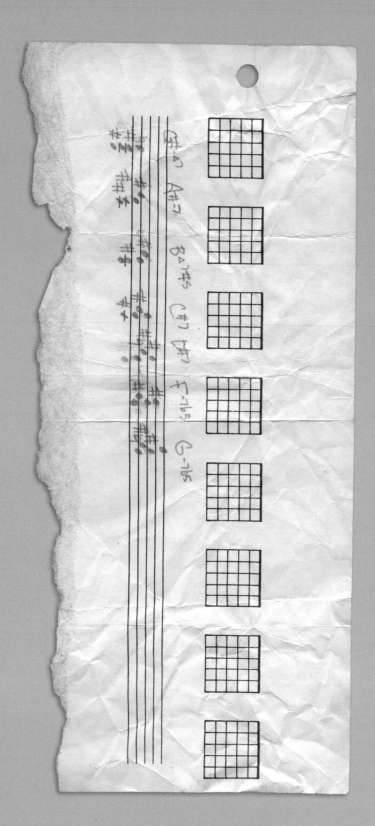
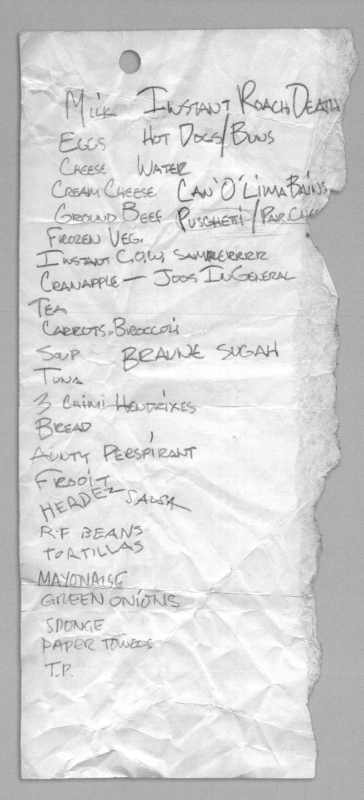

FACING PAGE: In an especially clever and creative note to his mother during his first trip to New York in 1990, Jeff fills her in on his new day job, folding clothes at a Banana Republic store near the Upper West Side apartment he was sharing with his platonic friend, actress Brooke Smith. Jeff's first Manhattan work experience would be brief and calamitous: falsely accused of shoplifting a blouse, he was forced to sign a form admitting to the crime and was fired forthwith.

DEAR **Mama**,

I HAVE BEEN SO 1. BUSY ✓___
                2. BORED ✓___
                3. DEPRESSED ✓___
I DECIDED TO SEND YOU THIS QUICK EASY FORM LETTER.

HOW ARE YOU? I AM 1. FINE___
                 2. EMPLOYED ✓___!
                 3. BUMMED OUT___
                 4. IN LOVE___
                 5. DEPRESSED___

LIFE IN NEW YORK IS 1. FANTASTIC___
                  2. DANGEROUS___
                  3. JUST WHAT I EXPECTED___
                  4. NOT WHAT I EXPECTED___
                  5. DEPRESSING ✓___

THE WEATHER HERE IS 1. COLD ✓___
                  2. HOT___
                  3. WET___
                  4. MUGGY___
                  5. DEPRESSING___

I WOULD LIKE YOU TO 1. SEND MONEY ✓___
                  2. WRITE ✓___
                  3. COME VISIT ✓___
                  4. GET LOST___!

(MISCELANEOUS NOTES)

BAGGED A JOB AT BANANA REPUBLIC 30-40 HRS/WK $6.50 AN HOUR, MUST FIND A WAITING JOB VERY SOON, BUT THIS WILL DO FOR THE MOMENT. HAVE TAKEN UP DRINKING TO DEEPEN MY VOICE, CAN'T STAND IT ANYMORE. EVERYONE HERE IS FALLING IN LOVE...SPRING...NOT ME, DUDE. DON'T FORGET MY POSTERS, MY KILLER ROCKIN POSTERS IN THE SEWING ROOM CLOSET WHEN YOU SEND MY STUFF CROSS-COUNTRY. LOVE YOU MADLY!

GOODBYE FOR NOW,

Jeffrey Scott

(SIGNATURE)

P.S. WE ARE THE MASTER AUTO RESCUE OUTFIT OF THE WORLD !!

HI-TECH EXPRESSIONS™

FACING PAGE: Beginning in the spring of 1992, Jeff began playing his first-ever solo performances at coffeehouses and small clubs in downtown New York, printing up flyers himself for gigs at Sin-é (the tiny Irish bar opened by immigrant Shane Doyle) and the SoHo space Skep. Jeff's performances gained must-see status in the city nearly overnight. The Jeff seen and heard was unlike any revealed before. Accompanied only by his white Fender Telecaster, which he'd borrowed from Janine Nichols at St. Ann's Church after his own guitar was stolen during a break-in at his Los Angeles apartment, he offered up sets that, in their earnestness and eclecticism, stood apart from the alternative-rock landscape of the time. No one else was covering songs by Dylan, Nina Simone, Elton John, and Bad Brains—and with an emotional investment that never remotely hinted at irony or sarcasm. By early summer, executives at major record labels had begun seeking him out.

Jeff Buckley

AT SKEP
527 BROOME ST. (6th AVE & THOMPSON ST.) AUG. 6th
9:00 PM $5.00

THE KNITTING FACTORY
47 E. HOUSTON AUG 13
CALL FOR DETAILS (212) 219-3055

AT SIN-E ~~~
122 ST. MARKS PL.
AUG. 2ND 10:30 & 7th,
14th, 20th & 27th @ 10 PM

Jeff Buckley

AT SIN-É
JUNE 1, JUNE 8 AND JUNE 20
(8:00)   (10:00)   (8:00)
....122 ST. MARK'S PLACE...

AT SKEP JUNE 13
..527 BROOME ST. (212) 219-2626...

AND IN JOHN ZORN'S COBRA
JUNE 5
AT THE ATRIUM .64 W. 11th ST...

7/7/92 THESE ARE THE FIRST WORDS I'VE EVER WRITTEN IN MY LIFE

LET ME FALL ASLEEP AT YOUR KNEES LIKE A CHILD
BREATHING IN THE FABRIC OF YOUR SIMPLE CITY DRESS
SOFT AND POOR SURRENDER ON MY DIRTY KITCHEN TILES
CAUSE I NEED TO FIND A WAY TO MAKE A JOKE OF ALL THE MESS
THAT I HAVE MADE
AND I NEED TO FIND A WAY TO KEEP YOU SAFE FROM ALL THE
TROUBLE
~~LOSES~~ I HAVE KNOWN
YOU ARE MY ONLY ~~ACTUAL~~ REASON
YOU ARE MY ONLY ~~ACTUAL~~ REASON FOR
YOU ARE MY ONLY REASON FOR THIS TRAIL I LAY TO
FIND ~~MY~~ WAY BACK HOME

LET ME RUN AWAY ACROSS THE EARTH AND BAT THE FIRES
I SET IN PEOPLES GARBAGE JUST TO HELP THEM SEE THE LIGHT
LET ME BREAK MY HANDS AGAINST THE FACES OF THE LIARS
WHO KNEW MY LIES AND STILL WOULD ~~TELL~~ WAKE ME ~~DOWN~~ UP TO FIGHT
AGAINST MY DREAMS
CAUSE I NEED TO FIND AN ANSWER TO THE TIES
I CAN'T UNTIE
AND I NEED TO FIND A WAY TO RIGHT THE ONES
~~ONES~~ I HAVE WRONGED
YOU ARE MY ONLY
YOU ARE MY ONLY REASON
YOU ARE MY ONLY REASON FOR THIS TRAIL I LAY TO
FIND ~~MY~~ WAY BACK HOME.

I'M SO FUCKING OLD I'M SO OLD AND TIRED. GOODNIGHT.

from The Pastel Paper Pad 7·27·92

"Come to See: Maria 10:10.pm
The Fortune Teller
113 7th Ave
Met up with a Fortune Teller On The Way Back from Dropping
Rebecca off at her Job
Was Walking Around the W. Village Looking
for Caffe Donatello ... I always Get Lost ... Walked up
7th Ave, Shouting To me from Her Wicker Chair Was a Fat Latina
in her late forties, Long Black Ponytail and a Red Sundress with
Floral Pattern. She sat in front of Her Neon-Signed Fortune
Telling Parlor ... Cracked Glass in The Front Door
She Told Me That Her Ankle
Had Been
Was Broken in an Accident at Her Church, She Showed Me Her
Big Leg ... Calloused Toes and Heel, A Horrible Scar Above
The Ankle, ..."Please Bring me a Bottle of Rubbing Alcohol and a
Roll of Paper Towels and I'll Tell you a Good Fortune

PAGES 80–81: Life in New York in 1992: new love, new sights, new sounds. Though Jeff complains of being "so old and tired" (at twenty-five), the summer of 1992 would be an enthralling time, as A&R executives at labels like RCA and Columbia met with Jeff and attended his shows. On August 6, a week and a half after this second entry, the first draft of Jeff's contract with Columbia Records was drawn up. Page 80 also contains the seeds of "So Real" ("your simple city dress"), which wouldn't spring into existence for another year.

PAGES 83–86: Almost as soon as record company denizens began making their pilgrimages to Sin-é, Jeff was instantly on his guard, worried he would be swallowed up in the corporate music cocoon. He eventually chose Columbia, owned by Sony Music, for both its team (including A&R executive Steve Berkowitz, whose knowledge of music history was formidable) and its fabled heritage (Bob Dylan, Bruce Springsteen, Billie Holiday, and many more). Nonetheless, Jeff was wary and, unlike many other musicians, wanted to know precisely what he was getting into, so he pored over the contract and offered up these questions to his lawyer and future comanager, George Stein. As seen on the following pages, Jeff clearly had many questions about his and Sony's obligations, artistic control, and financial responsibilities. As he notes in the section about cost overruns, "What protects me?" The final contract was signed on October 29, 1992.

Proposal (Subject to Contract)

Against my royalties

Cross Collateralized — when it comes down to recipient. They fill in debts from all possible album

Period 1 (3 Firm):

ALBUM 1: $100,000 Advance to artist.
Mutually approved album budget.

ALBUM 2: $50,000 Advance to artist;
Mutually approved album budget. *25,000 at beginning*
25,000 at end

ALBUM 3:   Recording fund: *25,000*
Minimum $250,000/Maximum $500,000 *25,000*
Balance after recording cost goes to artist. ✳

TOUR SUPPORT: $100,000 over 2 albums for tour shortfall
based on approval itinerary, fully recoupable.

Period 2 (Our Option):

ALBUM 4:   Recording fund:
Min: $300,000/Max: $600,000 ✳

Period 3 (Our Option) (for 2 Firm):

ALBUM 5:   Recording fund:
Min: $350,000/Max $700,000 ✳

ALBUM 6:   Recording fund:
Min: $350,000/Max $700,000 ✳

Period 4 (Our Option):

ALBUM 7:   Recording fund:
Min: $400,000/Max: $800,000 ✳

Vito Nixon

P8 6. First $100,000 - FEE OR ADVANCE?   Is ADVANCE RECOUPABLE
                                          BY SONY FROM SALES

6.02 ADVANCE OF $100,000 - 1ST

50,000 - 2ND   WHY DOES IT GO DOWN?

ONCE THE BUDGET IS FIXED ON 1ST ALBUM, DO I GET
BALANCE AFTER RECORDING COSTS? NO

P11 6.02 ∂ $50,000 ADVANCE IS REDUCED FOR ___ ...?   PROTECTS
                                                      US FROM BEING RAPE
                                                      INDEPENDANT
                                                      FEE CONTRACTOR

HEALTH INSURANCE? NO   NOT EMPLOYEE

                    AS LONG AS IT DOESN'T BREAK 100,000 1/2 OF IT IS RECOUPABLE
P17 8 A WHY SHOULD SONY HAVE TOTAL CREATIVE CONTROL WE PAY 1/2 MUTUAL DOESN'T
                                                                   WORK
ON VIDEOS FOR ALL 7 ALBUMS? SO THERE IS NO IMPASS

AT LEAST MUTUAL   WILL CONSULT! WILL RENEGOTIATE
                                 OTHERWISE NO VIDEO

MAYBE BREAK IT UP — ONLY AGREE FOR FIRST 2 ALBUMS
(MUTUAL) THEN RENEGOTIATE FOR VIDEO
· DO THESE ROYALTIES ONLY APPLY TO ALBUMS? WHAT RE: CD's? TAPES? DATS?

P 19 HOW IS IT TO MY ADVANTAGE TO SEE ROYALTIES FOR OPTIONAL ALBUMS NOW?
IS IT?

                                   PROMOTIONAL DEVICES
P 23 WHY DOES ROYALTY DROP FOR SINGLES? ESPECIALLY JAPAN ∓ GERMANY U.K.
                                        SMALLEST DROPS POSSIBLE
                                                                  STANDARD
P 24 INQUIRE ABOUT CLUB OPERATIONS — WHO DETERMINES RE: PARTICIPATION

P. 25 RE: ISSUE 1/2 ROYALTY RATE - WHY IS THAT DECIDED NOW? STANDARD

P. 26 9.04: B IN "6" AUDIOPHILE RECORDS — TALKS RE: CDS AT 80% ROYALTY RATE
DOES THAT APPLY TO ALL CDS? SO ALL YOUR ROYALTIES MENTIONED ABOVE
ALL JUST FOR ALBUMS NOT CD'S OR CASSETTES? STANDARD SCREW
                                           RENEGOTIABLE

∓: THIS ALL STANDARD 84? HOW NEGOTIATED?

P.26 COVERED VIDEOS WHY DOES IT STAY THE SAME FOR ALL? VIDEOS DON'T SELL

9:06

NET RECEIPTS / GROSS RECEIPTS

P.28 PLEASE EXPLAIN THE MEANING OF ROYALTIES FOR VIDEO
9:06

P.30 DITTO

P.31 ROYALTY RESERVE? HAVE RIGHT TO HOLD 35% OF ROYALTIES UNTIL SALES ARE SEEN

P.32 11:02 FOREIGN SALES - ROYALTIES. ASK SISTER RAY
WHAT RE EXCHANGE RATES

P.37 12 LICENSING FOREVER? YES STANDARD
MECHANICAL ROYALTIES?

P.44 13:07 A) INDEMNIFICATION OF SONY
PLEASE EXPLAIN

P.49 B) ADVANCE — ON VIDEOS. WHAT'S THE DEAL FOR EACH?
DOES THIS SAY THEY CAN'T RECOUP ON VIDEO ADVANCE
FROM RECORD SALES? YES

PUBLICITY? PROMOTION? — WHAT WILL THEY DO — WHO DETERMINES
← PUBLICIST   SEE 9:09   POSITIONING? IMAGE?
↓ DISTRIBUTION

DO I HAVE ANY RIGHT TO OWN PUBLICIST? WHO PAYS?
IF SONY - IS IT AN ADVANCE? I PAY FOR IT

ITEM

~~(scribbled out)~~

2.02.B1 SONY ENGAGES PROD.
IS THIS TO PROTECT SONY FROM COST OVERRUNS?
WHAT PROTECTS ME? CAN THE COST BE SET IN ADVANCE?

(GEORGES FEE FUTURE? IS HE ON RETAINER? HOURLY RATE?)

3.02.A1   12 MONTHS? HOW FIRM?

4.01.04 SONY HAS LINE ITEM APPROVAL OR/VETO OF BUDGET. STANDARD?
EVERY ITEM IN BUDGET THEY DECIDE. MAYBE GOOD FOR #1 OR 2 ALBUMS
BECAUSE OF MY INEXPERIENCE BUT NOT 3 AND OPTIONS

#25,000 IS THAT ENOUGH FOR PRE-PRODUCTION?

4.01.4.D   ANYBODY? EVERYBODY? FOR ALL TIME?

5.02.A   IS THAT A PUBLICIST WHO HIRES WHO PAYS

ADVANCE – NON REFUNDABLE
YET RECOUPABLE AGAINST ROYALTIES

GEORGE
   ON PERCENTAGE

RECORDS
15%
DEAL

TOURING
20% MGT. INTENSIVE
DEAL

PAGES 88–89: The business of Jeff Buckley is enough to fill several file drawers, as seen in this collection of work memorabilia in his archives. From left to right: the cover letter for his Columbia contract, the itinerary for his early 1994 tour to promote *Live at Sin-é,* and the official list of stage pseudonyms he used on his solo tour in late 1996.

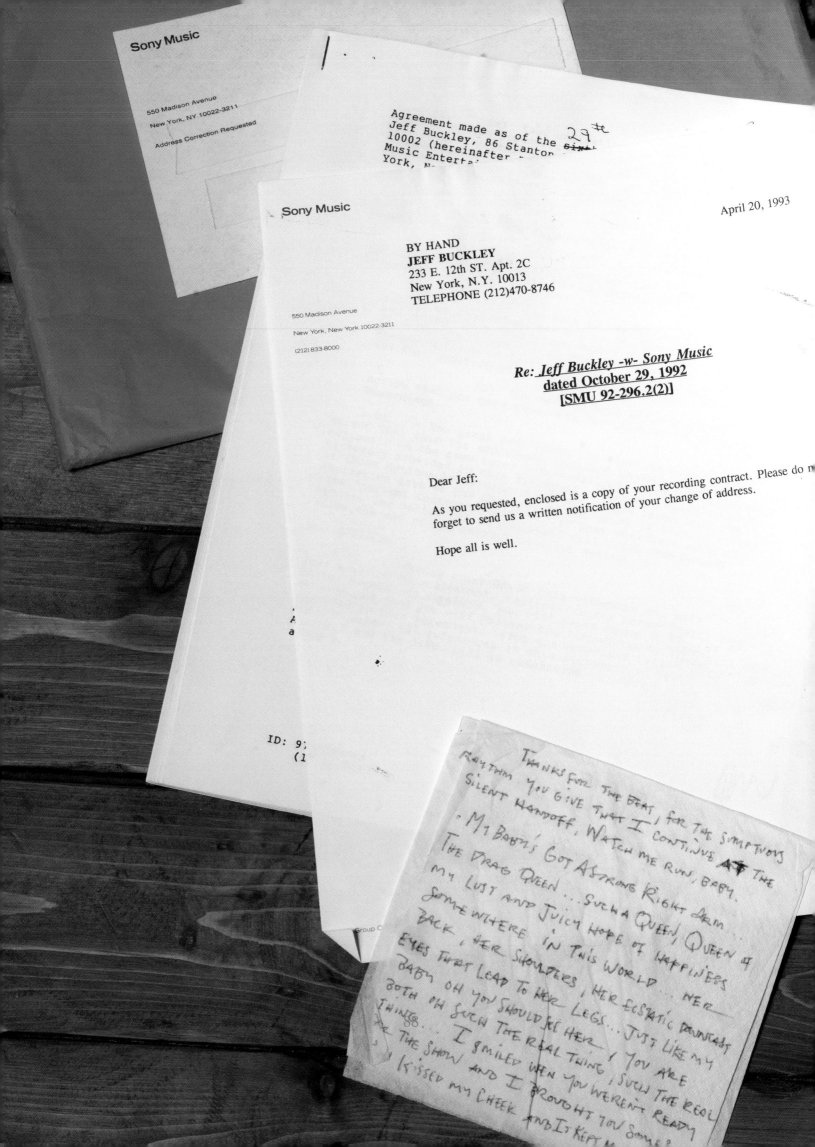

Sony Music

550 Madison Avenue
New York, NY 10022-3211

Address Correction Requested

Agreement made as of the 29th
Jeff Buckley, 86 Stanton
10002 (hereinafter
Music Enterta
York, N

Sony Music

550 Madison Avenue
New York, New York 10022-3211

(212) 833-8000

April 20, 1993

BY HAND
JEFF BUCKLEY
233 E. 12th ST. Apt. 2C
New York, N.Y. 10013
TELEPHONE (212)470-8746

Re: <u>Jeff Buckley -w- Sony Music
dated October 29, 1992
[SMU 92-296.2(2)]</u>

Dear Jeff:

As you requested, enclosed is a copy of your recording contract. Please do n
forget to send us a written notification of your change of address.

Hope all is well.

ID: 9:
(1

Group C

THANKS FOR THE BEAT, FOR THE SIMPTWONS
RHYTHM YOU GIVE THAT I CONTINUE AT THE
SILENT HANDOFF, WATCH ME RUN, BABY.
MY BABY'S GOT A STRONG RIGHT ARM...
THE DRAG QUEEN ... SUCH A QUEEN, QUEEN OF
MY LUST AND JUICY HOPE OF HAPPINESS
SOMEWHERE IN THIS WORLD ... HER
BACK, HER SHOULDERS, HER ECSTATIC DOWNCAST
EYES THAT LEAD TO HER LEGS ... JUST LIKE MY
BABY OH YOU SHOULD SEE HER , YOU ARE
BOTH OH SUCH THE REAL THING , SUCH THE REAL
THING ... I SMILED WHEN YOU WEREN'T READY
FOR THE SHOW AND I BROUGHT YOU SOME
I KISSED MY CHEEK AND I KEPT

WE'RE NO ALTERNATIVE... BUT... ROCK. FUCKING... IS... TO...

THE AMERICAN FALL TOUR
NOVEMBER 1994

JEFF BUCKLEY ITINERARY
JANUARY 1994

DAY:	DATE:	CITY:	VENUE:
FRI	JAN 14	VANCOUVER	TRAVEL DAY
1. SAT	JAN 15	VANCOUVER	RAILWAY CL
2. SUN	JAN 16	SEATTLE	PARADISIO
3. MON	JAN 17	SEATTLE	VELVET E
4. TUE	JAN 18	PORTLAND	LA LUNA
WED	JAN 19	REDDING	– TRAV
5. THU	JAN 20	SAN FRANCISCO	PARAD
6. FRI	JAN 21	SAN FRANCISCO	HOT
7. SAT	JAN 22	BERKELEY	ST
SUN	JAN 23	LOS ANGELES	–
8. MON	JAN 24	LOS ANGELES	
9. TUE	JAN 25	LOS ANGELES	
10. WED	JAN 26	LOS ANGELES	
THU	JAN 27	LOS ANGELES	
11. FRI	JAN 28	LA JOLLA	
SAT	JAN 29	TBA	
12. SUN	JAN 30		
13. MON	JAN 3		

ON THE ROAD......
IN A CAR, WITH A GUITAR(S
COUPLE OF PEOPLE.

(DECEMBER 6-16, 1996)
Presenting:

The Crackrobats
Possessed by Elves
Father Demo
Smackrobiotic
The Halfspeeds
Crit-Club
Topless America
Martha & The Nicotines
A Puppet Show Named Julio

I KNOW THAT IF I WAS AROUND SOMEONE WHO WAS REAL AND VERY PHYSICAL AND RECOGNIZED ABOUT, I WOULD PROBABLY VERGE ON ENVY AND I'D BE TOO REPRESSED FOR FEAR OF FUCKING UP IN FRONT OF THIS "SERIOUS" PERSON – INTIMIDATED. DON'T BE. BE SERIOUSLY INVOLVED WITH GROWING, WITH YOUR OWN DEVELOPMENT, AND NEVER FEAR. BE THE KIND OF PERSON WHO IS NATURALLY POWERFUL, POSITIVE, INGENIOUS, OPEN, TO THE HIGHEST DEGREE, BUT WITH NO INTEREST IN COERSION OR PRESSURE OR POWER OVER OTHER PEOPLE. THAT KIND OF POWER IS HOLLOW. IT CONTAINS NOTHING AND BRINGS YOU NOTHING IN THE LONG RUN. BE THE BEST. NO NEGATIVITY, NO WEAKNESS, NO ACQUIESENCE TO FEAR OR DISASTER.

Grandma,   11/27/92

                    HERE IS THE REST OF THE MONEY I OWE YOU.
I LOVE YOU I LOVE YOU I LOVE YOU I LOVE YOU I
LOVE YOU I LOVE YOU I LOVE YOU I LOVE YOU I LOVE
YOU I LOVE YOU I LOVE YOU I LOVE YOU I LOVE
YOU I LOVE YOU I LOVE YOU I LOVE YOU I LOVE YOU I
I LOVE YOU I LOVE YOU I LOVE YOU I LOVE YOU I LOVE
YOU GRANDMA I LOVE YOU! THANK YOU SO VERY MUCH...
I ONLY THANK THE ANGELS THAT I COULD EVER SEND THIS CHECK
OVER TO YOU. AND NOW I'M GLAD THAT IT CAN HELP YOU OUT JUST
IN TIME.... HEY! JUST IN TIME TO SPEND IT ALL! WHOOPEE.
                                             IT WAS SO
COOL FOR GEORGIE TO DROP IN TO TOWN — JUST AS I HAD
SIGNED WITH COLUMBIA, JUST AS MY STEP-STEPSISTER ANNIE AND
HER BOYFRIEND Käj (KAI) HAD DROPPED IN EN ROUTE TO SWEDEN,
NOT TO MENTION THE TONS OF THINGS I WAS DOING ALL AT ONCE
(REBECCA'S PLAY, MY OWN SHOWS) A TREMENDOUS AMOUNT OF WORK, I CAN TELL
YOU — EVEN IF IT WAS FOR A FEW HOURS AT AN IRISH PUB IN THE
EAST VILLAGE IT WAS STILL FANTASTIC TO SEE HIM AGAIN. I MEAN,
YOU KNOW, HE COMES IN THE ROOM AND SOME PART OF ME STILL
FEELS LIKE A LITTLE BOY WHO'S CALLED "BUTCH".
                                      HE SENT ME A BEAUTIFUL
PICTURE OF DYLAN IN A COWBOY SUIT. I SAID TO MYSELF "OH, MAN,
HERE WE GO AGAIN!" THE GUIBERTS SPARE NOTHING IN LAVISHING
THEIR CHILDREN IN TOTAL ADORATION AND CUTENESS. BUT
WHAT I MEAN TO SAY IS THAT WE HAVE A STYLE, A CERTAIN
STYLE ABOUT IT THAT LAYS ALL OTHER FAMILIES TO SHAME, COMPLETELY.
MAVENS OF CHILD-LOVE. I MEAN, I CAN WALK THE STREETS OF
NEW YORK, OR EVEN PARIS OR ICELAND OR CUBA AND I'LL
NEVER BE ABLE TO FORGET THAT MY FAMILY LOVES ME AND I LOVE THEM.
EVEN IF PEGGY DID DRESS ME LIKE A GIRL, I'LL ALWAYS LOVE HER.
          AND I LOVE YOU TOO, GRANDMA.!!!! OOOXXX
     TAKE CARE OF YOURSELF!! MERRY CHRISTMAS
                          LOVE, Scott

FACING PAGE: Flush with cash from his Sony advance, Jeff immediately repaid his grandmother, Anna Guibert, money he'd borrowed from her. His love and respect for the Guibert side of his family emerges in his appreciative comments about them, including "Georgie," Mary's brother George.

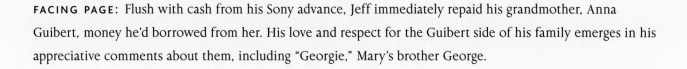

PAGE 92: In the months after Jeff signed with Sony, the company left him more or less alone, realizing he had to firm up his sonic direction and repertoire. Jeff used the time to throw himself into the experimental downtown theater and art world. But decisions about band members, material, and producers had to be made, and early into 1993, he was already feeling the pressure of living up to the expectations the industry was placing on him. In this entry, he touches on that pressure—but is thankfully sidetracked by a flu and the random selection of TV shows he forces himself to watch in his and Rebecca Moore's downtown apartment.

Jan 30 1993

On the fiery verge of responsibility, "Better get goin' boy!"
On the edge of obligation in song and sacred savage
And I caught the flu on ~~Saturday~~ Friday.
Lay languid watching my nothing flow out of me on Saturday
Feeling abandoned and less confident having pushed the
plastic off button on the TV remote control.
I watched nothing but Death today.
Death of innocents, Satanist prey and farm animals
I always always knew the Hippie heart-cult
was the toy of the Vampyre Nosferatu Nosfera-to everything, turn, turn,
turn...
Now they walk up to me and suck the sickly past from
the wounded neck of now with their childish mellow
Just a punk inside I know "Say boy can you sing?"
"No... 'cause I been in jail too long, Daddy Daddy-O."
I snap my fingers and the mouth of Hell itself opens wide
in front of the Hippie-casualty and he sees his own hand
on the flame-thrower gushing furie over Vietnam huts.

Jan 31
I don't want a woman, any longer, to have
to point out my hypocrisy for me.
I want desperately to be my own janitor.

THERE IS SKY ENOUGH FOR BOTH OF US WHEN WE FLY
AND IF THIS WORLD WILL SHUT US OUT ~~THEN~~ WE CAN SHUT
THE WORLD OUT TOO

7-8-93
I CAN SEE BY THE WAY YOUR GIRLFRIEND LOOKS AT
ME
THAT SHE THINKS I'M A FOOL AND A BORE
AND THAT I'M A BAD INFLUENCE ON YOUR GENTLE LIFE
BUT I'M OUT FOR SOMETHING MORE
I'VE GOT A FRIEND DOWNTOWN ON THE BOWERY
WHO KNOWS WHERE THE TRUTH IS BOUGHT AND SOLD
~~I HEARD THE NEEDLES~~
~~THE NEEDLES SAY THEY'LL MAKE ME INTO BARS OF PUREST GOLD~~
I HEARD THE NEEDLES SAY THEY'D SPIN MY NIGHTMARES INTO GOLD

YOU WERE SO DISTANT WHEN I SAW YOU LAST
LIKE A WEEPING CHINA DOLL IN A LONELY ~~FRAGRANT~~ SILKEN SLIP
NEW YORK SUMMER BLOWING HOT ON YOUR SKIN
LIKE A WEEPING CHINA DOLL IN YOUR FAVORITE SILKEN SLIP
YOU PLEAD IN A LANGUAGE ONLY I CAN UNDERSTAND
YOU WISH FOR FREEDOM FROM UNFRIENDLY WORDS
FAKING THEIR WAY INTO THE HOME OF YOUR HEART
DISGUISED AS PURE HEARTED STRANGERS, HUNGRY FOR
BREAD AND A LONG NIGHT IN LOVE WITH YOU.
AS I HOLD YOU YOU HARDLY HANG ON.

FACING PAGE: One of several nonmusic projects Jeff threw himself into during the first half of 1993 was the title role in a downtown production of Georg Büchner's nineteenth-century play *Woyzeck*, about a military barber who, in a fit of rage and jealousy, stabs his wife to death. "I decided to confront the role, confront the fear, slip into another voice and pretend to be a symbol made of real bones and flesh," he wrote to a friend at the time.

WOYZECK
by Georg Buchner

CAST (in order of appearance)

Andres	Chris Gordon
Woyzeck	Jeff Buckley
Marie	Christina Fallon
Margaret	Alicia Nashel
Drum-Major	Paul Scott
Showman	Kendra Barber
Sergeant/ 2nd Journeyman	Lloyd Wallisch
The Captain	Steve Landau
The Doctor	Algernon D'Ammassa
1st Journeyman/ The Knife Seller	Eli Bishop
Grandmother	Katie Fallon

Directed by
Linell A

Assistants
Devra Z

Master El
Adrienn

MANY T
Alan Ha
Colaiace
Norman

SPECIA
Josh Be

PAGES 97–98: Feeling he needed his own living and work space, Jeff moved out of the apartment he was sharing with Moore and into a place of his own in the East Village in the spring of 1993. Although he would feel guilty over leaving Rebecca, he was nonetheless captivated by the idea of a separate enclave, as these jottings in one of his smaller notebooks plainly reveal. The elation he feels over his "few-ture," as he calls it, is palpable. He refers to the album he is about to start making, as well as a hectic schedule of "albums, performance, live video treatments, everything." Especially striking is his stated plan to release two albums and an EP by the end of the year—wishful thinking for any musician but indicative of the creative rush Jeff was experiencing as his career as a major-label artist was beginning.

Mead

MEMO

BORN #N2XT6 420·8746
2q 8/31
233 E. 12th St. #2C
NY, NY 10003
TURN ON PHONE, SPRINT, ETC.
MOVE IN SATURDAY - IN TOTAL
FUNCTION #1 — MUSIC WORK PARADISE
#2 SEX TIME LANCHOLY MYSTIC O MECCA
OF SOUL POWER CREATION REFUGE OF LOVE
THE KEY TO 26?
WORK HARDER THAN 100 MICHAEL JACKSONS
RELEASE, PRODUCE, MAGICATE 2 CDS:
AND ONE BEAUTIFUL TOUR♥ TO BURY
YOUR HEART DEEP DOWN TO THE BOTTOM
OF LOVE AND PAIN AND UGLINESS AND BEAUTY
AND LIVE IN THE DEEPEST DREAM STATE POSSIBLE
BALANCED WITH LOVING DISCIPLINE OF DOOM

SINCE I EXPERIENCE
SELF-ESTEEM AS A
SEPERATE OR RATHER
COMPLETE INTEGRAL BEING
APART FROM MYSELF
AS WELL AS INSIDE
MYSELF — SELF ESTEEM
AS A GOD OR
GODDESS WITH
WHOM YOU HAVE
AN ONGOING
RELATIONSHIP

THE UPSTAIRS IS MY LIVING ROOM
MY KITCHEN, MY SEX ROOM, MY
THINKING ROOM.
THE DOWNSTAIRS
IS WHERE I DO MY LOVE
HOUR UPON HOUR WHERE I
CELEBRATE MY MUSIC MY WORK
THE UNDERWORLD.
5/7 THINKING ABOUT THE
MUSIC... THINKING OF BUTTERFLY
DANCING IN HER BEAUTIFUL BLACK
DRESS, HER LOUISE BROOKS HAIR-DO
SHINING LIKE THE TAIL OF A MAGIC
FOAL, SMOOTH BLACK LIQUID;

AT BEING A FULL FLEDGED WRITER AND POET IN MY VERY OWN RIGHT. 24 HOURS A DAY IN A GUTTERAL OUTPUT OF LOVE. WORK! I AM SO EMBARRASSED TO BE IN THE PRESENCE OF ALL OF THESE GREAT AMAZING GENIUS ARTISTS WITH NOTHING TO GIVE. SOMEDAY SOON I'LL BE SOMEONE WHO IS KNOWN NOT ONLY AS A GUY WHO SINGS, BUT ALSO THE LAST WORD IN POETRY, SURREAL HIPDREAM ABANDON, INNOVATOR SUPREME, ARTIST

AND THE HARDEST OF THE CORE. JUST LIKE DOUGHTY. BUT ONLY LIKE ME. IN ONE MONTH I'LL MAKE THE ALBUM'S MUSIC, IN MAY I'LL DEMO IT, AFTER IT'S RECORDED I'LL ASK SABBY TO LISTEN AND MAYBE HE'D LIKE TO HELP ME MAKE AN ALBUM. NO ONE WILL GET TO SEE ME MUCH SOCIALLY FOR THE NEXT 50 YEARS BECAUSE I'LL BE WORKING SO SO, SO SLAVISHLY HARD AND INDESTRUCTABLY DEEP... ER THAN THE OCEAN. LOVE!

ALSO... BESIDES WORKING LIKE A MADWOMAN FROM DAYBREAK TO THE WEE HOURS OF THE MORNING MAKING MATERIAL FOR THE FUTURE AND PRESENT TIME. HARD LABOR AND FREE CREATION OF SONGS, MUSIC, FORMS, ALBUMS, PERFORMANCE, LIVE VIDEO TREATMENTS, EVERYTHING... BUT FOR NOW ONLY FOCUSED ON ALBUM SONGS OVERFLOW W/... OVERLOVE OVERFAITH. OVERFLOW OVERWHELMED W/ THE FEW-TURE. SABBY & THE ONLY DRUMMER IN THE WIRL, W/ SUEDE IN '93.

AND THIS MONTH THE CIRCLE OF THE B-VOX IS BROKED AND SHATTERED AND GROUND INTO POWDER AND SNORTED LIKE A GRAM OF CHEAP BLO NEVER TO EXIST AGAIN I WILL DESTROY THE OTHER ONE. FOREVER! ALBUM? 2 THIS YEAR WITH ONE EP ON XMAS AND 1 MORE BEFORE JANUARY IS DEAD. AND IT SHALL BE _____

JULY 15 '93

Only the fucking
people who make this fucking business run my fucking
insect life, my beauty, my soul, my love for life and song
and all of humankind. Only those people behind the desks
with their budgets and their bullwhips make these questions
possible. Am I an oracle or a vegetable? Which one
can you sell more of and move faster? Which one takes
the most commands? Which one can you hack into easy
to eat, bite-size slivers that lack the sharp sweet
richness of flavor that you taste from the whole of
its body? Which one can you leave out to rot in the
wretched heat of the sun, 'til the flies shit their
maggots in to have their fun? Which one can you
forget without guilt when all is said and done?
Which one am I? Which one? Which one? Witch won?
Witch-one! Singer: Zero! What will my beautiful
Rebecca, ~~the~~ intoxicated with her compassion and her
wild unseeable flame, have to endure in this big
bossman's plantation? If they touch her, I will kill
them all. Poor little lonesome, how much more
can you take?

PREVIOUS PAGE: Like a gradually accelerating locomotive, plans to introduce Jeff to the world were in motion by the summer of 1993, and he was already feeling the stress. Those fears and concerns—for himself, his music, even Moore—spill out in this particularly apprehensive notebook entry. Despite the support he was receiving from the Columbia team, he remains riddled with doubt about whether he has made the correct decision in signing with the company. Four days later, he would walk into Sin-é for the recording of his first EP.

FACING PAGE: Ever eager to make to-do lists of his schedules, Jeff dashed off this revealing rundown in August 1993. To preserve an early, crucial part of his musical development on tape, Columbia decided to record him live at Sin-é on July 19 and August 17, and by the end of that month, he had recruited a rhythm section comprising two budding local musicians, bassist Mick Grondahl and drummer (and Texas transplant) Matt Johnson. As this entry shows, those events were merely the beginning of a productive summer and fall. While still performing at Sin-é and nearby venues like Fez (a club beneath a restaurant in the Village, run by Ellen Cavolina Porter), Jeff also made time for whittling down the Sin-é recordings to an EP (released in November as *Live at Sin-é*) before he drove up to Bearsville Studios in Woodstock to start his first studio album. Intriguingly, this timetable indicates that that album, *Grace*, would be released far sooner than it was. Although basic tracks would be completed at Bearsville with producer Andy Wallace, work on the album would eventually stretch into the early months of 1994, and *Grace* would not arrive until August 23, 1994.

BUCK LIFE

1. Sun. 8/22 PHILLY
2. WED. 8/25 SINÉ 10PM
3. THURS 8/26 CUCARACHA THEATRE 8:45PM
4. FRI. 8/27 SINÉ 10PM

5. MON - TUES. 8/30 - 8/31 MIXING LIVE EP

6. 9/1 WFMU LIVE RADIO SHOW 8:00PM
   WED.

7. SATURDAY 9/4 FEZ AT 10:30 OR 11:00PM

8. MON. 9/6 - WED. 9/15 TOUR

9. MON 9/20 - PREPRODUCTION FOR ALBUM

10. MON. 9/27 UP TO BEARSVILLE TO RECORD
    FOR 5 WEEKS

11. JAN. 94 ALBUM RELEASED

12 REAL WORK THEN BEGINS.

PAGES 102–103: Jeff's obsession with blues singer and slide guitarist Son House led him to purchase this prized National dobro, which he dubbed "God." As a joke to himself, he reversed the name on its case. Jeff can be heard playing the instrument on "Parchman Farm Blues," a warm-up outtake from the *Grace* sessions included on the legacy edition of that album, and "Poor Boy Long Way from Home" from the *You and I* collection.

FACING PAGE: Jeff had long sought to disassociate himself from Tim Buckley, but he remained unnerved by his father's limited presence in his life and by the troubling idea that record companies and music fans alike would only be interested in him for his bloodline. Those concerns spill out in this unsent letter to Larry Beckett, Tim's high school friend and longtime lyricist. Starting with Jeff's first trip to New York in 1990, Jeff and Beckett would exchange numerous letters over the years, and Beckett was never less than supportive and understanding of Jeff's struggles. Some of Jeff's fears, unfortunately, would manifest themselves in concerts where Tim Buckley fans would yell out the names of his songs.

THE REVOLUTION TO END ALL REVOLUTIONS, FOR ALL TIME, FOREVER, IT ISN'T AS FAR A JOURNEY AND AS BLOODY A BATTLE AS THE WORLD THINKS IT IS. IT'LL BEGIN AND END WITH A KISS. EVERYTHING IN THE MIDDLE IS ARMAGEDDON. HITLER, IN COMPARISON, WILL SEEM AS A FLEA BETWEEN THUMBNAILS. AFTER THAT, THEN WE CAN REALLY GET DOWN TO FUCKING BUSINESS, BABY.

THIS IS NO LONGER A LETTER TO YOU, LARRY. I'M WRITING TO SOMEONE WHO DOESN'T EXIST. I'M WRITING TO SOMEONE WHO UNDERSTANDS ME. YOU ARE SOMEONE WHO UNDERSTOOD MY FATHER. YOU MAY HAVE UNDERSTOOD HIM BUT HE STILL DIED LIKE A POISONED DOG WHO DIDN'T KNOW ANY BETTER, BUT KNEW HE SHOULDN'T O' BEEN SNIFFIN WHERE HE WAS A-SNIFFIN. YOU'RE NOT MY FRIEND... YOU'RE A GHOST. THEY WILL ACCUSE ME OF STEALING FROM MY FATHER. THEY ALREADY STAND IN BAITED JUDGEMENT, WAITING FOR MY FIRST MOVE, WAITING TO DUMP THEIR LOADS OF GARBAGE UPON ME. I FACE THEM LIKE THE MAN HE NEVER WAS AND SAY "THE ONLY THING I EVER STOLE FROM MY FATHER WAS A FLEETING GLIMPSE!!" THE ONLY

TIME TO TURN OFF THE FOOL
IN THE PRESENCE OF THE SMILE.
THE JUICES ... I WANT THEM
FLOWING AS WE SPEAK, I
WANT THEIR EYES TO BE CHARGE
-D WITH THE PROMISE, THE FANTASY
OF MY WHITE-HOT SEXY SIDE ...
I WANT TO LEAD THEM TO MY
WEB WITH EVERY WORD I
UTTER. NOT ACCESSABLE.
PREGNANT WITH MYSTERY SO
INTENSE, THE KIND THEY LIKE
TO TRY TO BREAK DOWN. I'LL
BE ALONE, A LONER, ALL ONE.
UNTOUCHABLE, YET VISITABLE,
UN DESPERATE.   WOUNDED.
SILENT ...   STRONG, FULL
OF LONGING AND POETRY AND HELP

FOR FRIENDS IN NEED OF A GOOD.
HEART ... BUT NOT ABLE TO BE
WATERED-DOWN, OR INTIMIDATED
BY ANYTHING.
          MY WORK IS
ALL ... AND THEY ALL WILL
BE CLAWING DOWN MY DOOR
TO TASTE MY FLESH AND LEARN.
TIME AFTER TIME AFTER TIME
AFTER. UNSENTIMENTAL. REAL.
NEW WOMAN, SENSUALLY ENDLESS,
FLUENT IN NEGOTIATING THE SHIFTS
AND NOT AFRAID TO ASK ADVICE
AND NOT EVER AFRAID TO GIVE
HEARTED HELP. AND MY SIN.

NO, NO, NO, NO, NO, N

PAGES 108–113: Particularly at this early stage of his recording career, songwriting did not come easily to Jeff. Perhaps his years as a teenage prog-rock guitar player were to blame, since that genre emphasizes musical dexterity and over-the-hills-and-far-away instrumental passages over conventional verse-chorus formats. Whatever the reason, Jeff would often grapple with lyrics, melodies, and traditional song structure. Few better examples of this struggle exist than the following six pages, which document the evolution of "Lover, You Should've Come Over," one of his original songs from *Grace*. On page 109 we see an early draft of its lyrics with almost entirely different words ("smell the rain," one of the few lines that would survive, would become "see the rain"). On the next several pages, a more organized structure, with further refined lyrics, begins tumbling into place, followed by chord changes and additional lyrics (worked out at Veselka, a coffee shop a few streets away from his apartment) and his own explanation of what he was trying to achieve. The song would continue to be refined in the studio, incorporating a harmonium introduction recorded in New York City months after the Bearsville sessions.

You Should've Come Over

Looking out the door I see the rain descend
Upon a crowd of mourners
Parading in a wake of sad relations as their
shoes fill up with water

NO, NO, NO, NO, NO, NO, NO

OH MAMA MIA MAMA MIA
MAMA MIA LET ME GO
BEELZEBUB HAS THE DEVIL PUT ASIDE
FOR ME, FOR ME, FOR MEEEEEEEEE!!
AH...
How many days til September 6th? None.
It is August 13th ... Friday
Tuesday the 17th ... Record at Siné
Wed. Through Sun. 18th - 21st

(YOU SHOULD HAVE COME OVER)

* OH LOVER YOU SHOULD HAVE COME OVER
WHILE THERE WAS ~~HUNGER~~ HUNGER IN YOU
AND NO WAY TO FEED IT
I WROTE MY HEART AND SENT IT OFF BUT SOMETHING
TOLD ME YOU WOULD NEVER READ IT
WHILE I INSIDE MY ROOM WITH DREAMS OF MY HEAD
UPON YOUR FURNACE HIPS
AND THE TOUCH FROM YOUR LIPS
MY LEGS CAN'T STOP MOVING AROUND AND THE
PHONE JUST WON'T MAKE A SOUND
OH LOVER, YOU SHOULD HAVE COME OVER
EVERY INCH OF ME, ITS FULL OF PAIN
MY BROKEN BONES THEY SMELL THE RAIN
AND THE RAIN I WANT TO COME DOWN FAST LIKE KISSES ON MY EYE
BUT IT PASSED ON EM AND LEFT ME DRY
I'M SO DRY
OH LOVER YOU SHOULD HAVE COME OVER.

* HER FACE IS THE VERY TEAR THAT
HANGS IN MY THROAT FOREVER
NOW IT COMES TO MY EYES
NOW IT FALLS ON MY COATSLEEVE
NOW IT WILL SLEEP IN THE RIVER

(1) LOOKING OUT THE DOOR
AT TIMES I WONDER
HOW THIS SEPERATION EVER STARTED
... SINCE YOU & I'VE PARTED
(2) NOTHING'S ABSOLUTE
OR SELF SECURE

YOU SHOULD HAVE COME OVER

V LOOKING OUT THE DOOR I SEE THE RAIN COME DOWN.
   UPON THE CROWD OF MOURNERS
   PARADING IN A WAKE OF SAD RELATIONS WHILE THEIR SHOES
   FILL UP WITH WATER
* ~~MAYBE~~ MAYBE I'M TOO YOUNG TO KEEP GOOD LOVE FROM
   GOING WRONG   BUT TONIGHT MY MIND IS ON YOU, OH ONLY YOU
   ~~THERE HURT, AT LEAST THEY DON'T SLEEP ALONE~~

V EVERY INCH OF ME IS FULL OF PAIN
   OH, YOU SHOULD'VE COME OVER
   MY BROKEN BONES CAN SMELL THE RAIN
   AND I'M ACHING TO BE COVERED

* AND THE RAIN I WANT TO COME DOWN FAST
   LIKE KISSES UPON MY EYES

CHORUS BUT IT PASSED ON BY, AND LEFT ME DRY
        OH LOVER YOU SHOULD HAVE COME OVER

V BROKEN DOWN A HUNGRY FOR YOUR LOVE
   AND NO WAY I CAN FEED IT
   WHERE ARE YOU TONIGHT, CHILD YOU KNOW
   HOW MUCH I NEED IT
* TOO YOUNG TO HOLD ON, TOO OLD TO JUST BREAK FREE AND RUN
   TOO OLD TO RUN

CHORUS OH, OH, OH LOVER YOU SHOULD HAVE COME OVER

CHORUS   AD LIB

        BREAK

LONELY IS THE ROOM, MY BED IS MADE, THE OPEN WINDOW
LETS THE RAIN IN
BURNING IN THE CORNER IS THE ONE WHO ONLY DREAMS
HE HAD YOU WITH HIM

* MY BODY TURNS AND YEARNS
FOR SLEEP THAT NEVER COMES

IT'S NEVER OVER
MY KINGDOM FOR A KISS UPON HER SHOULDER
IT'S NEVER OVER
ALL MY RICHES FOR HER SMILES WHEN I SLEPT SO SOFT
AGAINST HER
IT'S NEVER OVER
ALL MY BLOOD FOR THE SWEETNESS OF HER LAUGHTER
IT'S NEVER OVER
SHE IS THE TEAR THAT HANGS INSIDE MY SOUL FOREVER

* MAYBE I'M TOO YOUNG
TO KEEP GOOD LOVE FROM GOING WRONG

(CH.) OH, LOVER YOU SHOULD'VE COME OVER

CH.

CH.

CH.

LOVER Chorus

10:5

D/F#   G-6

| BLAH BLAHBLAHBLAHBLAH BLAH BLAH |

D/A   G/B   A/C#
OOOH   BLAH BLAH   BLAH
          BLAH BLAHBLAHBLAH | BLAH

C/E   B/D   A/C# G/B F#/A D/F#   E-9

LOVER YOU SHOULD'VE COME | OVER

~~[scribbled out title]~~

SOMETIMES A MAN LOSES HIS WAY
WHEN HE FEELS LIKE HE NEEDS TO HAVE HIS FUN
SOMETIMES A MAN IS TOO BLIND TO SEE WHAT HE HAS DONE
SOMETIMES A MAN AWAKES TO FIND AT LAST
THAT REALLY HE HAS NO-ONE.

I WANT THE ~~SUBJECT~~ IN THIS SONG TO BE ACHING FOR
HIS LOVE TO COME OVER TO HIS PLACE, TO MAKE LOVE.
TO SAVE THEIR LOVE FROM CERTAIN DEATH. SHE IS OFF
SOMEWHERE ... BUSY. HE IS A FALLEN MAN, HAS KEPT
HER WAITING LATE AT NIGHT, HAS CHEATED ON HER,
HAS DISAPPOINTED HER IN SOME WAY... THINKING THAT IF
SHE WOULD ONLY COME TO HIS ROOM, IF ONLY THEY COULD
BE TOGETHER TONIGHT, OF ALL NIGHTS, THEN THEIR LOVE
COULD BE SAVED. BUT SHE'S NOWHERE TO BE FOUND. OUTSIDE
IT IS RAINING AND JUST LIKE THE FEELING HE GETS WHEN
HE IS INSIDE HER BODY, HE WANTS IT TO COME AND OVERWHELM
HIS SENSES, LIKE HER KISSES UPON HIS SKIN. BUT THE RAIN
WILL NEVER TOUCH HIM ... WON'T MOISTEN HIS ACHING BODY,
~~HE~~ ACHES FOR HER. TONIGHT OF ALL NIGHTS — IF HE DOESN'T
HAVE HER IN HIS ARMS TONIGHT HE FEARS THAT HE WILL
LOSE THEIR BEAUTIFUL MAGIC. COME TO ME, LOVE ME, OR WE'LL LOSE
IT ALL.

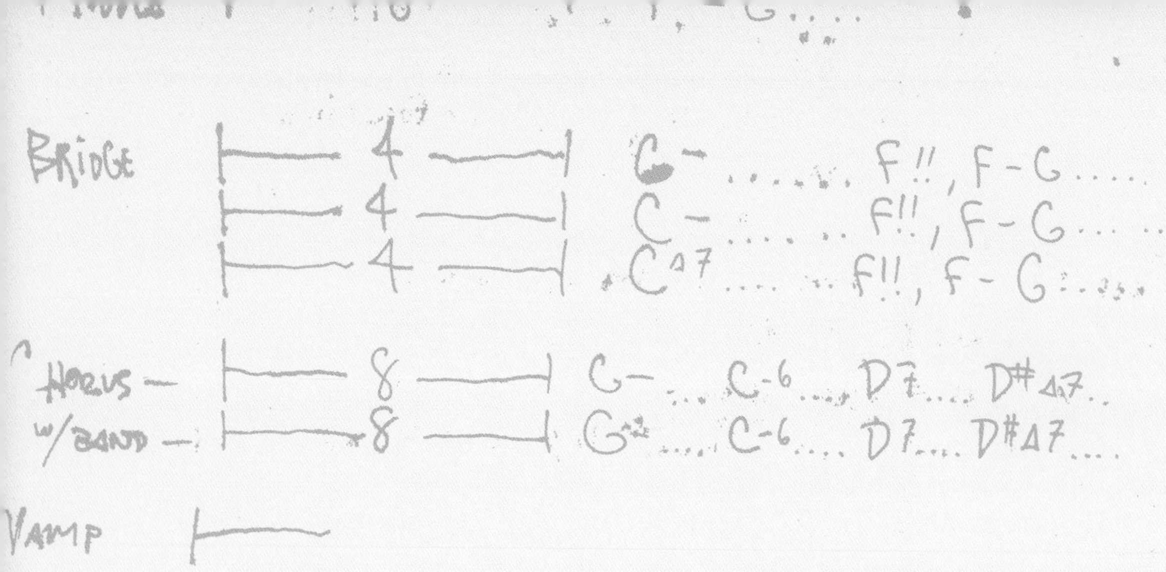

BRIDGE |—— 4 ——| C-..... F!!, F-G.....
       |—— 4 ——| C-...... F!!, F-G......
       |—— 4 ——| .C△7... F!!, F-G:.....

Chorus — |—— 8 ——| C-... C-6.... D7.... D#△7..
w/band — |——8 ——| G△2.... C-6.... D7... D#△7....

VAMP |——

FACING PAGE: After he signed with Columbia in the fall of 1992, Jeff treated himself to a few pieces of gear—a new acoustic guitar, a small amp, and, seen here, a used harmonium. A portable keyboard operated by way of a pump that pushes air into it, the harmonium is prevalent in Qawwali, the South Asian devotional music that made such an impression on Jeff when he first came to New York. Part of Jeff's devotion to Qawwali involved learning how to play the instrument, which can be heard on the introduction of "Lover, You Should've Come Over" (as well as on a cover of Van Morrison's "Madame George" cut during his 1993 session with producer Steve Addabbo). He also purchased language tapes to properly learn Urdu. Jeff could be seen walking around New York with this harmonium under his arm, wrapped in a blanket.

Song Titles

I BELIEVE I WAS CALLED

LAST NIGHT I HEARD THE NEEDLES PRAYING FOR MY SOUL

~~DREAM BROTHER~~ [crossed out]

YOU AND I -

BEAUTIFUL (LOSER) [NOT "LOSER" BUT SOMETHING FITTINGLY TRAGIC LIKE THAT...
'CAUSE I DON'T WANT IT TO SOUND LIKE LEONARD COHEN'S BOOK OR SOME KIND OF
COUNTRY SONG GENERICNESS - TITLE]
WONDERFUL LOSER .... BEAUTIFUL GIRL ALONE...

TIM BUCKLEY   — ANOTHER BEAUTIFUL LOSER. JEFFREY'S SON, TIMOTHY.

LOVER, YOU SHOULD'VE COME OVER -

SOMETIMES A MAN -

MILES OF DEATH - THE FOREVER WORK-IN-PROGRESS - WORK

ULTIMATE SOUND OF LOVE

MAGDA

DREAM BROTHER

FACING PAGE: In this undated 1993 entry, Jeff makes another list, this time of the most recent songs he's written or has begun. Several are familiar, including "Lover, You Should've Come Over" and "Dream Brother." "Sometimes a Man," the opening line of "Lover," indicates he may have had two separate songs in mind at one point for that lyric. An early version of the atmospheric "You & I" had been recorded at a demo session earlier that year with producer Steve Addabbo (and would later be released on the album *You and I*). "Ultimate Song of Love" refers to an earlier, never-recorded composition, "Song of Love," from several years before. "Miles of Death" — "the forever work-in-progress work," he writes — was a spoken-word piece he had debuted at St. Ann's Church earlier that year. The note about a song titled "Tim Buckley," though, remains a mystery.

NEXT PAGE: "Last Night I Heard the Needles Praying for My Soul" is one of the most powerful "lost" songs in Jeff's archive. He laments the "talk around town . . . all about my foolish behaviour" and returns to the idea of fleeting, inconsolable love that will waft through many of his lyrics. No mention of the song exists in Columbia Records' logs, making it possible that Jeff never found an appropriate melody for the lyric and never put it on tape.

Last Night I Heard The Needles Praying For My Soul

If I don't wise up soon I know I'll lose control
Last night I heard the needles praying for my soul

Last night I heard their voices wailing low in the dark
And they want me to be ~~their~~ ~~own~~ their ~~own~~ saviour
They know about me from the talk around town
And all about my foolish behaviour
~~I~~ better ~~keep~~ moving I can't stop moving

One wants to sleep in my eyes
Because they're wild from seeing too much
One wants to dance on my skin
Lend me his liquor and his ivory crutch
One wants to drink up my sex, Lord
If she can't kiss me, then nobody can
And one wants to ease my mind, forever
And tell me ~~she's~~ how lovely I am
And one wants my heart
And one wants my heart
And one wants my heart
And one wants my heart
And one wants my life
And one wants my life
And one wants my life
And one wants my life
And I try not to think of how their love
Would feel as good as gold
Last night I heard the needles praying for my soul

He is standing... Alone with the gifts he never gave you

9-16-93 2:00 A

Now there is nothing and no one to help you
Over and done is your youth and your fear
Gone in the distance is the mother you'd run to
Dead in the ocean is the father you'd lost
Out of the milky white mind of my child
Came stories of angels and cities of gold
And there in the bedroom, a house in the desert
His family went from him and there he grew old
When silver his hair grew from his troubles
And withered his face from grief and remorse
And dim did his eyes become from their lone struggle
To constantly lose and discover his course
With no-one to care if he cried at the table
Remembering gestures and words of calm joy
And stories between the grey days as a child
The ink on his letter did his tears destroy
As he wrote to the landord "Dear Sir, I regret
To relay my bad news to the men of your employ
That my money is low but could you please let
Me propose that we come to agree on a deal
Where I send you this monday a part of my rent
Next month a small check can finish it off, seal
The debt off for good until my room is lent."
The sun hid the dark night away from the hills
At six o'clock sharp and the doves woke to sing
The old man awake, but he slept full of pills
And when the mail came, the man said not a thing.

FORGETHER

	5	6	7	8	9	10	11
INTRO					OK		YES
V I					ick	TRERICK	
CHORUS I					ick		
INSTR.							
V II							
CHORUS II					Sloppy AND out of tune		
SOLO							
V III							
CHORUS 3							
4							
5							

10/11/93

Will there ever be a voice who speaks exactly what
the truth is?
    Will there ever be a beginning, a doorway, not
a gold encrusted gate, but a plain old brown wooden
thing creaking on open for you to walk through?
    I hope that there is never a day on earth without
Death's door of rebirth.
    Death of ashen ideas, weak from their struggle on the stage,
watching their prepared lines flow out of the punctured hole in their
will
Until all that is left is panicked improvisation, falling flat
without the fuel of passion and acid love
Exposed as a vulgar ghost of an idiot
Worse than an idiot
A sexless schoolmaster, bleating lessons from his
cliff-edged lips. All arbitrary order and punishing penis - the Godfather.
Either you live as a song, or rot to death as
a special effect. Either you fly through thick life, a beautiful
aching crawl through its muddy music — or you die as a device.
I don't need incense and a degree to write down my soul.
I don't need acceptance from the outside to sing my love.
I need to relentlessly dig down dig down until my muscles are
rock and my eyes are stars and my breasts are heavy with milk.
I need to learn the language of my dreaming, night after night.
To speak it out, to move boulders off the road with it. To kiss with it.
To never leave its side for a millionth of a second.
And I find that I don't want to be closer to God in heaven,
I want to know my real father and mother who are humanity?
Earth. The one who is law and the one who knows all.
My real father is my word. My real mother is my music.
My mother's child by my father is my voice. My parents are all
benevolent, all-loving, helpful and challenging and so, so much in love.

10/24/93

IM SO ANGRY ALL THE TIME ATT MYSELF
SO FRUSTRATED ALL THE TIME. AND NOW I KNOW WHAT
TO DO. PROVE TO MYSELF THAT I AM A REAL ARTIST,
HELP MYSELF TO STAY AWAKE.

C, IF SHE TRIES TO GET INSIDE I WON'T LET HER

SO YOU SEE ME AS I REALLY AM
A RAILROAD TRACK ABANDONED

1. ALWAYS KEEP NOTEBOOK AND PEN WITH YOU
AT ALL TIMES.
2. NEVER DO ANYTHING THAT WILL TAKE YOU
AWAY FROM WRITING EXCEPT EAT SLEEP SING OR MAKE LOVE
3. WRITE A SONG A DAY EVERY DAY. FOREVER AND PUT
IT DOWN ON 4-TRACK

12/7/93

ITS A SAD WORLD...
THIS INNOCENT FEELING INSIDE CARRIES SUCH BIG SADNESS.
I LOST MY LOVE. SHE IS LOCKED OUTSIDE MY HEART
AND IT DOESN'T MAKE SENSE!!
I WISH I COULD READ MY DREAMS MORE CLOSELY
AND FIND SOME ANSWERS. FIND SOME INNER GIFT TO POINT A
WAY TO CHANGE MY HEART. SOMETHING. ANYTHING AT ALL.
I LOVE MY BUTTERFLY. WHY AREN'T WE LOVERS ANYMORE?

PAGES 122–123: With the basic tracks of *Grace* in the can, Jeff lays out his creative goals in the fall of 1993—a song a day and continued journal writing—and grapples with his breakup with Rebecca Moore. The reference to "a railroad track abandoned" will eventually make its way into "Opened Once" several years later.

FACING PAGE: A tribute to Paul McCartney tucked away in one of Jeff's smaller notebooks. Paul and Linda had a special fondness for Jeff, since Linda had known and photographed Tim Buckley in the '60s. When Linda heard that her friend Danny Fields would be attending the 1991 "Greetings from Tim Buckley" concert, she gave Fields a note to pass along to Jeff. Two years later, when Paul was the musical guest on *Saturday Night Live*, he and Linda invited Jeff to attend the live broadcast. Both Paul and Linda would visit Jeff backstage at his concert at Roseland in New York in 1995.

PAGE 126: Jeff purchased this flowery Fender Telecaster (seen here next to a pair of his Doc Martens) in an antique store or flea market in either France or Belgium during his 1995 tour of the Continent. In the same store, he bought a piece of art depicting a man holding a beer, which became one of the logos on his laminated tour passes (see page 153).

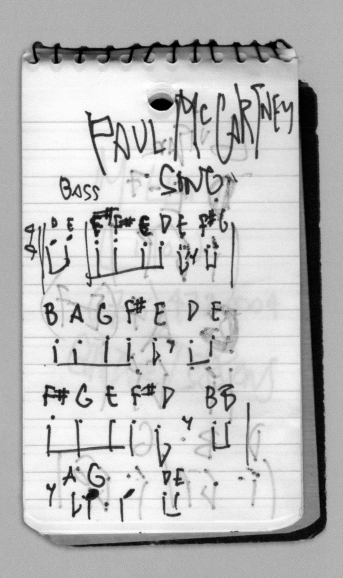

Can you do
own terribly
droll Neil
Young
impersonation
for us?

P-L-E-A-S-E

Dear Bob,   Wetlands Niteclub, Thanksgiving, NY '93

                    I DON'T KNOW HOW TO START. LAST SATURDAY
MY MAN STEVE BERKOWITZ BROKE IT TO ME THAT YOU
WERE TOLD OF SOMETHING I'D SAID FROM A STAGE .... AND THAT
YOU HAD FELT INSULTED. I NEED ~FOR~ YOU TO LISTEN TO ME.
                    I ~HAVE NO WAY~ OF KNOWING HOW MY
~WORDS~ WORDS WERE TRANSLATED TO YOU, IF THEIR WHOLE
MEANING AND CONTEXT WERE INTACT. BUT THE TRUTH IS
THAT I WAS OFF ON A TANGENT, ON A STAGE, MY MIND
GOING WHERE IT GOES, TRYING TO BE FUNNY. IT WASN'T
FUNNY AT ALL. AND I FUCKED UP. I REALLY FUCKED UP.
AND THE WORST OF IT ISN'T~~~ THAT YOUR BOYS WERE AT
THE GIG TO HEAR IT ... THAT DOESN'T REALLY BOTHER ME.
IT ~JUST~ KILLS ME TO ~KNOW~ THAT ~~WHATEVER THEY TOLD YOU
IS WHAT ~I YOU THINK~ I THINK OF YOU, NOT THAT I LOVE YOU, NOT
THAT I'VE ALWAYS LISTENED TO YOU AND CARRIED THE MUSIC
WITH ME EVERYWHERE I GO, NOT THAT I BELIEVE IN YOU.
AND ALSO THAT YOUR SHOW WAS GREAT. IT WAS ONLY
THE ~SUPPER CLUB~ CROWD THAT I WAS CYNICAL ABOUT
AND THAT'S WHAT I WAS TRYING TO GET AT WHEN I SAID
WHAT I SAID. AND I'M SORRY THAT I'LL NEVER GET TO
MAKE ~ANOTHER~ A FIRST IMPRESSION.
                              YOU WERE REALLY GRACIOUS TO
ME, TO ~EVEN~ ALLOW ME BACKSTAGE TO MEET YOU. I'LL NEVER
FORGET WHAT YOU TOLD ME AS LONG AS I LIVE; I'M VERY
VERY HONORED TO HAVE MET YOU AT ALL. ~~~~~~~~~~~~~~
~~~~~~
I'M ONLY SAD THAT I DIDN'T GET A CHANCE TO TELL YOU BEFORE
ALL~ THIS INTRIGUE. THE INTRIGUE IS NOT THE TRUTH.
~~~~~~~ LOTS OF EYES WILL READ THIS LETTER BEFORE ~~~~
   IT GETS TO YOU, BOB, WHICH I ACCEPT. SOMEDAY YOU'LL
KNOW ~EXACTLY~ WHAT I MEAN MAN TO MAN. ALWAYS BE WELL.

                                              Jeff Buckley

PAGE 127: A note passed along from a fan, date unknown.

FACING PAGE: In November 1993, Jeff met Bob Dylan, one of his heroes, backstage at a Dylan show in New York. Not long after, during a gig at the club Wetlands, Jeff talked about that encounter and went into what he felt was an affectionate Dylan impersonation. Unbeknownst to him, though, members of Dylan's crew were in the audience and misinterpreted Jeff's comments as a dig at their boss. When Jeff heard what had happened, he wrote this letter, which, according to Columbia executives, was eventually passed along to Dylan. (To ensure Dylan got the message, Jeff also read the letter aloud at one of his club shows.) A copy of the note was later discovered in Dylan's archives.

PAGES 130–131: Undated 1993 poems containing the seeds of "Lover, You Should've Come Over" and what would later become the completely rewritten "I Woke Up in a Strange Place."

In This World would I rather
Stray from the multitudes, die in solitude
Live in lonliness, speak in secrets, invent in code,
Because I love my own soul... and protect my love
with my life from this sad, painful world?
Or would I be an honest slayer of life like
the rest.
    I woke up in a strange place
The door was open with the dust blowing in
And the smell was so strange
    from the rug where I lay
    I woke up in a strange house
My mind was a blur and some red on my chin
Music so loud that I
Spit up my beer
There was no one around
And somehow I could remember
Only your words to me, only your voice,
    Like the day I was born
My Jeans stick to my thighs and there's sweat in my shirt
So what about innocence
Act like you're rough and you know where it hurts
And you know how to use it
    I woke up in a strange room
With someone elses shelves filled with keepsakes and books
The bed is so drab and the sky filled with sex
And this love being spoiled by too many cooks
    I remember my host was nice enough
But I could see she wasn't a friend
She gave me some gifts
And a plastic cassette
And kissing her cheek I smelled her cigarette

~~WHY SHOULD BE LONESOME~~

Sometimes a man loses his way
When he feels like he needs to have his fun
Sometimes a man is too blind to see what he has done
Sometimes a man awakes to find at last
That really he has no-one.

I want the SUBJECT ~~of~~ of this song to be aching for
love to come over to his place: To make love.
~~their love from certain death. SHE is off~~
~~Day. He is a song~~

And stepping to the street
I threw it in the garbage can
I never want to see my face
In the mirror again.
I woke up in a strange place
Feeling it was too late for everything
That I ~~had~~ missed my turn, that every move I
made was useless
That I'd ~~been~~ left behind.
I woke up feeling strange.
And I saw through every lie and I could
call out every trick
~~Every ?????? ??????, A ???? ???? and Dick~~
There's the smile looking fake and the love turning sick
Disappointment is a gash on the jaw labeled "Beauty"
Don't reach out to hold me
Just stand there and empty that language out Quick

PAGES 133–136: The creation of "Dream Brother," the climactic track on *Grace*. During band rehearsals that preceded the sessions, Jeff, Grondahl, and Johnson began working up a swirling melody that built from a caressing introduction into a Zeppelin-gone-to-India frenzy. Late in the *Grace* sessions, Jeff returned to the unfinished song, which only had a title, "Dream Brother." The lyrics, which made elliptical references to his friend Chris Dowd as well as to Jeff's own father, were clearly important to Jeff, as these pages of early drafts demonstrate. With few exceptions—an "angel dark and uncaring," which would be a "dark angel" in the final version—most of these words would not appear in the finished song. This process is representative of the way Jeff would often compose lyrics—spewing images, phrases, and emotions onto a page, then riffling through them and editing them down to a more concise form. The schematic on page 135 finds the skills Jeff gleaned from his time at Musicians Institute bursting out, as he works through the chords and arrangement.

~~Forget Her~~

My head in my hands and her lips on
the mouth of another
My head in my hands and her kiss on the
lips of another
My head in my hands and her nights in
the arms of another

Dream Brother on the mind of the road
~~Words~~ ©
Sleeping w/ his arms around the ~~waist~~ of wanderlust
And his tears scattered round the world
She'll never love you more
Than the girl she was before
She'll never love you more than the woman she was before
Dream brother with your eyes to the ground in vain
in a permanent search for the answer to your pain
Dream of her day in and day out with a song of her name
Ringing out in the night drift
Forever in the air
Without the whisper of your words
in her butterscotch hair
Without her
Every song is about her
And for all the times you told me I was doing wrong
I want you to be strong now your love is gone
Snow is on the house where I am
Snow on the houses in Arkansas
San Francisco freak show bubbling sweaty chocolate melting
corpses wax between his toes freakshow with eyes for
brunette late night game

AND YOUR BABIES IN THE CRADLE
WAITING FOR YOU
LIKE I WAITED FOR MINE
AND NO, HE NEVER CAME
AND NO, HE NEVER CAME

MY HEART IS CLOGGED WITH A SLEEPLESS SHAME
AND THE BLOOD IS STAMPEDING MY SLUMBER
WHEN A ROOM IS A PRISON FOR A SOUL HOT WITH BLAME
THEN THE ROAD IS A KISS TO REMEMBER
I KNOW YOU ... I KNOW YOUR SECRETS
YOUR TROUBLES FOLLOW THE WINE INTO YOUR SMILE
AND I'M WATCHING FROM ABOVE YOU
ALL THE NUMBERS PUT UPON YOU
THAT YOU HAVE TO PAY IN FULL ALL THE WHILE
OUR FATHERS WILL NEVER BE AT PEACE WITH US
OUR LOVERS WILL NEVER REST WITH EASE WITH US
AND DEATH WILL KEEP OUR MOTHERS EVER FEARING FOR
THE DAY THEY MUST LET GO
BUT THE SKY IT HOVERS OVER WITH THE SINGING SETTING
SUN SO HEAVY BREASTED AND WITH FUTURE'S FRAGRANT MOUTH
WITH ALL HER PROMISE OF THE UNSEEN SPARKLE
THE LIFE WE KNOW, NOT KNOW
YOU ... I'M JUST LIKE YOU
YOUNGER BUT STILL WATCHING OVER
DREAMING THAT THE ANGEL DARK AND UNCARING
TRIPPED YOU AND DRUGGED YOUR SWEET MIND WITH HIS ENVY
SIMULTANEOUSLY DOES HE KEEP YOU ASLEEP AND AWAKE
POOR LITTLE LONESOME HOW MUCH MORE CAN YOU TAKE?
FEELING THAT YOU TRUST NOT A SOUL BENEATH THE SUN
BUT HERE IS ONE
HERE IS ONE

Dream Brother

Intro

Verse I |——— 6 ———| F - G ... F - G ... G - F - Ab ....

~~●●●●●~~ |——— 4 ———| Bb ... C ... F - G ...

|— 2 —| F - G

Verse II |——— 6 ———| F - G .... F - G ... G - F - Ab ...

|——— 4 ———| Bb ... C ... F - G ...

|——— 4 ———| Bb ... C ... F - G ...

~~●●●●~~

Chorus |——— 4 ———| G- ... C-6 ... D7 ... D#Δ7 ...

|——— 4 ———| G- ... C-6 ... D7 ... D#Δ7 ...

Middle |——— 8 ———| F - G ...

Bridge |——— 4 ———| C- .... F!! , F - G ...

|——— 4 ———| C- ..... F!! , F - G .....

|——— 4 ———| CΔ7 ... F!! , F - G .....

Chorus — |——— 8 ———| G- ... C-6 D7 ... D#Δ7 ...

w/Band — |———8———| G- ... C-6 D7 ... D#Δ7 ...

Vamp |———|

You're my Confidence
You drink some poison stranger
You bleed a stranger poison
All the babes backstage who dance into the devil for you
Never will bring you satisfaction
And the one you lost with her skin so fair
Is free again with the wind in her butterscotch hair, her green eyes
And she'll never need you more   bloom goodbyes
Than the woman she was before

Don't be like the one who made me so old
~~while the ~~ Don't be like the one who left
~~behind his name~~ Behind his name
Cause they're waiting for you like I waited for mine
And nobody ever came

Sleeping with his arms around the hips of fate
And his tears scattered round the world
~~his false power~~
Angel go tell him these dreams; my cold black visions

Show him his troubles like a cloud of rain
~~that cut a festering rate~~
~~show him the danger of sin~~
~~believe in the waters~~
Be his ~~demons~~
Show him his babies in a helpless state of
Never knowing fully his voice
And knowing what it is to be his children
Dream Brother with his eyes to the burning sun

Mead

COMPOSITION

100 sheets • 200 pages
9¾ x 7½ in/24.7 x 19.0 cm
wide ruled • 09910

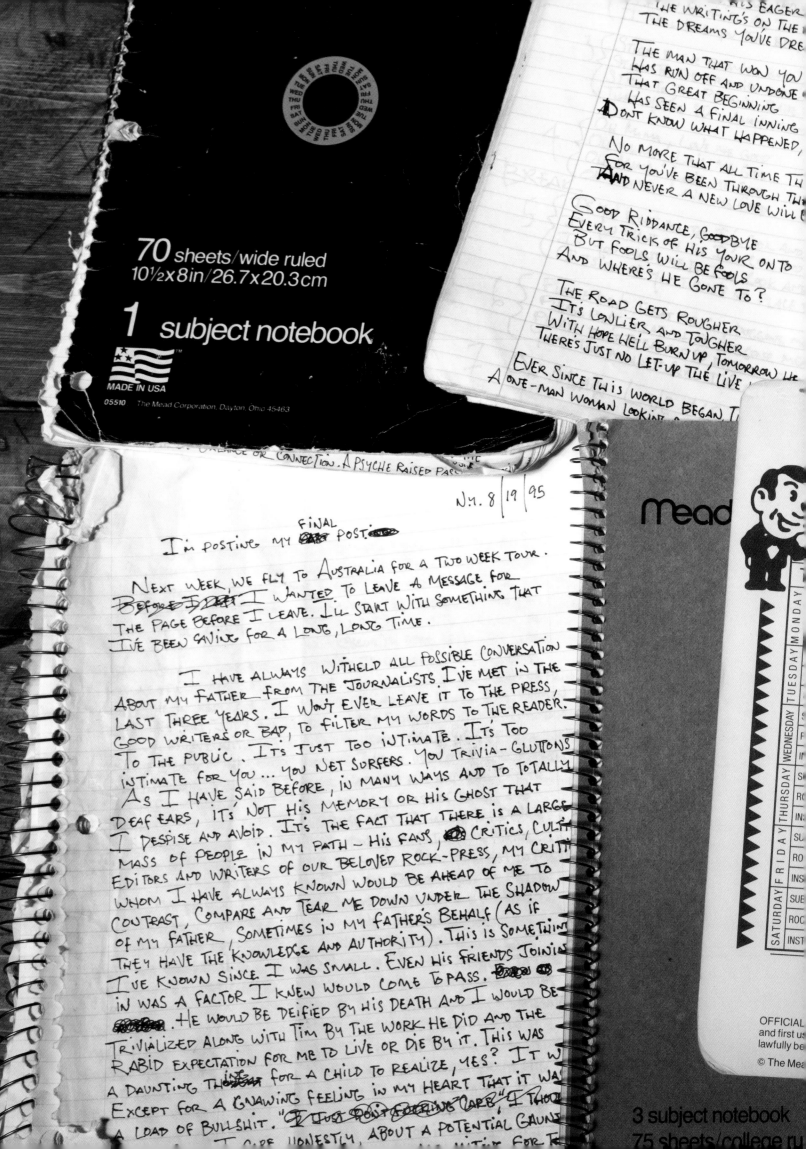

N.Y. 8/19/95

I'm posting my FINAL ~~post~~ post.

Next week, we fly to Australia for a two week tour. ~~Before I left~~ I wanted to leave a message for the page before I leave. I'll start with something that I've been saving for a long, long time.

I have always witheld all possible conversation about my father from the journalists I've met in the last three years. I won't ever leave it to the press, good writers or bad, to filter my words to the reader. It's just too intimate. It's too intimate for you ... you net surfers. You trivia-gluttons. As I have said before, in many ways and to totally deaf ears, it's not his memory or his ghost that I despise and avoid. It's the fact that there is a large mass of people in my path — his fans, critics, cult editors and writers of our beloved rock-press, my critics whom I have always known would be ahead of me to contrast, compare and tear me down under the shadow of my father, sometimes in my father's behalf (as if they have the knowledge and authority). This is something I've known since I was small. Even his friends joining in was a factor I knew would come to pass. He would be deified by his death and I would be trivialized along with Tim by the work he did and the rabid expectation for me to live or die by it. This was a daunting ~~thought~~ for a child to realize, yes? It w... Except for a gnawing feeling in my heart that it wa... a load of bullshit. "I just don't ~~feeling care~~" I thou... T.C. be honestly, about a potential gaunt...

s eager...
THE WRITING'S ON THE...
THE DREAMS YOU'VE DRE...

THE MAN THAT WON YO...
HAS RUN OFF AND UNDONE...
THAT GREAT BEGINNING
HAS SEEN A FINAL INNING
DON'T KNOW WHAT HAPPENED,

NO MORE THAT ALL TIME TH...
FOR YOU'VE BEEN THROUGH TH...
AND NEVER A NEW LOVE WILL...

GOOD RIDDANCE, GOODBYE
EVERY TRICK OF HIS YOUR ONTO
BUT FOOLS WILL BE FOOLS
AND WHERE'S HE GONE TO?

THE ROAD GETS ROUGHER
IT'S LONLIER AND TOUGHER
WITH HOPE HE'LL BURN UP, TOMORROW HE...
THERE'S JUST NO LET-UP THE LIVE...

EVER SINCE THIS WORLD BEGAN T...
A ONE-MAN WOMAN LOOKIN...

70 sheets/wide ruled
10½ x 8in/26.7x20.3cm
1 subject notebook
MADE IN USA
05510   The Mead Corporation. Dayton, Ohio 45463

mead

3 subject notebook
75 sheets/college ru...

OFFICIAL
and first u...
lawfully b...
© The Mea...

HAVE ALL GONE ASTRAY.

LL A CRAZY GAME

SAME

IS PERFECT WHERE HER RIVAL FAILS
TO MANICURE HER NAILS
NEVER SEEN WITH PIN-CURLS IN HER HAIR ANYWHERE
THE OTHER WOMAN ENCHANTS HER CLOTHES WITH FRENCH PERFUME
THE OTHER WOMAN KEEPS FRESH CUT FLOWERS IN EACH ROOM
AND THERE ARE NEVER TOYS THAT SCATTERED EVERYWHERE
AND WHEN HER OLD MAN COMES TO CALL
HE'LL FIND HER WAITING LIKE A LONESOME QUEEN
CAUSE WHEN SHE'S BY HIS SIDE
ITS SUCH A CHANGE FROM OLD ROUTINE
BUT THE OTHER WOMAN WILL ALWAYS CRY HERSELF TO SLEEP
THE OTHER WOMAN WILL NEVER HAVE HIS LOVE TO KEEP
AND AS THE YEARS GO BY THE OTHER WOMAN
WILL SPEND HER LIFE ALONE....

OUTLAWS
CRIMINALS
COPS
PROMOTERS
ATTORNEYS
DRUG LORDS/MAFIA

ALL CONTROLLED BY
THE MOB M.O.B.

THREE LITTLE WORDS
BETWEEN ALL LOVERS
AND SO-CALLED FRIENDS
HOLD US TOGETHER
IN THIS WORLD
IM SO SORRY
IM SO SORRY
IM SO VERY SORRY
FRIENDS WILL MAKE US SAINTS
PATRON SAINTS OF LIARS
WHO WE LOVE AS OUR OWN
THE TIES THAT BIND HAVE ROTTED
UNDEPENDABLE FRIENDS
THE NIGHT I MET YOU
I FELL ASLEEP WITH A SMI
I DREAMED I WAS CAUGHT
AND YOU SWAM TO ME WITH K
THERE WAS A MESSAGE ON
ANKLE BONE
THE TARGET WHERE I DROVE
DAGGER HOME

DREAM BROTHER
ETERNAL LIFE
LAST GOODBYE
LILAC WINE
HALLELUJAH
LOVER YOU SHOULD'VE COME OVER
FORGET HER
CORPUS CHRISTIE
GRACE
MOJO PIN

* EVERYBODY HERE WANTS YOU

Bloom inside,
My beautiful flower
If you feel your blood moving under your skin
Then let it kiss every inch of you
Let the friction of its rushing through
your riverbed
Arise like applause in your breast
And sparkle like kisses upon your belly.
Close your eyes and fly
Stretch your legs and sing
Because inside you the sea is swelling in love with
the moon
No such thing as self defense or bondage
Or regret for the past, the ocean only
Lives and creates and flows
But always in love with the moon
Speak out to me

My beautiful sparrow
In the morning you fly over a city
of lunatics walking in pain and waiting for betrayal
All you know is the wind
The rhythm of the fragrance of the world
Only you can sing me awake
Sing it to me with the small of your back
Sing it to me with the heat of your lips
Kiss me where you want and the song is all
I can hear
Inside you the sea is swelling over
Spilling over my head
And I stay submerged
Waiting for your rose to open to me
And your song to sink into my skin.

12/7/93

THERE IS A MUSIC OF THE SKIN
AND IN THE EXPANSE OF MY BODY'S MOIST DESERT PLAIN
THERE IS BEING MADE BY THE WIND
A LOVE SONG EPIC ~~XXXX~~ IN YOUR NAME
MY THIGHS LIKE THE DUNES OF DEATH VALLEY
IN RADIANT WINTER MAGIC
THAT NO MAN EVER SEES.
      WHAT A SONG IS BEING MADE FROM MY PALMS
THE HUSH OF IT SLIDING ACROSS MY SHOULDER
   IN WISTFUL PANTOMIME
OF YOUR BODY'S SLY LULLABY
      YOU KNOW YOU'RE A WOMAN
BY THE WAY YOUR MESSAGE BUILDS FROM BELOW
TO FLOAT FROM YOUR FINGERS
   AND FEED MY MOUTH WITH FEMALE
      FRAGRANCE IN SWEET IMPATIENT ANGER
MY TONGUE IS A FRUIT OF THE MIND OF EROS
IMPARTING LIGHT UPON EVERY WORD EVER UTTERED
MERELY BY SLIPPING ITS WORDS
      ACROSS YOUR SEX
OVER AND OVER SO ITS EASIER FOR YOU
TO UNDERSTAND   STAND STILL
   I WANT TO TELL YOU SOME MORE
      OF MY SECRET
            YOU'LL NEVER

         TELL

            LOVE

FACING PAGE: In November 1993, Columbia released *Live at Sin-é* in the US (Big Cat, a British indie, handled its release in the UK). To promote the record, Jeff and driver Reggie Griffith embarked on a solo tour of the States, beginning in the middle of January 1994 and ending in March. (He would return to New York March 1 and 2 to continue working on *Grace* before hitting the road again.) This page stands as the only surviving journal entry about those shows: the first time most of the country—from Seattle and San Francisco, down to Dallas and Austin, and up through Alexandria, Virginia, Washington, DC, and Asbury Park, New Jersey—saw and heard Jeff onstage.

PAGE 146: Jeff's wallet was in itself a miniature tour through his world. Main Street Music & Video was one of his favorite Northern California music stores as a teenager, and his California driver's license and Loara High School and Musicians Institute ID cards document the next phases of his life. Allen Ginsberg's business card is a significant memento of the time he met the poet during the recording sessions for the Hal Willner–produced *Closed on Account of Rabies*, an album of stories and poems by Edgar Allan Poe read by various artists.

PAGE 147: Jeff's black Hagstrom electric guitar, purchase date unknown.

ROAD 1/19/94 SINE TOUR

DRIVING FROM PORTLAND TO REDDING, CALIFORNIA...
ON INTERSTATE 5... ~~OFF TO THE RIGHT A MAMMOTH~~
~~MOUNTAIN OF~~ UP AHEAD, A MAMMOTH BILLOW OF STEAM FLOATING
UP TO THE GRAY SKY ABOVE, STEAM SO PURE AND WHITE
MASSIVE MASHED-POTATO SLOWNESS... TWISTING IN ACHINGLY
~~ACHINGLY~~ SLOW DOWN MOTION... UP... UP... UP... TURNING...
UP... TURNING ROUND AND ROUND LIKE A SLEEPING WHALE
IN AN OCEAN OF AIR, FLOATING TO THE SURFACE. MOVING
CLOSER IN THIS SPEEDING CAR I SEE A MOUNTAIN OF ORANGE
SAWDUST... A LUMBERMILL, A PAPER FACTORY?... A FACTORY
ON THE COUNTRYSIDE... ~~too~~ A THOUSAND FOOT PILE OF
STEAMING SAWDUST... HEAT EMANATING FROM THE INNER
BELLY OF THE PILE... A PILE. SO FUNNY. IT IS A PILE
BUT IT'S TOO LARGE REALLY, IT IS AN INDUSTRIAL BY-PRODUCT
AND IT IS ALSO A STEAMING LAND MASS — STRETCHING FOR
A QUARTER MILE, OF SAWDUST, ORANGE AND NATURAL BROWN
THE COLORS OF SLAUGHTERED TREES... SO BREATHTAKING AND BEAUTIFUL,
ALMOST WASTEFUL. IMAGINE THE SHAVINGS ARE THE ENDLESS
DUNES ON A SAWDUST PLANET... STEAM RISING INTO THE DREAMY
GRAY COLD, A SKY DARK LIKE DEATH, LIKE MAGIC.
TRUCKS PLUMMETING ROUGHLY AHEAD THROUGH THE AIR,
SPEEDING OVER MY SAME HIGHWAY... JUST AHEAD OF
MY CAR... SNUFFING OUT BLACK BROWN FUEL EXHAUST
OUT OF DOUBLE SATAN — HORNS, CHROME PIPES HOT TO THE
TOUCH, STEAMING FULL SPEED LIKE MAD BULLS. MAN WILL ALWAYS
CREATE ETERNAL WONDER INADVERTENTLY. MOTEL ORLEANS.
MY INK IS DRYING IN THE PEN. ALMOST FELL ASLEEP.

③ STAGE : iF THERE ARE ANY SPOTLIGHTS ON STAGE, THERE WILL BE FOUR.

④ MUSIC — THINGS HAPPEN IN OUR MUSIC THAT SHOULDN'T BE POSSIBLE, THAT HAVE NO WAY OF HAPPENING.

BUT WE DO MAKE THEM HAPPEN.

SUCH BEAUTY HAS NEVER BEEN HEARD OR SEEN BY ANY LIVING THING

SUCH DEPTH HAS NEVER BEEN EXPLORED BY THE MOST CELEBRATED THINKERS OF OUR TIMES.

SUCH BRUTE VIOLENCE HAS NEVER CUT SO DEEP INTO ANY SOUL THROUGH ANY ART FORM BY ANY OTHER ENTITY.

SUCH RUTHLESS CONVICTION, SUCH NAKED PASSIONATE EMOTION, SUCH WORSHIP OF TRUTH IS ENOUGH TO KILL ANY MAN OR WOMAN INSTANTLY SIMPLY BY THE SHEER FORCE OF ~~THIS INTENSITY,~~ ~~OR DEEP CONSCIOUSNESS~~.

SUCH SUCH SUCH SUCH A BITCHin BAND, Y'KNOW?

FACING PAGE: Undated note in preparation for the *Grace* tour. The first comment is indicative of Jeff's concerns that he and his band (which by then also included guitarist Michael Tighe) be considered a unit, not simply a leader and his sidemen. The mention of "things . . . that shouldn't be possible" alludes to the ways Jeff was envisioning a set that would largely consist of *Grace* songs but, to the consternation of some Sony executives, retain the improvisational feel of his solo performances.

NEXT PAGE: Jeff readies himself for the nomadic roadwork to promote *Grace* by writing out the "Warrior's Creed," the anonymous credo of a fourteenth-century samurai.

A Warriors Creed

I HAVE NO PARENTS: I MAKE THE HEAVENS AND EARTH MY PARENTS.

I HAVE NO HOME: I MAKE AWARENESS MY HOME.

I HAVE NO LIFE OR DEATH: I MAKE THE TIDES OF BREATHING MY LIFE AND DEATH.

I HAVE NO DIVINE POWER: I MAKE HONESTY MY DIVINE POWER.

I HAVE NO MEANS: I MAKE UNDERSTANDING MY MEANS.

I HAVE NO MAGIC SECRETS: I MAKE CHARACTER MY MAGIC SECRET.

I HAVE NO BODY: I MAKE ENDURANCE MY BODY.

I HAVE NO EYES: I MAKE THE FLASH OF LIGHTNING MY EYES.

I HAVE NO EARS: I MAKE SENSIBILITY MY EARS

I HAVE NO LIMBS: I MAKE PROMPTNESS MY LIMBS

I HAVE NO STRATEGY: I MAKE "UNSHADOWED BY THOUGHT" MY STRATEGY.

I HAVE NO DESIGNS: I MAKE "SEIZING OPPORTUNITY BY THE FORELOCK" MY DESIGN.

I HAVE NO MIRACLES: I MAKE RIGHT-ACTION MY MIRACLES.

I HAVE NO PRINCIPLES: I MAKE ADAPTABILITY TO ALL CIRCUMSTANCES MY PRINCIPLES.

I HAVE NO TACTICS: I MAKE EMPTINESS AND FULLNESS MY TACTICS

I HAVE NO TALENTS: I MAKE READY WIT MY TALENT.

I HAVE NO FRIENDS: I MAKE MY MIND MY FRIEND.

I HAVE NO ENEMY: I MAKE CARELESSNESS MY ENEMY.

I HAVE NO ARMOR: I MAKE BENEVOLENCE AND RIGHTEOUSNESS MY ARMOR.

I HAVE NO CASTLE: I MAKE IMMOVABLE-MIND MY CASTLE.

I HAVE NO SWORD: I MAKE ABSENCE OF SELF MY SWORD.

— ANONYMOUS SAMURAI, FOURTEENTH CENTURY.

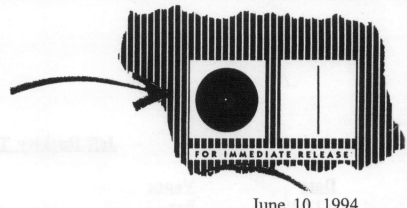

FOR IMMEDIATE RELEASE

June 10, 1994

Tour Press Contact:
Renee Pfefer
212.833.4424

JEFF BUCKLEY EMBARKING ON NATIONAL TOUR OF INTIMATE VENUES

Singer's First Album To Be Released August 23

Columbia Records artist **Jeff Buckley** is bringing his music to a series of small American venues in anticipation of the release of his first full-length studio album, **GRACE**, due in-stores on August 23.

Jeff Buckley has built a growing word-of-mouth reputation for his solo performances. Singer/songwriter/electric guitarist Buckley has, up until this tour, performed almost exclusively as a solo artist. For the past two years, he has been performing mainly in tiny clubs, cafes, and coffeehouses in Lower Manhattan. He undertook his first extensive touring outside of Manhattan earlier this year playing North American dates January through mid-March. Weaving together influences as seemingly diffuse as folk, heavy metal, free jazz, Mid-Eastern chanting, European *chansons* and hymnody, Buckley's music is both structured and improvisational.

Recorded late last year at Bearsville Studios in Woodstock, **GRACE** was produced by Andy Wallace (Paw, White Zombie, Soul Asylum) and features Buckley on guitars, vocals, harmonium, and other instruments. Accompanying Buckley on tour will be his rhythm section from **GRACE**--Mick Grondahl on bass and Matt Johnson on drums--as well as recently-recruited second guitarist Michael Tighe.

[more]

COLUMBIA RECORDS PRESS & PUBLICITY

550 MADISON AVENUE, NEW YORK, NY 10022-3211 212/833-7080/FAX: 212/833-5401 • 2100 COLORADO AVENUE, SANTA MONICA, CA 90404 310/449-2500/FAX: 310/449-2506 • 34 MUSIC SQUARE EAST, NASHVILLE, TN 37203 615/742-4345/FAX 615/244-2549

Jeff Buckley Tour Itinerary

Date	Venue	City/State
6/17-19	Fez	New York, New York
6/20	Last Call Saloon	Providence, Rhode Island
6/21	Local 186	Boston, Massachusetts
6/22	Johnny D's	Boston, Massachusetts
6/24	Iron Horse	Northampton, Massachusetts
7/1	Gem Theater	Detroit, Michigan
7/2	Summerfest	Milwaukee, Wisconsin
7/5	Hothouse	Chicago, Illinois
7/6	Green Mill	Chicago, Illinois
7/8	Cedar Cultural	Minneapolis, Minnesota
7/9	Gabe's	Iowa City, Iowa
7/11	Jazzhouse	Lawrence, Kansas
7/12	The Hi Pointe	St. Louis, Missouri
7/14	Bug Theater	Denver, Colorado
7/15	Salt Lake City Bar & Grill	Salt Lake City, Utah
7/19-20	Velvet Elvis	Seattle, Washington
7/22	La Luna	Portland, Oregon
7/24	Starry Plough	Berkeley, California
7/25	Above Brainwash	San Francisco, California
7/27-28	Ivar Theater	Los Angeles, California
7/29	Hahn Cosmopolitan Center	San Diego, California
7/31	Mill Street Theater	Phoenix, Arizona

Further dates to be added...

####

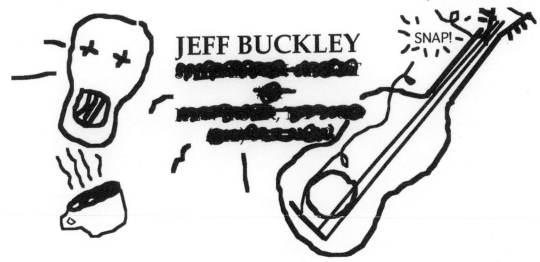

JEFF BUCKLEY

SNAP!

Lynn,

You probably don't remember sending me your letter by now. Maybe you do. It's been so long, though, I apologize.

A very huge kiss and a thank you for everything you said to me. It was a mild, satanic nightmare that first night at Green Mill. So were the events leading up to it. I promise (myself, you) not to let myself get into such a childish escape-route again. Tequila can not sing a ninety minute show. So, I fired it from the gig. And I'm such a sorry drunk on it, anyway. Cuervo is for weeping, blithering poet-boy in Mexico: My Panamanian blood was aching for a good tears 'n' tantrum because of the outside pressure. But, I found the next day that the only good antidote is unstoppable song straight from the bones. Anything else just goes into the urinal at the end of the night.

FACING PAGE: While critically well received upon its release in August 1994, *Grace* still needed to be actively promoted, and Jeff and his band embarked on a tour that would stretch out to over a year and a half. The work would prove to be artistically rewarding but physically and emotionally punishing, as fans saw for themselves when Jeff took the stage of the Green Mill in Chicago on November 8, 1994. Rattled by a call from a Sony executive who upbraided him for dissing MTV in an interview, Jeff hit the bottle before the show and gave a disastrous, inebriated performance. Five months later, during a break in rehearsals before the group resumed touring, Jeff caught up on his fan mail and wrote this belated, apologetic letter about the Green Mill show to a fan in the audience that night.

PAGE 157: Unfinished, undated lyric poem taking "whitebread conservative drunks" to task. No musical track for these lyrics has been unearthed.

TODAY. I MUST BE A RECOVERING PASSIVE-AGRESSIVE PERSONALITY.
HOW CAN PEOPLE SIT ON A TRAIN AND NOT NOTICE EACH OTHER?
HOW CAN PEOPLE RESIST THE URGE TO CONNECT SOMEHOW?
NOT COMPULSIVELY, TOTALLY WITHOUT TACT OR GENTILITY
BUT SOMETIMES STRANGERS DO RECOGNIZE EACH OTHER.
OF COURSE, I'M TALKING ABOUT YOUNG FEMALES. NOT
TO FUCK OR TO FUCK WITH BUT MAYBE JUST TO SATISFY
CURIOSITY ... OR MAYBE MY HORMONES ARE STILL WORKING
OVERTIME, JUST LIKE MY BEAUTIFUL FILTHY MIND, AND I SEEK
SOME VERY LIGHT ENTERTAINMENT. CAN PEOPLE FEEL MY
EYES ON THEM AS I DO THEIRS ON ME? DO WE ALL KNOW
THAT WE'RE HERE IN THIS SOCIAL PRISON SYSTEM? WHY AREN'T
WE PREPARED TO HAVE MORE FUN BEING HUMAN BEINGS?
WILL WOMEN EVER OUTGROW THE SCARS INFLICTED UPON THEM
BY A WORLD RULED BY MEN? MUST MY FANTASIES BE STUCK
WORKING OVERTIME? LIVING IN THE ABSTRACT IS A CANCER AND
A HELL, MY LOVE, AND THE LEVELLING OF HEATED DAYDREAM TO
THE EDICTS OF BLESSED REALITY IS A SAD AND NECESSARY EXECUTION
TO WITNESS... THE BEHEADING OF A TORTURED BLONDE HAIRED BOY-
CHILD. AND ALL OF THE GARBAGE THAT WAS STUFFED IN HIS SKULL
IS NOW CARRIED TO THE PYRE TO BURN AND ADD TO THE STENCH
OF ~~XXXXXX XXXXX~~ ALL THE OTHER LITTLE DEATHS CAUSED BY THE IMPOTENCE OF
HIS JUDGEMENT, THROUGHOUT HIS LIFE. HIS OVERGROWN LIFE.
RAISED BY A SPANK-WIELDING KISSING MACHINE. MY HAIR
LOOKS LIKE SHIT AND I'M FEELING EMBARRASSED AND UGLY ALL-
AROUND.

Pigs in Office

Come on ask me over
Don't think just groove with that motor
Black rain, Black sun, Black flower
Moving over and under your bonfire

You're right I'm here for your children
To throw them to the acid freaks and the punks
It's better than living as puppets
Of your famous whitebread conservative drunks
We're gonna take over
~~We with steal your fortress~~ fresh from copping
In the back of our jitney cabs and sing
We smell the blood of ethnic cleansing
Through your official fax machines

I mean you, I mean you, I mean you Pigs in office

I am the filthy elixir, a hatchet for your ear
Don't you remember me baby I'm employee of the year
You call me a liar a devil and a whore
I am everything you say and so much more 2x

We have no time for you any longer
You pop the hard-on as we suffer
No tears no mercy or compassion
I'm the whore whos knock you straight to a whole other gutter
Blood in glorious explosion
Pornographic death painted on the sky
Watch us, ~~listen and~~ weep and listen
Get ready to shake hands with the other side

Pigs in office

I know you'll grow to hate me as I live on.

PAGES 159–164: After wrapping up the summer European leg of the 1995 *Grace* tour, Jeff had a rare period of free time between July 19 and August 23. Two years had lapsed since he had recorded *Grace*, and the need to record new material was mounting. But during this break, Jeff clearly had other things on his mind, namely family. In these extraordinary pages, written "in a bar . . . with two shots of tequila in me," he uncorked his feelings about his family heritage. In some of his most impassioned writing, he lays bare his thoughts on Tim Buckley's life and recorded legacy; Buckley family members; Tim's friends, whom Jeff had tracked down to learn about his father's life; and his views on the comparisons to his father that he knew would haunt him. Grappling with both his mother's and father's lineage, he tries to grasp why Tim left him and Mary when Jeff was so young. Judging from the beginning of the entry ("my final post") as well as the way it addresses "you Net surfers," it appears Jeff was considering posting this piece online. In the end, he may have considered it too personal and instead relegated it to his notebook.

I'm POSTING MY ~~ONE~~ FINAL POST. ~~VICE~~

NEXT WEEK, WE FLY TO AUSTRALIA FOR A TWO WEEK TOUR.
~~BEFORE I LEFT~~ I WANTED TO LEAVE A MESSAGE FOR
THE PAGE BEFORE I LEAVE. I'LL START WITH SOMETHING THAT
I'VE BEEN SAVING FOR A LONG, LONG TIME.

    I HAVE ALWAYS WITHELD ALL POSSIBLE CONVERSATION
ABOUT MY FATHER FROM THE JOURNALISTS I'VE MET IN THE
LAST THREE YEARS. I WON'T EVER LEAVE IT TO THE PRESS,
GOOD WRITERS OR BAD, TO FILTER MY WORDS TO THE READER.
TO THE PUBLIC. IT'S JUST TOO INTIMATE. IT'S TOO
INTIMATE FOR YOU ... YOU NET SURFERS. YOU TRIVIA-GLUTTONS.
AS I HAVE SAID BEFORE, IN MANY WAYS AND TO TOTALLY
DEAF EARS, IT'S NOT HIS MEMORY OR HIS GHOST THAT
I DESPISE AND AVOID. IT'S THE FACT THAT THERE IS A LARGE
MASS OF PEOPLE IN MY PATH - HIS FANS, ~~MY~~ CRITICS, CULTISTS,
EDITORS AND WRITERS OF OUR BELOVED ROCK-PRESS, MY CRITICS -
WHOM I HAVE ALWAYS KNOWN WOULD BE AHEAD OF ME TO
CONTRAST, COMPARE AND TEAR ME DOWN UNDER THE SHADOW
OF MY FATHER, SOMETIMES IN MY FATHER'S BEHALF (AS IF
THEY HAVE THE KNOWLEDGE AND AUTHORITY). THIS IS SOMETHING
I'VE KNOWN SINCE I WAS SMALL. EVEN HIS FRIENDS JOINING
IN WAS A FACTOR I KNEW WOULD COME TO PASS. ~~XXXX~~
~~XXXX~~. HE WOULD BE DEIFIED BY HIS DEATH AND I WOULD BE
TRIVIALIZED ALONG WITH TIM BY THE WORK HE DID AND THE
RABID EXPECTATION FOR ME TO LIVE OR DIE BY IT. THIS WAS
A DAUNTING THOUGHT for A CHILD TO REALIZE, YES? IT WAS.
EXCEPT FOR A GNAWING FEELING IN MY HEART THAT IT WAS ALL
A LOAD OF BULLSHIT. "~~I JUST DON'T FUCKING CARE~~" I THOUGHT.
    HOW COULD I CARE, HONESTLY, ABOUT A POTENTIAL GAUNTLET
OF REVERENT HIPPIES. LOOKING DOWN AT ME WAITING FOR THE
TIME WHEN THEY WOULD EITHER STICK ME ON THEIR LAZY PARADE FLOAT OF
DAYS-GONE-BY, FLOATING NOWHERE, OR GIVE ME THE THUMBS DOWN

CLUCKING THEIR TONGUES; BOTH WITH EQUAL GLEE. WHAT FOR?
TO WHAT FRUITFUL END? FOR WHO'S SALVATION? MY FATHER
WAS DEAD. I ALMOST JUST BARELY TOUCHED HIS LIFE, I WAS
SO CLOSE. BUT I LOST HIM. I SAVOUR THE MORSEL TO THIS DAY.
THE TASTE IS ALMOST GONE. I WAS STUCK WITH HIS CULT, HIS
BLURRY MEMORY, BLURRED INTO OBSCURITY EVER AFTER BY SECOND-
HAND STORIES, CONJECTURE, BURIED JEALOUSIES, GUILT, SECRETS,
ACCUSATIONS AND SO MUCH PAIN ... SO, SO MUCH ... AN OCEAN OF PAIN.
ALL THE INCREDULOUS SOULS LEFT BEHIND IN A FLASH. HIS WOMAN
AND HIS SON, JUDY AND TAYLOR, LEFT BEHIND. WITHOUT TIMOTHY
FALLING IN LOVE WITH THEM, JUDY'S HEART WOULD STILL BE PARALYZED
BY THE DEATH OF HER FIRST HUSBAND. TAYLOR WOULD STILL BE MUTE
AND IN SHOCK FROM THE DAY HE WATCHED HIS NATURAL FATHER
DIE IN FRONT OF HIM. TAYLOR WAS IN A STATE OF SHOCK AND
SPOKE TO NO-ONE FOR YEARS BECAUSE OF IT. IMAGINE IT. DEVISE
YOUR OWN HORROR AND PLACE IT UPON YOUR FATHER OR MOTHER.
YOU ARE NINE YEARS OLD. WATCH THEM DIE. CAR ACCIDENT IN MEXICO.
WHEN TIM FELL IN LOVE WITH JUDY AND TAYLOR HE FILLED
THEIR LIVES UP AGAIN, JUDY HAD A HEART REOPENED AND RENEWED.
AND TAYLOR ... HE WOKE UP AGAIN. HE WAS BEING RAISED BY
A LONG-HAIRED LOVER-FREAK ... SLIGHT DISCIPLINARIAN ... IN LOVE
WITH HIS WOMAN AND HER SON. HE SOON MARRIED JUDY AND ADOPTED TAYLOR.
THE BUCKLEY ARTICLES WILL TELL YOU OF A TROUBLED MARRIAGE. VIEWS
FROM THE OUTSIDE, MY FRIEND, MAYBE TRUE, MAYBE FALSE OR SOMEWHERE
IN BETWEEN. SO WHAT, THEY WERE TROUBLED PEOPLE. LISTEN TO
ME, IT WAS HIS LOVE THAT RESCUED JUDY AND TAYLOR FROM BEING
FROZEN BY TRAGEDY. AND IT WAS THEIR LOVE THAT RESCUED MY FATHER FROM HIS
GUILT LONG ENOUGH FOR HIM TO ALLOW HIMSELF TO
SET THINGS RIGHT IN HIS LIFE. NOT TO MENTION THE REST OF MARRIED LIFE,
THE GOOD AND THE BAD. I KNOW SO MUCH OF IT AND I STILL AFTER ALL OF THESE YEARS
ONLY COME UP WITH LOVE BETWEEN THEM.

HE LEFT HIS MOTHER BEHIND. HIS
SISTER. HIS DERANGED FATHER. MY GRANDFATHER, TIMOTHY JR.

With a father like this man, it is no wonder that Tim Buckley was afraid to come back to me. So afraid to be my father because his only paradigm for fatherhood was a deranged lunatic with a steel plate in his head. I'm sure that he was ashamed of leaving my mother and me... I know the circumstances and though I have felt abandoned sometimes, I understand him... I understand that he had no choice... But I know that he must have been scared shitless to ~~think he might~~ think possibly become like his father. Scared shitless ~~to treat~~ of treating me the way his father treated him and his family. Can you imagine the ~~heartbreak~~? The useless, shitty torture day in, day out? When I was twenty-three, I began to track down my estranged Buckleys: Elaine, Kathleen & Timothy Charles Jr. My grandma, my aunt and my grandfather, respectively. When I was twenty-four, I found Elaine and Kathleen. They are beautiful. I never found my grandfather. He is now reunited with his late son, ~~Joseph~~.

Elaine explained one day, as we sat in the bleachers at the Monterey Jazz Festival on our big date together, about Tim's father. He came back with a steel plate in his head from a landmine that exploded under him, near him, during combat when he was in Korea. He came home to his family and was pretty much all right. One day, years later, at his job, the workers had gone on strike and scab labor had moved in... My grandfather was the foreman... It was raining and there was a leak in the roof. Nobody knew how to fix it, or wouldn't, and he climbed up to the roof to do it himself. A real hardass. The only thing was that his leather soles slipped on the wet roof and he slid down on his back, to the ground, landing squarely on the back of his neck. He was never the same, my father's father. My mom and my dad both had the shit beat out of them, by their fathers, throughout their teens. Escape, escape, escape, escape, escape sweet Timothy and Mary. In November of 1966 I was born.

THEY HAD MARRIED BRIEFLY AND HAD DIVORCED BEFORE
I WAS BORN... MY MOM WAS 18 AND MY FATHER WAS 19.
THERE ARE NO PICTURES OF MY FATHER IN HIS CHILDHOOD.
MY GRANDMA ELAINE DESTROYED THEM OUT OF ANGUISH,
OUT OF LOSS, OUT OF PAIN. I DON'T REMEMBER WHEN
IT WAS SHE DID IT, EXACTLY. IT DOESN'T MATTER.
                                        TIM WOULD ALWAYS
GIVE A CALL TO ELAINE FROM THE ROAD, OR FROM N.Y. (THE FAMILY
WAS BASED IN ORANGE COUNTY, CA.) THEY SHARED A DEEP
CONNECTION, A DEEP, DEEP LOVE. HIS FATHER WAS JEALOUS OF
THE BOND. NOT TO MENTION TIM'S TALENT. MY GRANDFATHER,
KATHLEEN TOLD ME, HAD A BEAUTIFUL VOICE. IRISH TENOR. BEAUTIFUL.
TOO MUCH OF A MILITARY HARDASS TO DEAL WITH HIS OWN AND HIS SONS
TALENTS. I WISH IT WERE OTHERWISE. I WISH ALL OF THIS
FUCKING SHIT ~~WAS~~ WAS OTHERWISE. I LOVE YOU, YOU POOR
FUCKING BASTARDS. WHERE ARE YOU NOW? I WISH I KNEW
WHERE YOU ARE RIGHT NOW. I MISS YOU SO GODDAMN MUCH.
I'VE BEEN WONDERING ABOUT YOU, ALL MY LIFE.
                                        KATHLEEN IS A SEATTLE
RESIDENT AND A POET. WHEN I FIRST MET HER, I FOUND
OUT WHAT MY GRANDFATHER LOOKS LIKE. ELAINE SAYS THAT SHE'S
THE SPITTING IMAGE, BIG BLUE EYES, BROAD IRISH CHEEKBONES,
BROWN HAIR, IRISH IRISH IRISH. SHE LOVED TIM. LOVED HIM.
LOOKED UP TO HIM, TINY BABY SISTER THAT SHE WAS. HATED IT WHEN
HE MOVED OUT OF THE HOUSE. DEVISTATED WHEN HE DIED. DESTROYED.
ABANDONED. ELAINE'S HEART WAS SHATTERED. THAT WHICH HAD BEEN EVENTUALLY
CRUSHED HAD MIRACULOUSLY BEEN SHATTERED TO PIECES.
                                        I'M IN A BAR
RIGHT NOW WITH TWO SHOTS OF TEQUILA IN ME. NO ONE CAN
SEE ME TRYING NOT TO FUCKING CRY. I'M TRYING TO SUMMON
THE HARDASS. TWO MORE SHOTS ON THE WAY. I'M FEELING THE
CLEFT IN MY CHIN WITH THE TIPS OF MY FINGERS. THE OLDER
I GROW, THE DEEPER IT GETS.

Over the years
I have contacted and talked with every character in the play. Almost all. It's becoming irrelevant. I've spoken with friends of his, old lovers (mostly by accident ... a couple of them approached me post-gig on my first solo tour ... bizarre but enlightening) Around Halloween, 1989, I met Lee Underwood. He was the guitarist in Tim's best combos way back in the day. He is your T.C.B. III Archivist. Told me plenty of history. It was his personal view, yes, but so, so important. I'm glad he was so forthcoming with the stories because I must've seemed pretty bizarre: black-death rock-loser, very mohawked, stick legged wierdo at his door ... asking another stranger about his dead father. All of his stories are now rock journalism. You can find it on your own, computer-children of the night. He always mentioned "Tim's Good Looks," "Tim's Charm with the ladies," "Tim's Vocal Technique-Epiphany" — Cathy Berberian and the lot. "Tim said, always said, he'd never live to see thirty." "Tim liked booze and reds." "Tim pushed the boundaries." Please excuse my superficiality because there was so much more. It's just that you can find it all yourself. Watch ... take all of it, cut it out of the magazines and put it together on a table. Lee has a Tim Buckley mantra 1,000 words in length. I have violated the code of the mantra many times. "Do not question the mantra. Do not contradict the mantra. Do not leave the temple without crossing yourself and kneeling before the scroll containing the downbeat article." I love, love fucking love this man! No one has been closer to the creative process of the Buckley ouvre, especially the God-given brilliance of your Lorca-Blue Afternoon-Starsailor holy trinity period. He was there. He was down. I swear to God that I am serious. I just can't be a disciple to my own father. Fuck it. He just made some stuff that I didn't dig so much. It's human. I wanted to be his son, not his follower.

AND ALSO, IT'S MY HUMBLE OPINION THAT THE UNDERWOOD,
COLLINS - HOLY TRINITY PERIOD JUST SIMPLY ROCKED. LEE
ROCKED. CHECK OUT THE ELECTRIC PIANO ON LORCA. HAH!! THE VOCAL! HAH!
SO FUNKY. THAT SONG IS NASTY FUNK. NIGHTMARE SEX FUNKY.
IN THE CONTEXT OF TIM BUCKLEY LAND ... WHICH I KNOW
~~MORE~~ MORE THAN A FEW THOUSAND OF YOU DWELL ... THAT WORK
TIM DID WAS IT. THAT WAS IT. IN MY MEMORY OF MY
FATHER, WHEN I DIE, YOU CAN ALL REMEMBER MY ADMIRATION
OF THAT PERIOD. THEY HIT IT. THEY CERTAINLY HIT SOMETHING
THAT NO ONE CAN TOUCH. FOR ME, LEE'S PRIDE IS SANCTIFIED. LOOK,
~~I CAN'T~~ THIS IS THE KIND OF PERSON I AM: GYPSY WOMAN
AND BUZZIN' FLY IRK ME. ALTHOUGH I APPRECIATE THEM ...
I JUST DON'T GET TO THEM, CHEMICALLY. ~~GIVE~~ GIVE ME "THE RIVER"
GIVE ME FUCKING "MONTEREY", GIVE ME "MOUNTAIN" DON'T GIVE ME
HOBO'S AND BLAH BLAH BLAH. GIVE ME LARRY BECKETT AT HIS
HORNY BEST. HORNY HORNY POET-MAN. YOU CAN'T WRITE WORTH
A DAMN UNLESS YOU ~~ARE~~ ON FIRE FOREVER. CAN I GET A WITNESS?
ANYWAY ... IT'S JUST MY PERSONAL OPINION!
IT'S JUST MY PERSONAL OPINION
OF MY FATHER'S WORK.
I'M HIS SON, YES, BUT WE COME FROM TWO DIFFERENT WORLDS.
I AM FROM A COMPLETELY DIFFERENT WORLD FROM YOU ALL.
FROM MY FAMILY. FROM YOUR PARENTS. FROM MY LOVER.
"LOOK AT THE FOOL". OH GOD, I JUST CAN'T GET THROUGH IT.
AND I AM OVERCOME WITH THE DESIRE TO GRAB HIM AND KISS
HIM AND PLEAD FOR HIM TO PLEASE LET ME BE IN YOUR BAND FOR
AWHILE SO WE CAN STOP THIS WHITE FUNK WIERDNESS, WE DON'T
NEED HERB COHEN ANYMORE. "STARSAILOR" WASN'T A FAILURE, IT WAS
AN UNTOUCHABLE BEAUTY AND I THINK YOU MUST STOP THINKING OF
DYING AND START DANCING WITH THAT LUSCIOUS BEAUTY YOU CREATED.
BECAUSE SHE IS HOT WHILE SEX WAITING TO HAPPEN AND YOUR STUDIO CATS FROM
L.A. AIN'T GONNA GET YOU THERE. I'LL HELP YOU EVEN IF I FAIL.
BUT THEN ... I LOVE HIM ANYWAY. LET'S BOOGIE. GET ON TOP IF YOU MUST.
MY LIFE WITH MY GHOST FATHER IN A NUTSHELL. SIX TEQUILAS LATER.

PAGE 165: Especially when writing songs, Jeff frequently turned to this Gibson acoustic, which was outfitted with pickups for added sonic versatility.

FACING PAGE: One of Jeff's favorite guitars, this Gibson Les Paul Custom was bought on the road in Wisconsin in 1994. During downtime on a quiet Sunday afternoon, Jeff and a crew member ventured out to a musical instrument store and found the guitar, buying it for about $700.

PAGES 168–173: "I Woke Up in a Strange Place," a splattered-imagery rocker Jeff and his band played regularly on their Australian tour in early 1996, was another original that came together over the course of months. The first three of the following pages contain additional verses not included in the take heard on the posthumous live album *Mystery White Boy*. The version on page 170 includes a planned chorus—"Sexy, sexy lack of escape / I'm drunk on you til the end"—that was abandoned. For all the work that went into the song, Jeff ultimately did not tackle it during sessions with producer Tom Verlaine in New York in 1996, nor was it included in plans for his Memphis sessions the following year.

Woke Up in A Strange Place

V1

THE GHOST CAME TO VISIT WITH MY KEYS IN HIS POCKET
KISSED ON MY MOUTH WITH HIS EYES ROLLING OUT OF HIS SOCKET
MEMORIES CRUMBLED ~~UNDER~~ UNPER ~~SOLID~~ STEEL RESISTENCE
I WAS TORN OUT LIKE A PAGE FROM THE BOOK OF EXISTENCE

CHORUS

I WOKE UP IN A STRANGE PLACE
MY MIND A BLUR AND SOME BLOOD ON MY CHIN
I MADE A CALL FOR A BLACK DEATH CAB
MY DESTINATION IS MOVING ON IN
AND I REMEMBERED THE WORDS YOU TOLD ME
THEY CAME DOWN SO HARD, SO PLAIN
FATE WILL FIND, YOU MY LOVE, IN YOUR GLASS OF CHAMPAGNE

V2

LOVE CAME CALLING AS A COUNTERFIET MISTRESS
STEALING FROM THE POCKETS OF HER SADO MASOCHIST
MOUTHING FALSE ~~PRAISE~~ PRAISE LIKE A TONGUE ON CRYSTAL-METH
HER CIGARETTE SMELLED LIKE THE FEAR IN MY CHEST

V3

I LIED TO MY HOST THAT I KNEW HOW ~~FAR~~ FAR I COULD GO
BUT I EMPTIED MY GUTS OUT ON HIS BRAND NEW STEREO
HE PAID ME TO GO UPSTAIRS AND SPEND THE NIGHT WITH HIS FRIEND
I NEVER WANT TO SEE MY FACE IN THE MIRROR AGAIN

CHORUS

I WOKE UP IN A STRANGE PLACE
MUSIC SO LOUD THAT I SPIT UP MY BEER
I TOOK A RIDE IN THAT BLACK DEATH CAB
MY DESTINATION IS ALMOST HERE
EASY NOW, THE CAR IS SPEEDING UP FOR MY LAST CHANCE
CRASH INTO FREEDOM
FATE ~~~~ IS GONNA FIND YOU BOY IN YOUR GLASS OF CHAMPAGNE

BREAK

V/IV SWEAT POURS DOWN I'M THE BACKSEAT SLEEPING
SHE WATCHES THE PHONE FROM HER EMPTY BED WEEPING
THE GHOST GUNS THE MOTOR ON OUR WAY TO THE PROMISED LAND
A DRAWBRIDGE ABANDONED AND THE FUCKER LEADS NO WHERE

CHORUS THIS IS A SONG TO THE DISLOCATED
WHO'RE BORN TO LOVE BUT ARE DOOMED TO BE HATED
BECAUSE THE LIES OF THE SPIRIT POSSESSED YOU
BECAUSE THE EYES OF YOUR LOVER RESIST YOU

LISTEN UP BOY, I'M SHOUTING FROM THE BOTTOM OF A BARREL
HEADING DOWN THE RAPIDS

STEADY NOW, KEEP YOUR AIM SOLID AS YOUR TEMPLE TURNS
TO KISS THE PISTOL
HEED THESE WORDS OF MINE, WHEN YOU MISPLACE YOUR MIND,
FATE IS GONNA FIND YOU IN YOUR GLASS OF CHAMPAGNE

THE PEOPLE WHO COME TO YOUR SHOWS

THEY DON'T COME TO GET THEIR MINDS BLOWN

THEY CAME TO GET THEIR HEARTS TORN OUT.

4/20/97

Woke Up in a Strange Place

✓ I left the ghost with my keys in his pocket
Kisses on my mouth with his eyes hanging out its sockets
Memories crumbled under steel resistence
I was torn out like pages from the book of existence

Sexy, sexy lack of escape
I'm drunk on you 'til the end

CH: I woke up in a strange place
Mind a blur and some red on my chin
I'm in the bottom of a black death cab
Some destination must be moving on in

✓ Some other bedroom and a counterfiet mistress
Stealing from the pockets of her sado-masochist
I felt so divided but my body said its best that you rest
Her cigarette tasted like the fear inside my chest

Sexy, sexy lack of escape
I'm drunk on you til the end

CH: I woke up in a strange place
Music so loud I spit up my beer
I'm in the bottom of a black death cab
Some destination must be already here

Easy now, the car is speeding up for my last chance
Crash into freedom
Fate is gonna find me down in my glass champange

V
Sweat pours down you're in the back seat sleeping
She waits by her window on her empty bed weeping
Driving straight upwards, all ~~but~~ you know is in the present tense

This is the time when all your best intentions
Become accidents

CH:
And you'll wake up in a strange place
Dull as a junebug in a light fixture
You can't remember just how you came
Into this house or who's it is

Listen to me, the road leads nowhere
And it comes down so hard and so plain
Fate is gonna find you down in your glass of champange

STEADY NOW, ~~KEEP YOUR~~ EYES ON THE TARGET
AS THE TEMPLE TURNS TO KISS THE PISTOL

I WOKE UP IN A STRANGE PLACE
MUSIC SO LOUD I SPIT UP MY BEER
~~NO~~ I TOOK A RIDE IN A BLACK DEATH CAB
MY DESTINATION IS ALMOST HERE
EASY NOW, THE CAR IS SPEEDING UP FOR THE LAST CHANCE CRASH
IN TO FREEDOM
FATE IS GONNA FIND ME IN MY GLASS OF CHAMPAGNE

SWEAT BREAKS THE ~~COMFORT~~ COMFORT OF YOUR BACKSEAT SLEEPING
SHE WATCHES THE WINDOW FROM HER EMPTY BED WEEPING
THE GHOST GUNS THE MOTOR TO THE LAND THAT HE PROMISED
A DRAWBRIDGE ABANDONED AND THE FUCKER LEADS NOWHERE

WHERE HAVE I BEEN?
SEARCHING FOR GOLD IN THE BONFIRE
AND WHO AM I NOW?
WILL I RETURN TO HER ARMS ~~ROOM~~ ALIVE
LISTEN NOW, I'M SHOUTING FROM THE BOTTOM OF A
BARRELL HEADING DOWN THE RAPIDS
GOODNIGHT, LADY, I'M DYING NOW FOR WHAT I DID ... (BREAK)

THIS IS A WARNING TO THE DISLOCATED
WHO ARE BORN INTO LOVE BUT ARE DOOMED TO BE HATED
BECAUSE THE LIES OF THE SPIRIT POSSESSED YOU
BECAUSE THE EYES OF YOUR LOVER RESIST YOU

THERE IS A LIGHT
YOU HAVE SEEN FROM YOUR DOOR
THIS IS THE DEATH OF THE MAN YOU WERE BEFORE

THERE WAS A TONE I HEARD
ALL NIGHT LONG, IN THE DISTANCE, IN THE STREET
IT HELPED ME FINALLY SLEEP

WHEN THEY PULLED HIS HEAD
AWAY FROM THE STEERING WHEEL, IN THE MORNING
THE TONE IN MY HEAD DISAPPEARED
AND I CAN SLEEP NO MORE AT NIGHT

HAVE YOU BEEN DRINKING AGAIN?
TELL ME THE TRUTH
YOU GOT SOMEPLACE TO SLEEP TONIGHT?
DO YOU NEED ME TO BE YOUR FRIEND?
WE ALL NEED TO BE LOOKED AFTER, SOMETIME
DO YOU NEED ME TO PLAY YOUR MOTHER?
DO YOU NEED ME TO PLAY YOUR GIRLFRIEND?
HAVE YOU BEEN TRIPPING ON X AGAIN?

Demon John

I threw out my plans of escape, papers with numbers and names,

I cast off my limp-wristed shame

I wore white to catch the lipstick souvenirs

In a massive make-out session with the gods.

My hand LEFT trembling cut the flesh of my calves

To drain the fear from my walk

My dream catalogue is NOW ^defaced with idiot porno cartoons

And I got rid of it in secret

We have probably COUGHED ON THE breathed its ashes by now THEY'RE FLOATING THROUGH THE AIR OF THE CITY

Stream of soul murder, by the light of THE sun 2x TO HELP US DIE, HELP US DIE, HELP US.

Stone cold stupid, by the light of the sun 2x

So long defensless young sonny-jim and the ~~BLOOD~~ DESPERATE

Hand that begs WITHIN ~~FOR ALMS~~ your winning smile

~~ESCAPE THE BAR-SIDE SHOWDOWN DISSECTOR~~

You will be stained by the alcohol run-down of forgotten

Demon John or some other master of unmasking

You will not escape the bar-side showdown dissector

Casual nightmares come down in waves of disaster

And bliss the actress bliss the assassin bliss the abyss BLISS THE ACCESSORY TO MURDER, BLISS YOU'RE NOT AWARE

And you freeze on the eyes of Demon John

Bliss we follow single-file to harvest cotton in the heat

For wedding clothes we will never wear

Demon John : When you take the riddle from my hand

It will be time for you to leave, but you look so

Fucking ~~GOOD~~ WASTED you'll probably stay here all night.

I was red in the eyes with tequila

The night I got a load of Demon John

His generosity rotting the marrow

FACING PAGE: Early, undated take on the impressionistic "Demon John." Jeff would record a longer version on the four-track in his Memphis home, with the goal of cutting a full band version in the summer of 1997.

NEXT PAGE: Jeff begins expressing his concerns about the eagerly awaited follow-up to *Grace* in this undated entry from 1995.

"ONE FOR THE MONEY
CHOP CHOP CHOP"

DON'T MAKE THE MISTAKE
OF LETTING THEM PUSH YOU
INTO BREAKING ~~THE YOUR~~ THE GROOVE
WITH..... YOUR SOUL
DON'T LET THEM MAKE
YOU RELEASE IT BEFORE ITS READY
OR THAT SHIT WILL FOLLOW
YOU LIKE A GHOST, WHEREVER YOU GO
FOR THE REST OF YOUR LIFE
UNTIL YOU DIE

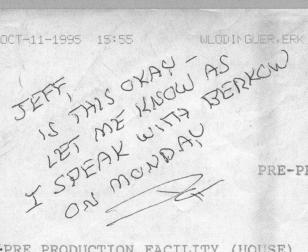

JEFF,
IS THIS OKAY —
LET ME KNOW AS
I SPEAK WITH BERKOW
ON MONDAY

JEFF BUCKLEY
PRE-PRODUCTION/RECORDING BUDGET
1995/1996

*PRE PRODUCTION FACILITY (HOUSE)		
(6 MONTHS @ $1,100)		$6,600
*SOUNDPROOFING		1,500
*UTILITIES (HEAT,LIGHT,WATER)		1,500
*TELEPHONE/FAX		3,000
CATERING		3,000
STUDIO RENTAL (NOT INCL. MASTERING)		60,000
EQUIPMENT RENTALS		10,000
MUSIC SUPPLIES		2,000
*REHEARSAL P.A., CABLES,MISC.		10,000
PRODUCER'S FEE		50,000
ENGINEER'S FEE		35,000
*BAND COMPENSATION:		
MATT JOHNSON	$10,000	
MICHAEL TIGHE	10,000	
MICK GRONDAHL	10,000	30,000

ADDITIONAL MUSICIANS		7,500
RECORDING COORDINATOR (GENE BOWEN-FLAT FEE)		5,000
PER DIEMS (45 DAYS,$40/DAY,7 PEOPLE)		12,600
PAYROLL TAXES (@ 15%)		6,375
TRUCKING/TRANSPORTATION		4,000
UNION DUES (AFM)		4,000
CONTINGENCY (@ 5%)		12,604

TOTAL		$264,679

+ TAPE   5,000.00
NEW TOTAL   269,679.00

* DOES NOT INCLUDE LODGING IF BAND IS OUT OF TOWN

PREVIOUS PAGE: By the end of 1995, Jeff's label and management were eager for him to return to the studio and start cutting a new album. During band practice in Sag Harbor, New York, in the fall of 1995, drummer Matt Johnson had informed Jeff that he was leaving the group; the fact that Johnson is listed here shows Jeff was still keeping management in the dark about the shaky status of his band during this period. These plans for a full-fledged sophomore album launch, like others during this period, would not materialize.

PAGES 179–181: Preliminary drafts of the tormented "Moodswing Whiskey," a prominent part of the set during Jeff's final tour of Australia in early 1996. Jeff would discard many of these lines, although the use of the words "beautiful" and "loser" would return in the final rendition.

~~YOU'RE BLANKING OUT AT CHRISTMAS TIME~~

NO MORE BLANKING OUT AT CHRISTMAS TIME
NO NEED TO RESIST
THEY'LL PRY THE BOTTLE FROM YOUR HANDS
LOST IN A KISS
WITH YOU MOODSWING WHISKEY, YOU MOODSWING
                                                      WHISKEY

LIGHTS YOUR EYES AND CHEATED AND IT LIED
LAUGHED AS IT STOLE HER
BURNS YOUR TONGUE JUST LIKE THE
SWEAT FROM HER SHOULDER
   YOU MOODSWING WHISKEY, YOU ~~MOODSWING WHISKEY~~ ARE LOVE THE DESTROYER

YOU WERE BORN BY PURE ACCIDENT
TIED TO A STONE
EYES TRAINED ON THE LEMON PEEL
YOU WISH WERE A GUN
YOU'RE GOOD THING QUITS ~~YOU~~ ME, YOU'RE GOOD THING QUITS ME

YOU'RE TIRED OF FINDING ALL YOUR WEDDING RINGS
TRAPPED IN THE HEATER
SPRAYING WATER ON THE FLOOR
OF YOUR SEX-STARVED ROOM

I RAISE MY GLASS TO ALL THE
HEADLESS ACROBATS
FACES CRUSHED AND DEAD IN THE
CIRCUS DUST

WHO TRIED TO FLY IN THE FACE OF GRAVITY
FOR THE PRICE OF ADMISSION

HERE'S TO THE LOSER
WHAT HAS IT LOST YOU NOW
HERE'S TO THE LOSER
WHAT WAS IT LOST YOU
WAS IT BEAUTIFUL

I AM A MAN ENCLOSED IN QUOTATION MARKS
EVER SINCE I TOOK A DRINK OF YOU

MOODSWING WHISKEY FLOODS MY BRAIN
I DIDN'T MEAN TO WRECK THIS TRAIN
I NEED HER IN MY BED AGAIN

I'M SICK OF FINDING WEDDING RINGS
TRAPPED IN MY HEATER
I'M SICK OF WAKING ON THE FLOOR
OF THIS SEX-STARVED ROOM

You smell of blood and bring the rain
The taste of tin and break champagne
~~Its made a mess of things again~~
Its made a mess of things again

Moodswing Whiskey Oooh Moodswing Whiskey

~~That Ill run another round~~
~~around the~~
One more thing when you buy that one last round
Make sure your baby's out of town
One look from you you'll both go down

In Moodswing History Moodswing History

Because your hate to live inside your shell
And everybody elses shell as well
One bottle gone and I'm back to the well

In Your Moodswing Hits Me Your Moodswing Whiskey

WE ARE BORN TO LIVE
WE ARE BORN TO UNDERSTAND
WE ARE BORN TO CARRY A **CURSED** PATTERN
AND BE TRANSFORMED BY PAIN

TIME WILL BRING US
WHERE NEED TO BE
A PLACE WHERE WE CAN
~~ACCEPT THIS LOVE~~
MY TRUE SELF IS ~~NOTHING~~ WHAT BROUGHT
ME HERE TO GIVE MYSELF TO YOU
A PLACE WHERE WE COULD ACCEPT THIS LOVE
YOUR EYES AND BODY
BRIGHTENED — SILENT WATERS DEEP
~~THE SOUL YOU KEEP~~

OR ANY DAY YOU WANT
~~THE ~~

MAYBE ~~SOMEDAY~~ ~~I DON'T KNOW HOW OR WHEN~~
I HAVE NO ~~WONDER~~ HOW OR WHEN
RIGHT TO

FACING PAGE: "We are born to carry a cursed pattern and be transformed by pain," Jeff writes in an early draft of "Morning Theft," undated 1996.

NEXT PAGE: As Jeff and his band were heading into the last leg of their *Grace* tour dates, Jeff had more time to work on songs, like this preliminary, truncated draft of what would become his anti-media diatribe "The Sky Is a Landfill." At this stage, he was still toying with his imagery: "the landfill of souls" would become "the garbage dump of souls," and "death is no mystery to me now" would be revised to the more life-affirming "this power is no mystery to us now." The song would be among those recorded with producer Tom Verlaine in mid-1996.

MORNING THEFT

SKY IS A LANDFILL

SKY BLUE SKY

Landfill

Damn your hurry to die
To feed the landfill of souls in the sky
This City's ripped the shelter
Of illusion from my brow
Death is no mystery to me now

Leave your spirit suicide
The cancer you won't remove
Cast your funeral rose inside
And bury the need to prove
Our mutilation is to gain from the system

I see you take another drag
10 more dead souls to raise the flag
The sky is a landfill

We share our bodies in disdain for the system

Morning Thing

I Gotta Stay Up With The Rising Sun
I'm ~~Right~~ Up Close ~~To~~ Watching All Of It Done
~~Faster~~ Running Up The Mountains & The Just Begun
Vision Ever Open
~~Take Pity On Me Down~~ ~~From~~ The Pacified Haze
~~Dealers~~ ~~Something~~ ~~Full~~ Full Speed Away
Comfort In The Arms
Of The Decadence Grey
Funeral Songs Through
All Of My Days
My Spirit Ever Weakened
Come The Moments Of ~~The~~ Hunger
Bullets ~~Fire~~ Through My Mind
Ripping Holes Of Desperation
~~And Life Slipping By Me~~
And Life Slipping By
Slipping Right By Me

Moments Like Ladders Lead Nowhere
Lead Somewhere
Leading One Way
Moments Breed Hours
Ten Lifetimes
Ten ~~Lifetimes~~ Straight Lines
~~Only~~ Only One Way
One Way
One Way
I'm Looking Into A Heart
That Won't Know From Where It Came
In The Deepest Corridors
There Lives The Tiny Blue Flame
And All The World Is A Forest
I Bite The Apple I Gather The Branches

CASE 2   212 956-3335

JEFF BUCKLEY

CASE 1

PEYOTE RADIO THEATRE INC
C/O DE-EL ENTERTAIN
P.O. BOX 20131
COLUMBUS CIRCLE STA
NEW YORK, NY 10023-
212 714-8264

BUCKLEY

15   FRAGILE FRAGIL

PAGES 186–187: Jeff loved the trashy tone on his Ibanez Talman guitar and used it on some of his later recordings, including "Nightmares by the Sea." The smaller of the three cases on the right held the TASCAM DAT (digital audio tape) recorder seen on page 222. Peyote Radio Theatre, the name he coined for his tour production company, started as the title of a series of pretend radio shows left on his outgoing voicemail.

8:45 — 10:45
1 SONG – 15 MINUTES EACH
MEDITATE ON SONG FOR FULL 5 MINS
7 SONGS
LEAVE AT 11:00PM

FACING PAGE: Notes for what would become "Morning Theft," the ballad (partly inspired by his relationship with Cocteau Twins singer Elizabeth Fraser) attempted during the unsatisfying Verlaine sessions.

You're a woman, I a calf
You're the window, I'm a knife
We come together making chance into starlight

Meet me tomorrow night
Or any day you want
I have no right to wonder just how or when

And though the meaning fits
There's no relief in this
I miss my beautiful friend

I have to send it away to bring us back again

FEEL NO SHAME FOR WHAT YOU ARE
THIS IS THE SHAPE OF THE SOUL IN PURITY

FEEL NO SHAME FOR WHAT YOU ARE
IT'S THE HUMAN
THE GIFT IS SHINING THROUGH THE TROUBLED DARK

FEEL NO SHAME FOR WHAT YOU ARE
THE RHYTHM OF THE BLOOD THAT BRINGS THE RAIN

FEEL NO SHAME FOR WHAT YOU ARE
THE SHAKING OF THE STRING THAT SINGS THE SONG

FEEL NO SHAME FOR WHAT YOU ARE
~~THE WOMB THAT HOLDS THE LIGHT OF FUTURE~~
THE WOMB THAT BRINGS TO EARTH THE VOICE OF LOVE

FEEL NO SHAME FOR WHAT YOU ARE
THE BRIGHTER HOUR AWAITS YOU TURNING WISE

FEEL NO SHAME FOR WHAT YOU ARE
WORDS CANNOT DEFINE WHAT IS FROM THE HEART

FEEL NO SHAME FOR WHAT YOU ARE
LOWER THAN THE WILL TO LIVE YOU LIFE

FEEL NO SHAME FOR WHAT YOU ARE
~~[scribbled out]~~ THE TRUEST MOMENT HOLDS THE THRILL

FEEL NO SHAME FOR WHAT YOU ARE
ONCE YOU HAVE A TASTE YOU WON'T GO BACK

Preliminary draft for "New Year's Prayer," which would be recorded with Tom Verlaine during the early *My Sweetheart the Drunk* sessions in the spring of 1996. This version is far more lyrically fleshed out than the rendition Jeff would ultimately put on tape, and also more uplifting: "The gift is shining through the troubled dark" would be deleted in favor of images of an electric chair and a funeral.

PAGES 192–194: As he would sometimes remark in interviews and in his journals, Jeff loved to take a seat somewhere and observe whatever was happening around him, but he was also occasionally pulled into a situation. Although hardly a seamy part of town, Jeff's East Village neighborhood was home to its share of prostitutes and urban decay, as Jeff discovered when he came across a ravaged hooker on his block. "There is nothing more nauseating than human shame," he writes. These pages demonstrate his empathy for underdogs as well as his penchant for descriptive phrasing (and a degree of overwriting). The end note—"Stop smoking Stop hesitating Start flying!"—is another sign of his creative struggles during this period, as he sought to finish writing new songs and recruit a new drummer for his band.

I WALKED OUTSIDE TODAY AND PASSED A SHALLOW STAIRWELL
TO AN APARTMENT BUILDING, WHERE THERE LAY A ~~NICE~~
PROSTITUTE WHO HAD JUST BEEN FUCKED AND LEFT THERE
WITH HER PANTS DOWN. SHE WAS SLEEPING OFF SOME JUNK
AND THE WAY SHE WAS SPRAWLED AT THE BOTTOM IN
BROAD DAYLIGHT MADE ME WANT TO STOP AND HELP HER. SO I
DID; MR. MOTHER THERESA OF 12th ST., I AM SHE.
      WALKED DOWN THE FOUR STEPS TO WHERE SHE LAY, FACE
POCK-MARKED AND PINK-WHITE WITH MAKEUP, EYES HALF-LIDDED
UNDER ~~BLOOD REASON SUNGLASSES~~ (4EO6) ROCKSTAR SUNGLASSES
~~RED BRACELETS WERE~~ JUNK-SCABS ALL UP AND DOWN HER
FOREARMS. I SAID, "HEY, WAKE UP ARE YOU ALRIGHT?"
SHE SAID NOTHING AND STARTED TO CRY LIKE A CHILD
WAKING UP FROM A BAD DREAM AND WHINED ~~XXXX~~ OUT
SLOWLY AND PAINFULLY, "UUUH, ... I'M SICK!" I SAID "UH,
HUH," AS SHE COLLAPSED INTO MORE CRYING IN A WAY
THAT BEGAN TO RING MORE AND MORE HOLLOW, I FELT BAD
JUST LOOKING AT HER IN COMPLETE AGONY ~~XX~~ WANTING JUNK
WANTING MONEY, WANTING TO DIE, WANTING TO ROT HER
WHOLE LIFE BECAUSE SHE WAS A PIECE SHIT, HER FATHER/PIMP
ALWAYS TOLD HER SO.. SHE STOPPED THE WHINING BIT AND
HER FACE SLACKENED OUT OF ANY EMOTION AND SHE SAID
I JUST... I JUST NEED SOME MONEY... I NEED
MONEY..." AND I WAS LOOKING AT HER FACE, AMAZED
AT THE DAMAGE AND PREMATURE AGING THAT THE LIFE
OF A WHORE CAN BRING TO A FACE. HER EYES WERE EMPTY
AND GREY AS THEY LOOKED AT ME OVER THE RIMS OF HER
SHADES. SHE BEGAN TO USE HER BODY TO ENTICE ME AND
BEGAN TO SLOWLY SMILE, A SMILE THAT MIGHT HAVE
BROUGHT SOME LIFE AND BEAUTY TO THOSE EYES A LONG
TIME AGO BUT WAS NOW JUST AN OBSCENE VISAGE OF A NEW
INITIATE ~~FROM~~ TO HELL. HER BODY WAS SHIT. HER CUNT HAD SOMETHING
BAD GROWING FROM IT, LIKE BREADMOLD ALL MY LIFEFORCE WANTED TO
CLEANSE HER AND RESTORE HER ...BUT I AM NOT HOLY. AND I AM NOT A SAINT.

WHEN SHE BEGAN TO EYE ME UP AND DOWN WHEN
I SAID "WELL, WHAT CAN I DO FOR YOU, YOU WANT
ME TO CALL SOMEONE? CAUSE I CAN'T SPARE ANYTHING
RIGHT NOW." SHE JUST SQUIRMED AROUND SOME MORE LOOKING
UP AT ME, SHE WAS SO EVIL LOOKING, SHE KNEW SHE HAD
BEEN BEAUTIFUL ONCE AND IT WAS THE ONLY THING THAT
KEPT THE MEN COMING MORE COMFORTABLE LIKE, NOT FURTIVE
AND REPULSED BY THE ACT, NOT PIGS FUCKING IN SHIT
THERE IS NOTHING MORE NAUSEATING THAN HUMAN SHAME
THERE IS NOTHING SO ABSOLUTE AS THE FINAL STATE OF
HUMAN SHAME WICH IS DEGREDATION, SELF-MUTILATION,
DECAY, FEAR TO THE POINT OF INSANITY, DESPERATION
IN ACTION, THE HUMAN REDUCED TO GANGRENOUS LUNATIC
CLAWING BLOODY STREAMS IN THE FLESH OF ITSELF AND THE
FLESH OF ANY WHO COME TO ITS AID. WE ARE ALL LIKE THIS IN
SHADES.

       THIS IS JUST WRITER SHIT.
THE REAL DEAL IS THAT I SAW A PROSTITUTE
ON MY STREET WHO WAS TOTALLY SPRAWLED OUT WITH
HER JEANS RIPPED DOWN. HER ASS LOOKED SO YOUNG
AND HER FACE LOOKED SO OLD. I HELPED HER, SHE
TOTALLY NEEDED HELP SHE LOOKED SO DESTROYED.
HER BODY WAS SO SCARRED FROM JUNK AND
SHE HAD JUST BEEN NODDING OUT ON SOMEONES
DOORSTEP AFTER HAVING A CUSTOMER, LIKE
HOW SOON AGO DID THAT HAPPEN, ITS LIKE 3:00pm
IN BROAD FUCKING DAYLIGHT. THEY HAD JUST
FUCKED LIKE, HALF AN HOUR AGO, AND THE
NEIGHBORS WOULD PROBABLY BEAT THE SHIT OUT
OF HER CAUSE THEY'VE BEEN GETTING SO
VIOLENT WITH THE HOMELESS AND THE WHORES
BECAUSE THEY'VE TAKEN ENOUGH OF THEIR EXISTENCE
THEY'VE GROWN ANGRY JUST LOOKING AT THEM AND
NOW THEY'VE DECIDED TO DO SOMETHING ABOUT IT.

WHAT ARE THEY GOING TO DO WHEN THEY FIND OUT
THAT THE FIREMEN AND THE HASIDIM MEN AND
THE BUSINESSMEN AND THE COLLEGE BOYS AND THE
SLEAZEBAGS AND THE CRACKHEADS ALL LOVE
TO FUCK THOSE GIRLS AND THEY ALL NEED TO KEEP
COMING BACK. YOU MIGHT AS WELL FACE IT, IN
TIME IT WILL MAKE SURE THE MAYOR GETS YOUR
STREET REPAVED, YOU SHOULD BE GLAD, YOU SHOULD BE
MORE APPRECIATIVE OF YOUR NEIGHBORHOOD
STREETWALKER. SMILE "HELLO" TO THEM WHEN YOU
STEP OUTSIDE IN THE MORNING AND BID THEM GOODNIGHT
WHEN YOU COME BACK HOME. THEY NEED TO FEEL GOOD ABOUT
WHAT THEY DO ... THE WHORES CAME TO MY STREET
A YEAR AGO OR TWO. I LOVE TO SEE THEM
EVERY DAY AND EVERY DAY THE STREET LOOKS A LITTLE
NICER, THE TREES ARE REGULARLY MAINTAINED BY THE CITY
AND BETTER YET — ON ALL THE PROFESSIONAL STREETS —
THE STREETS HAVE BEEN A—REE—PAVED! AND THEY
ARE NOT DOING ANYTHING WRONG

STOP SMOKING STOP SMOKING
STOP HESITATING
START FLYING!

B

MY BABY'S GOT A STRONG RIGHT ARM

I GOT A GIFTED LETTER
ONE SUNNY SUMMER DAY
MY BABY'S GOT A STRONG RIGHT
TO WRITE ME THIS-A-WAY

OH NOT ANOTHER DEAR JOHN LETTER
FULL OF OL' CLICHÉS
NO SHE'S THE ONE WHO ~~RACKS MY HEART~~ RACKS MY HEART
IN A DIRTY, SHALLOW, GRAVE

SHE BUILDS HER MUSCLES ALL NIGHT LONG
AND OFFERS YOU HER TOWEL
YOU FEEL JUST LIKE A ~~NO~~ DEAR GIZELLE
THE LIONS DISEMBOWELED

~~SHE~~ SHE TELLS YOU ALL THE WAYS AROUND
YOUR GARDEN THAT SHE LIKES
I THINK THAT YOUR'E ~~LIKE~~ A BUBBLE
HEADING CLOSER TO THE SPIKE!
YOU PROWL AROUND ALL NIGHT LONG
WHILE SHE THINKS WHAT SHE LIKES.
SOME PIMPS WEAR PURPLE LEATHER AROUND WHILE SOME RIDE ON BIKES, MELTON TRAFFIC

SOMETHING FOR THE SCRATCH!

It's way beyond obsession
~~When I start to wear her clothes~~
~~When~~ I wear my lover's clothes
But no one seems to notice ME

My feet
don't fit
her ~~high heels~~
~~God dammit~~
all my
toes

I ~~do~~ paint between my toes   ~~when~~ I wear
on the subway   whith flowers
                                between
I'm holding on   my toes

And when she turned away
I put my finger to my head
I heard her laugh as it came back
Just hanging by a thread.

She had to make a date with someone else
I did adore
Thank god she didn't leave her drugs
I just don't know what they're for.
She pleaded ~~with~~ me, to let this be
~~nothing else~~ the only thing that
makes you happy

So play me something unashamed
So beautiful and pure
Don't let ~~a~~ your smile become ~~your mouth~~ a frown
Just stay there like you are

PAGES 198–203: In late 1995, Jeff was invited by *Interview* magazine to speak with one of his musical idols and continual inspirations, Nusrat Fateh Ali Khan. Most of the resulting article would consist of a question-and-answer session with the two men, but Jeff was able to use some of his observations here for his liner notes to Nusrat's *The Supreme Collection Volume 1* anthology (released after Jeff's death). The way Nusrat embodied "not 'playing' music but becoming music itself" spoke to Jeff and the rapture and release he sought from his own music making.

for INTERVIEW MAGAZINE
11/9/95 N.Y.

JUST A FEW REFLECTIONS ON NUSRAT FATEH ALI KHAN.
NOT ROCK-CRITIC SUPERLATIVES, BUT A FEW IMAGES ABOUT
THE MAN I'D WANT YOU TO KNOW, FROM MY DEATHBED, WERE
WE THERE (EASY, CHRISTGAU!)
                                        IN
                        BORN ~~FROM~~ A ~~LARGE~~ REGION
WHERE MUSIC IS OWNED AS A BIRTHRIGHT, LIKE BREATHING
OR WALKING OR EVEN THOUGHT, BY EVERY MAN, WOMAN AND
CHILD, THIS MAN IS HELD AS THE BRIGHTEST STAR OF QAWWALI
MUSIC IN ALL OF PAKISTAN. THAT'S NOT "BRIGHT", BABY THAT
IS "BLINDING". ALL QAWWALI MUSICIANS ARE EXCELLENT, MIND YOU,
FOR THEY ALL, BY DEFINITION, MUST SING FROM A HEART TOTALLY
                    A RELENTLESS OPENING TO THE DIVINE
INFLAMED WITH ~~THE PASSIONATE LOVE AFFAIR WITH~~, A HEATED, PASSIONATE
                        FOR THEM THERE IS NOTHING ELSE. THEY ARE LOST
LOVE FOR ALLAH (GOD). ~~THE GREAT POETS OF THIS CULTURE~~, FOREVER.
                        A VOCAL   SIX CENTURIES
AND KNOW THAT THIS IS ~~AN~~ ART OVER ~~600 YEARS~~ OLD, THE
                            ONLY PASSED DOWN   FATHER
MECHANICS OF WHICH HAVE BEEN ~~SOCIAL~~ FROM ~~SON~~ TO SON
(SOMETIMES DAUGHTERS) ORALLY, WITH NO WRITTEN MANUAL OF CURRICULUM
OR WHATEVER, BY SUFI MASTERS OF THE HIGHEST ORDER.
                                        TRUE
NUSRAT FATEH ALI IS OF THIS LINEAGE. QAWWALIS DON'T
SING, THEY ARE MADE TO SING, NOT "PLAYING" MUSIC BUT
BECOMING MUSIC ITSELF. YOU SHOULD COME TO THE GIG
AND SEE WHAT THAT FEELS LIKE.
    OUT OF STATIC ANTIQUITY INTO
~~A BRAND NEW STYLE ART~~ - NUSRAT HAS SINGLEHANDEDLY
            THE
INNOVATED ~~HIS~~ FORM TO A BRILLIANT EXPLOSION OF LIGHT.
NOT MERELY AN ARTFORM, BUT A LIVING TESTAMENT TO THE
GIFT OF MUSIC LINKING ALL HUMANS TO THE DIVINE. OUTWARD
                                        AWARENESS &
AND UNASHAMED IN EMOTION, ROCK SOLID SKILL AS IF TO BRAVE

THE ~~flaming~~ MOUNTAINSIDE THAT IS THE FACE OF THE BELOVED. ALL CRASHING
THROUGH AT THE CLIMAX INTO TOTAL CLARITY AND ABANDON.
JOY TO THE POINT OF HAPPY TERROR. HAPPY THAT THIS GIFT
IS SLOSHING AROUND IN EVERY POOR BASTARD ACROSS THE UNIVERSE.
YES, I KNOW THAT I'M SOME YANKEE ROCK-GUY AND A TOTALLY HIDEOUS WHITEBOY
FAN OF QAWWALI AND OF KHAN, BUT I'VE SEEN THIS MAN TELL IT
LIKE IT REALLY FUCKING IS THROUGH FOUR SEPERATE PERFORMANCES
SINCE 1990 AND I AM JUST CALLING IT LIKE I SEE IT.
I WOULDN'T LIE TO YOU: THIS IS THE MAN, THIS IS THE MAN,
THIS IS THE MAN.

THE SOUND OF LOVE OPENS DOORS. THE INNER DEVOTION OF
HIS HEART HAS OPENED THE DOORS OF HIS OWN DEVELOPMENT
FROM A SMALL CHILD, IN PAKISTAN WHO WAS DEEMED TOO SOFT ~~~~ TO EVEN SING TO CARRY ~~~~ ON THE
WITH ANY AUTHORITY AT ALL, TO AN IMMOVABLE MASTER FAMILY TRADITION OF QAWWALI
OF THE ART OF SONG, SOARING HEALING PENETRATING MUSIC THAT
RIPS THE SKY OPEN, SLOWLY REVEALING THE RADIANT FACE OF
THE BELOVED. I'M NOT JOKING. THIS IS NOT POETRY OR
CRITICAL HYPERBOLE. THIS IS WHAT YOU GET WHEN YOU PAY FOR
YOUR TICKET AND SIT DOWN AT THE BIG. HOW CAN A MAN
FLY EFFORTLESSLY THROUGH THE AIR AND STILL LOOK ~~~~ LIKE HE CARRIES THE ANCIENT
WEIGHT OF SIX-HUNDRED YEARS THAT IS THE ART OF QAWWALI
HAPPILY ON HIS SHOULDERS? THE SIGHT OF IT IS BEAUTIFUL
AND FREE AND FREEING. NUSRAT FATEH ALI KHAN AND THE
TEN OTHER MEN IN HIS ENSEMBLE DO NOT ~~~~ PLAY MUSIC,
THEY ARE ~~~~ MUSIC ITSELF. THE AUDIENCES ARE ~~~~ SLEEPWALKING

SCHOOLS OF SOULS HOOKED FROM THE MOUTH AND PULLED
GLORIOUSLY DOWN INTO WELLS OF EXALTATION AS A ~~A FEW~~ FEW
MUSIC
~~ROCK~~ CRITICS SIT AND SCRIBBLE AWAY, HEAD DOWN TO THE
NOTEPAD. BY THE END OF THE NIGHT NO ONE IS IMMUNE
TO ~~THE MUSIC AND~~ THE SPIRIT THAT CLOUDS THE AUDITORIUM,
                              TURN
ALL EYES AND EARS STRAIGHT TO THE STAGE, STRAIGHT TO
THE STORY BEING UTTERED INTO THEIR BONES. THERE IS A
                                          SOUND
VOICE SINGING LIKE IT'S THE LAST ~~WORDS~~ YOU'LL EVER HEAR
                         FLOAT AWAY   GUTTERAL
BEFORE YOU DIE AND ~~FLOAT~~ INTO HEAVEN OR HELL. THAT ~~FUCKING~~
SILVER FLAME
~~COLOR~~ OF MELODY AND ECSTASY IS SHOOTING ~~OUT OF A~~ FROM THE THROAT OF
A MAN WHO IS SO DEEP INSIDE THE MUSIC THAT HE DOES NOT
EXIST ANY LONGER. THAT MAN IS NUSRAT FATEH ALI KHAN.
                                                    AFTER
AND ~~I FUCKING LOVE HIM SO MUCH~~ AFTER SIX YEARS OF LISTENING TO HIM AND FOUR CONCERTS
THAT HEALED THE FUCK OUT OF ME, I FINALLY GOT TO SAY "HELLO."
TO THE MAN.

MUSIC AND MUSICIANS, LOVER AND BELOVED, THE DIVINE AND THE FAITHULL, THE MUSIC OF NUSRAT FATEH ALI KHAN, SUNG IN URDU, A LANGUAGE I WISH I KNEW, AND THAT YOU WILL, BECAUSE A TRANSLATION WOULD BE POINTLESS AS IS THE INHERENT FUTILITY OF EXPLAINING THE UNEXPLAINABLE. ~~THIS IS A MUSIC INVENTED BY AMIR KHUSRAU, A SUFI MASTER WHO LIVED BACK IN THE 13th CENTURY. BEFORE THERE WAS AMERICA, REMEMBER?~~ IN THE WEST, THERE ARE ~~RADIO~~ TELEVISION PREACHERS WHO ARE ABLE TO TRANSFORM THE LANGUAGE OF THEIR HOLY SCRIPTURES INTO FIRE AND BRIMSTONE LITANIES OF JUDGEMENT, OF ~~XXXXX~~ UNWORTHINESS BEFORE THE CREATOR AND THIS EARTH AS MERELY A SPIRITUAL DESERT OF SACRIFICE, ATONEMENT AND SHAME. THE ART OF THE QAWWALIS RENDERS ALL RELIGIOUS DOGMATISM AS USELESS; THE WHITE-NOISE BABBLE OF ~~XXX~~ POLITICIANS DISGUISED AS MYSTICS. THE QAWWALIS FOLLOW THE SUFI TRADITION OF ~~XXX XXXXX~~ OBSERVING THE UNMOVABLE SPIRIT ~~WITHIN XXX~~ OF ALLAH WITHIN ALL THINGS EVERYWHERE. ~~XXXXX XXX~~ THE BEAUTY OF GOD IS IN THE WIND, IN THE MOVEMENT OF THE OCEAN, ~~XXXX~~ IT IS IN THE EYES OF A WOMAN GAZING AT HER LOVER, POURING THE DEEP RED WINE OF LOVE FROM HER EYES LIKE TWO CRYSTAL CUPS. THEIRS IS A GOD WHO DANCES AND WHO LOVES AND WHO LONGS TO SING OF LOVE. ~~XXXXX~~ THE QAWWALI IS THE LIVING MOUTHPIECE OF HIS LOVE FOR ALL OF CREATION AND IN TURN THE MESSENGER THAT CARRIES THE REPLY OF JOYFUL DEVOTION BACK TO HIS DOORSTEP. TRANSCENDING BEYOND LANGUAGE, BEYOND RACE AND STATION IN LIFE. NON-DENOMINATIONAL AND I MEAN THAT THIS GOD IS MUSIC; ALL INCLUSIVE, BENEVOLENT AND LIFE-AFFIRMING, UNASHAMED HUMAN EMOTION.

Nusrat Fateh Ali Khan is of this tradition. His distinction among all other Qawwalis ~~[crossed out]~~ is his ability to bring his background in classical India ragas along with the ~~[crossed out]~~ brilliant Qawwali tradition of the Ali Khan family ~~[crossed out]~~ (which stems back to the thirteenth century & the birth of Qawwali itself) ~~[crossed out]~~ only to stretch their ~~[crossed out]~~ antiquated form fully to embrace the present day. Somehow the hardcore sensibility of Qawwali has not diminished in character ~~[crossed out]~~ or beauty as Nusrat has pulled the form out of medeivel times and into the age of electric guitars ~~[crossed out]~~, video music channels and the nuclear bomb. And all the time ~~[crossed out]~~ his devotion as a muslim ~~[crossed out]~~ and a Sufi speaks so clearly, so timelessly, it is difficult to fathom who is the pilgrim and who is the anachronism when in his presence;

With these two volumes of Qawwals from 1988, you will have the pleasure of hearing the voice of Mujahid Mubarak Ali Khan, Nusrat's uncle and teacher. Farrukh at me knowingly, muttering, "Nus-rat...Fa-teh...A-li...Khaaan," like he had just scored the wine of the century. I felt a rush of adrenaline in my chest, like I was on the edge of a cliff, wondering when I would jump and how well the ocean would catch me: two questions that would never be answered until I experienced the first leap. That is the sensation and the character of Qawwali music, the music of the Sufis, as best as I can describe it.

In between the world of the flesh and the world of the spirit is the void. The Qawwal is the messenger who leaps empty-handed into the abyss and returns carrying messages of love from the Beloved ~~(God)~~. These messages have no ~~words~~ words, per se, but at the high point of a Qawwali performance, they come in bursts of light into the hearts and minds of members of the audience. (Of course, by that time the whole house is either hanging from the rafters, or dancing) This is called Ma'rifat, the inner knowledge, and it is the aim of the Qawwali tradition to bring the listener into this state: first through the beauty of the poetry and the weight of its meaning; then, eventually, through the Qawwal's use of repetition; repeating key phrases of the poem until the meaning has melted away to reveal the true form to the listener. I've seen Nusrat and his Party repeatedly melt New Yorkers into human beings. At times I have seen him in such deep states of trance while singing that I am sure that the world does not exist for him any longer. The effect it has is gorgeous. ^These men do not play music, they are music itself.

The texts from which ~~traditional~~ Qawwali *is* ^usually are sung, come ^from either the works of the `POPULAR` ~~FOLK SONGS~~ `OR` great Sufi poets: Bhulle Shah (1680-1753), Shams Tabrez (d.1247), Shah Hussain (1538-1599), and the ~~greatest~~ `REVERED MUSICIAN` ^COURT ~~poet and scholar~~, Amir Khusrau (1253-1325), who was the inventor of Qawwali itself. These texts are devotional, of course, meaning poems of worship for Allah (Hamd) ~~or~~ the prophet Muhammad (N'at-i-Sharif). ^There are also love poems (ghazals), where a more secular romantic interplay is happening between man and woman (which I can dig). The Qawwals, however, see ghazals as metaphors for the love affair between Man and the Divine. ^They don't care about which meaning is derived from where. In the true Sufi way, through their music, any ~~knowledge~~ `GIFT` that is needed by the `RECEIVE` listener is there for the listener to ~~absorb~~. For the true Qawwal, all ~~meanings of~~ `REVELATIONS WITHIN` the music exist simultaneously and there is no need or purpose for religious dogma. There is only the pilgrimage to the light within the heart, which is the home of God. There is only a pure devotion and a fierce virtuosity to grow wings and soar through music. To plant a kiss on the eyes of Allah and then sing His loving gaze back home into the hearts of Men.

IT is THE `GOSPEL` OF ISLAMIC ENJOY.
`MYSTIC` ~~AND THE~~ CODE OF THE SUFIS INDIAN CULTURE,
~~AND THE UNDILUTED ~~ ~~OF EXISTENCE~~ `CODE`
DISTILLED IN `MUSICAL` RHYTHM
MELODY, SILENCE, MEANING
AND THE `MEANING` CONTAINED DEEP
WITHIN ITS MATERIAL BODY.

Jeff Buckley

CAROLINE
989 - 2929

N.Y. DEC '95.

AND HIS BELOVED FRIEND
ALi (MANQABAT)

NUSRAT'S STYLE OF QAWWALI ~~no. of~~ `INDIA` ~~it is the gospel of Islam~~ `IS` `OF THE` ~~less it is THE GOSPEL~~
THE ART AND CULTURE OF ~~MEDIEVAL~~ `ANCIENT, IC ORDER`
`THE MYSTIC` ~~CODE~~
OF SUFI MUSLIMS AND THE ^`SIMPLE` `UNDILUTED`
JOY OF HUMAN EXISTENCE `ALL` DISTILLED
`LIVING` INTO MUSICAL CODE; RHYTHM, MELODY, ECSTASY
SILENCE, POETRY, ITS ~~MEANING~~ `BEAUTY` AND THE
~~BEAUTY~~ ~~MEANING~~ CONTAINED DEEP WITHIN ITS
MATERIAL BODY. ~~NUSRAT IS THE GREATEST~~
~~messenger of our age~~.

PAGES 204–205: As a child of the mix-tape era, Jeff used the format to make compilations and keep track of song drafts and his own live recordings. If a blank tape was nowhere to be found, he wasn't averse to dubbing over whatever was lying around, as he did when he recorded a demo of one of his new songs over a Dave Matthews Band cassette.

FACING PAGE: Preliminary version of "Haven't You Heard," also written during the turbulent 1996 period.

HAVE YOU HEARD THIS TALK ABOUT EYE-CONTACT
GONNA BE THE DOWNFALL OF THIS TOWN
FIRST THE PHOTOGRAPHS TAKE YOU TO THE RIGHT-HANDS
LEADS YOU TO THE AUTHORITY MOLD···

PARANOIA WILL WRITE THE WORLDS PRAYER
MAKE SURE THAT YOU FIT IN THE RIGHT HOLES
MESMERIZED YOU WITH ONE FINAL OFFER
DOWN FOR THE MIND CONTROL?

AS YOU GO ABOUT YOUR BUSINESS PROPER
SOMEONE FEELS LIKE A GOD IN THIS TOWN
WANTS TO HOOK YOU WITH MENTAL PERSUASION
TAKE YOU DOWN UNDERGROUND

TAKE THE BUZZ OUT OF YOUR CONVERSATION
THROW YOUR SOUL INTO THEIR PSYCHO-WARD
JUST A LOOSE-WIRE SHOCK TO YOUR TEMPLES
NO MORE REBELS ~~crossed out~~ BRAINWASHED THOSE DEVILS

LAST THING THAT YOU SEE WILL BE THE ~~crossed out~~ TRAINER
TEACH AND TORTURE YOU NOW FIVE IS FOUR
~~BEATS TO~~ ~~crossed out~~ ~~BEAUROCRATS~~ ~~crossed out~~
SUCK YOUR LIFE WITH THEIR VIRUS CALLED LANGUAGE
~~crossed out~~ TAKE THEIR TESTS IN YOUR BLUE UNIFORM

TAKE THE I OUT OF AUTOMATION
OH BEHOLD THE AUTOMATON
~~HAVEN'T YOU HEARD?~~ ~~crossed out~~ HAVEN'T YOU HEARD
~~crossed out~~ OUR FINAL DOWNFALL ONE AND ALL

(Voice)

You read a country song like Christoper Walken
...read first the rhythm...let it be natural
intimacy,
relax yourself in its chasse and see how it works
with you inside. Also, stop talking so much.

Assignment #4
Choose a poem to memorize and recite
in class. Make it one of the poems from class.

Also, turn in dream poem next week

FACING PAGE: Notes from the poetry class Jeff took in the spring of 1996: an upcoming assignment and his advice to himself to "stop talking so much."

PAGES 210–211: "All that I want is to jump unsafe into the pit of despair and sing," Jeff writes in this April 1996 entry. His tormented words ("my throat is dry and my hair is thin") reveal the way he would often spill the contents of his mind into his journals in search of salvation and inspiration.

DO YOU REMEMBER ME DO YOU DO YOU REMEMBER ME I DON'T REMEMBER HAVING THE PLEASURE. DID I MEET THE KING DID I KISS THE QUEEN I'M GLAD I DIDN'T GO TO BED WITH HER I'M GLAD THAT MY LIFE ISN'T LIKE THE PORNOS NO MORE. I DON'T KNOW HOW TO WRITE THIS SONG I DON'T KNOW HOW IT GOES IT GRIFTED ME OUT OF TWENTY YEARS AND STILL THE CLOCK RUN FORWARD AND STILL MY LOVE FOR THEE... TWENTY NINE AND THIRTY YEARS OF PAIN CONFUSION AND GUILT AND CONFUSION AND PRETENSE TO CONTROL OVER MIND AND VOLITION AND LOSS OF DIRECTION BUT STILL THIS DRIVE TO FIND GREATNESS THROUGH MUSIC BUT IT LOOKS LIKE THE TRAPPINGS HAVE WORKS UP MY ARM SO FAR I DON'T KNOW THAT I'M DRUGGED I HAVE EARS THAT RING AND YEARS THAT CLING AND CLING TO MY PAST AS IT HOLDS ONTO MY SHOULDERS WHEN ALL THAT I WANT IS TO JUMP UNSAFE INTO THE PIT OF DESPAIR AND SING HOWLING SING FLYING AND COMPLETELY IN LOVE IN THE GREASED TUNNEL OF AWARENESS AND HEALING AND SHIT CLEARING FIRE AS A BREATH FROM MY THROAT. AND NOW IS THE TIME I THROW THAT CIGARETTE SHACKLED LUNG OUT OF MY LIFE AND WRITE MY WAY OUT OF THE FESTIVAL GROUNDS, OUT OF THE THEATRES, OUT OF THE CONCERT HALLS, OUT OF THE CAFES AND CLUBS AND REHEARSAL ROOMS AND OFF OF THE MEDIA EYE SURFACE BACK INTO MY HEART FOR THE WRITE FIRST WRITE TIME WRITE IN WRITE A WRITE LIFETIME MY THROAT IS DRY AND MY HAIR IS THIN AND MY MIND IS TOO UNFAIR AND TOO QUICK TO UNFAIRLY COMPARE MYSELF WITH THE LATEST EASY ENEMY. TIME, TIME, AGE, AGE, VOICES, VOICES, GHOSTS, GHOSTS, OTHERS, OTHERS, I LOVE YOU, I LOVE YOU, I LOVED YOU, I WANTED YOU, I GUTTED IT AND SPILLED IT'S BLOOD AND I KISSED YOUR SCARS AND I KISSED THE SCARS OF MY BEAUTIFUL WIFE BEFORE I AGREED TO LEAVE HER TO HER LIFE TO ANOTHER ONE, TO GROW OLD TOGETHER, TO FILL HER BODY WITH A PRECIOUS SON, WHY NOT SAY IT MAN NO ONE WILL EVER FUCKING KNOW YOU EXISTED. NO ONE WILL EVER KNOW YOU EXISTED. YOU NEVER EXISTED. WHY PRETEND YOU EXIST NOW? WHY PRETEND TO RESIST? WHY PRETEND THAT YOU KNOW? ONLY THE LIVING DEAD ARE EMPTY ENOUGH TO BE STUFFED WITH THE TRUE FLESH. AND TONIGHT I KNOW THAT I'LL NEVER GET OUT ALIVE.. ♡

PEOPLE OF THE WORLD ARE THE TRUE MORONS OF THE HISTORY OF EARTH.
I HAVE NEVER BEFORE REALIZED THAT THE ONLY TRUE HIGHNESS OF
MANKIND HAS BEEN ITS SOLID STEEL COMMITMENT TO CONFUSION AND DENIAL
AND PAIN AS A CONSTANT STATE OF MIND THROUGHOUT ITS EXISTENCE.
PEOPLE ACKNOWLEDGE NOTHING OF WHAT THEY SENSE, INTUIT, THINK,
FEEL, LONG FOR OR NEED. LEAST OF ALL THE LIVING BREATHING
LIFEFORCE LOVEFORCE THAT IS NOT GOD OR A GOD BUT THAT IS
OF "GOD" AND ALSO OF MAN OR ELSE IT COULD NOT BE OF GOD.
I NOW TAKE ALL WORDS OF WASTELANDKIND AND REESTABLISH
THEM UNDER THE TERMS OF THIS BEDROOM. THE ONLY PLACE WHERE
THE LANGUAGE MADE SENSE. FUCK ME JEFF FUCK ME BABY SUCK ME
JEFF SUCK MY PUSSY OH GOD OH GOD YES OH YES OH GOD OH YES
YES YES JESUS … OH KLEENEX … OH FUNERALS OH GREAT MUSICLESS
WASTELAND DON'T LET ME COME INTO YOUR HOMES BECAUSE I
WILL ONLY SAY THE TRUTHS YOU NEVER WANT TO HEAR AND MY
COMMITMENT TO THIS BEAUTY OF OURS IS OPENLY HOSTILE TO THE
NEEDLESS DULLARY OF YOUR GRAYLIFE SONG ETERNITY … IF BLOODRED
IS THE ONLY COLOR AVAILABLE TO SPLASH ACROSS THE BLANK FACE OF
THE WORLD THEN IT JUST SO HAPPENS THAT I PUMP PRIMAL HOURS
OF ENDLESS GALLONS OF LIQUID FIRE LOVE INTO THE SKY IT STAINS
THE CLOUDS IT IS HEATED TO A SICKENING BOIL BY THE SUN AND IT
RAINS RICH RED RAINDROPS OF BLOOD FOR MILES AND MILES
OVER MILLIONS OF ZOMBIE PICNICS AND SHIT COVERED FOOD CROPS
AND THE LIFE OF THE EARTH WILL SUCK MY BLOOD INTO ITS FRUITLESS
TISSUE THAT YOU ROBBED IN THE FIRST PLACE AND THE FOOD OF THE EARTH
WILL SQUIRT BLOOD INTO YOUR MOUTHS AND THE MEATCOWS WILL ONLY
BE USED TO YIELD FRUITJUICE AND FIELDSIDE CONVERSATION AND THE
LAST WILL BECOME INCOGNITO AND THE FIRST WILL GET THE FIST.
AND THEN I WILL LOOK TO THE SKY FOR COMETS AND NOT TO YOUR
STREETS FOR BODIES. WHEN BLOOD FROM THE EARTHS MUSIC
BLEEDS FROM YOUR SEXHOLES AND NOTSEXHOLES AND SKIN PORES ARE
PINK WITH BLOOD THEN YOU WILL BE THE LAST TO KNOW.

4/11/96 3:00 AM NM

Turn your face away from the screen
It will tell you nothing more
Don't suck the milk of flaccid
Bill K. Public's silent reign of terror
On the people that the public can ignore

His ~~×××××××××~~ Shaftway Doctrine is so
~~×××××××××××~~ devised
To kill EVERY ~~××~~ mind that moves
Moving with grace that men despise
And women have learned to lose
Throw off your shame or be a slave to the system

Clearer days and crowds of eyes
Becoming the mind that moves
Moving with grace that men despise
And women have learned to lose
We share our bodies in disdain for the system

FACING PAGE: Another early stab at "The Sky Is a Landfill."

NEXT PAGE: To keep Columbia executives apprised of the progress of his second album, Jeff faxed this list of songs to the company's office in July 1996. This note is the first reference in Jeff's archives to the use of *My Sweetheart the Drunk* as a title for the still-unrecorded album. "Edna Frau" was a song written and sung by bassist Mick Grondahl, but little remains of "Shoe Creep" and the unfinished "Dendrils of Death." Despite the indecision and fruitless rehearsals and recording sessions during this time, Jeff's use of exclamation marks is clearly a way of convincing Sony — and himself — that the in-flux album is finally on track.

PAGE 215: In exaggerated handwriting that indicates the anxiety he is feeling at the time, Jeff reflects on his meeting with Dylan and the bard's mention of Tim Buckley during their brief conversation.

My Sweetheart The Drunk

···· Vancouver !

··· The Sky Is A Landfill !

··· Murder Suicide Meteor Slave !

··· I woke Up In A Strange Place !

···· Shine !

··· Skyblue Skin ! ··· Edna Frau !

···· Demon John ! ··· Dendrils Of Death !

···· Moodswing Whiskey !

··· The Pleasure Seeker !

··· Shoe Creep !

··· Ever Since Then (Opened Once) !

··· Morning Theft !

··· You And I !

··· I Know We Could Be So Happy, Baby
      (if we wanted to be) !

I AM LOOKING AT MYSELF

THE DYLAN CHILD SOUNDS AT TIMES
LIKE HE'S APING HIS FATHER.
THE WORDS ARE THIN
" NEVER KNEW HOW TO ACT."
GOOD LINE BUT IT SOUNDS WIERD
WITH THAT GRUFFNES AND LILT
FEELING A BIT LIKE A FADED
IMPRINT OF THE ORIGINAL

AM I LOOKING MYSELF
IN THE MOUTH HERE?
HE NEEDS TO WORK HARDER
ON HIS TOTAL CRAFT. BREAK AWAY
TO PIECES.
BECAUSE HE'S TOO PRETTY
AND NOT TOO BEAUTIFIED INSIDE.

How do I know this isn't a lie. No one is going
to save you this time. When you get your shit together
by the time you get your shit together, will be smothered
with sand.

I kissed his hand saying
Thank you sir
Please see that I'm released
And he walked out of my life
~~Forever~~

Miles of death
Stretch across the sky
Like some pretty young thing
With nothing in the eyes

My Timothy and my darling
Mary I'm sorry I dragged your names into this thing
This is supposed to be a business
But in my blood theres so much love and forgetfulness

I Pardon Cool Richard if only in my heart at UCLA, He burns in hell
Even had to
Lee Underworld helped me drink the world of you
And Wu became a woman after you left this world
Is strong and beautiful and kind and always watches out for me.
Because of a beautiful man from Wales Llew Llewellyn
Taylor found a woman, Kathleen has found her muse
Elaine, am I finding a groove just before I fall to my doom?
I don't know what she sees when she looks into me.
But I know that it isn't you.
I've got seven more years to go
You can't let anybody know, my dears
The special place where I chose to die

JUST GOT SOME SHOCK TREATMENT
SIX MILD BLOWS TO THE MIND

It's something you don't realize
You're funny that way
Hatred and fascination
Hatred and fascination

For the cultures closest to ~~god~~ the earth
For the lovers throughout history of the same sex
For the feminine in all things
For the body itself
For the surrender and courage of the heart.

Decode that fucking
Evangelist
Devil
Doctrine

11/13/96

Do not borrow style from
another artist!! Like George Carlin
and Gavin Rossdale did from Lenny Bruce
and the Pixies... Both of those results are flat.

You   are   you

Sing   from   you

Fed from both outside and inside

Fuck   outside opinion and fear

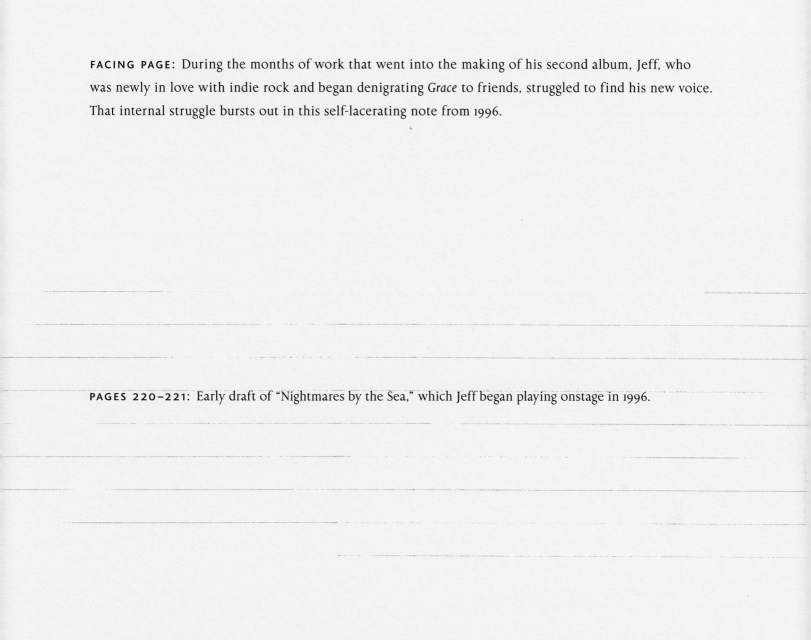

FACING PAGE: During the months of work that went into the making of his second album, Jeff, who was newly in love with indie rock and began denigrating *Grace* to friends, struggled to find his new voice. That internal struggle bursts out in this self-lacerating note from 1996.

PAGES 220–221: Early draft of "Nightmares by the Sea," which Jeff began playing onstage in 1996.

PAGE 222: Notoriously paranoid that any mistakes he made during a performance would be preserved for history, and wanting his audience to be fully present for the experience of his music, Jeff was actively against the idea of fans taping his shows on their own. However, he did want the shows recorded for his own use, and those tapes were made with this TASCAM DAT recorder.

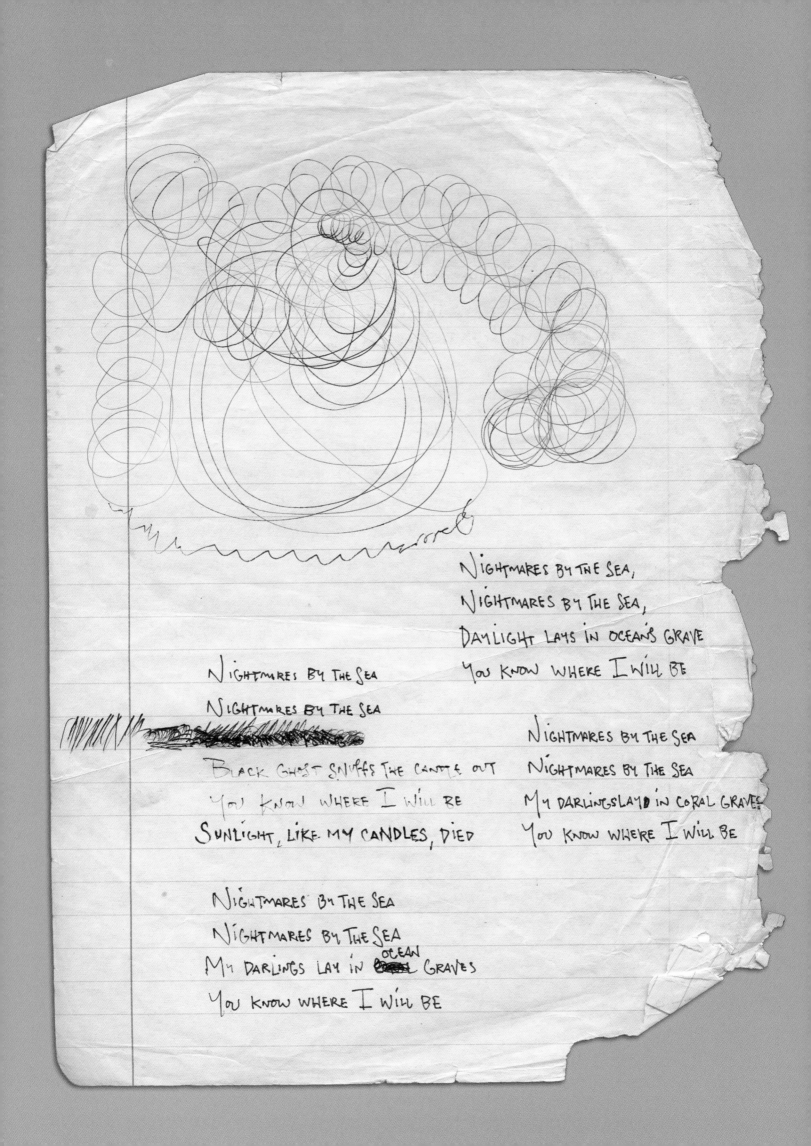

NIGHTMARES BY THE SEA,
NIGHTMARES BY THE SEA,
DAYLIGHT LAYS IN OCEAN'S GRAVE
YOU KNOW WHERE I WILL BE

NIGHTMARES BY THE SEA
NIGHTMARES BY THE SEA

BLACK GHOST SNIFFS THE CANDLE OUT
YOU KNOW WHERE I WILL BE
SUNLIGHT, LIKE MY CANDLES, DIED

NIGHTMARES BY THE SEA
NIGHTMARES BY THE SEA
MY DARLINGS LAYD IN CORAL GRAVES
YOU KNOW WHERE I WILL BE

NIGHTMARES BY THE SEA
NIGHTMARES BY THE SEA
MY DARLINGS LAY IN OCEAN GRAVES
YOU KNOW WHERE I WILL BE

THE THINGS YOU SAY ARE STOWED AWAY
AND THEY HAUL THEM OUT ON MARKET DAY
AND FIND OUT ALL THE THINGS YOU DID
WHEN YOU GO TO THE TABLE FOR MEAT

7/9/96 3:00 AM

I've felt this season before
As a child playing dead near the road
One curious blankfaced summer
Unaware that this flesh would erode

My child-heart raced without record
Of judgement toward self, sight or smell

11/16/96

By the time I find
The scheme of the rhyme
The meaning has fled
From my PEACOCK ~~BRAINSTEAD~~

PAGE 223: In September 1990, having returned briefly to Los Angeles after his first visit to New York, Jeff decided the time had come to put some of his songs on tape. Playing all the guitar and bass parts and using a drum machine, he recorded what he dubbed *The Babylon Dungeon Sessions*, the title a joke on the subterranean San Fernando Valley studio where it was made. The tape included early versions of "Last Goodbye" (then called "Unforgiven") and "Eternal Life." His LA influences were also heard in the hardcore-punk style "Radio" and the metal-propelled "Strawberry Street."

FACING PAGE: As seen here, Jeff's thoughts could be scattered over months of journals. The July entry at the top of the page indicates he may have considered turning parts of his creative writing project "Fullerton Road Trick" into a song.

KISS IN THE HEREAFTER   # SKY BLUE SKIN

REJOICE IN THE HEREAFTER

EVERYONE'S WAITING

THE DOOR IS UNLOCKED FOR YOU

SLEEP IS FOR US COURAGEOUS AND NEW

IT GLOWS IN THE HEREAFTER

YOUR FEATURES ARE CHANGING

IN THE ULTIMATE LIGHT

THEY SEE OUR GHOSTS ON THE SIDEWALKS AT NIGHT

WE KISS IN THE HEREAFTER

G-   Ab

ROSE PETALS CLINGING TO THE HILLS OF YOUR BREAST

  G-   F-

LIPSTICK ROSES EMBLAZON MY CHEST

  Eb   G-

ROSE PETALS SOAKED ON THE ROOF OF MY MOUTH

                              G-

I KNOW THESE STAINS WILL NEVER COME OUT

TURNAROUND

STAINED IN LOVE HEREAFTER STAINED IN LOVE STAINED IN LOVE

SEND ME YOUR SWITCHBLADE

I'LL MAKE ROOM IN MY HOUSE

IT FLIES FROM THE DARKNESS

AND ENTERS OUR MOUTHS

~~~~~~~~~~~~~~~~~~~~~~~~~~~

~~~~ REJOINED IN THE

              HEREAFTER

IT'S STRANGE TO REMEMBER IT NOW .... THE REASONS YOU MAKE UP FOR WHAT HAS NO

CONTROL .... THE KNIFE WANDERS THROUGH ME SO SLOW ... IT CUTS BETWEEN US AS WE

GROW ... AND CHANCES ARE YOU WOULDN'T EVEN RECOGNIZE THE MAN I AM NOW ....

SKY BLUE SKIN

1 {
THE DOOR IS UNLOCKED FOR YOU, YOUR FEATURES ARE CHANGED

WE ARE GLOWING IN THE ULTIMATE LIGHT

THEY'LL SEE OUR GHOSTS ON THE SIDEWALKS AT NIGHT

KISSES BATHED IN LIGHTS OF LOVE HEREAFTER
}

2 {
PICTURES SCENTED, LOCKS OF HAIR SURRENDERED

AND FIGURES SHAPED IN CANDLE WAX I'VE MADE

INVOKING OUR MEMORY

THE PAST WILL NOT REMAIN

BUT FADE LIKE THE PAIN OF LOVE HEREAFTER
}

3 {
SEND ME BACK MY TREASON, MY BROKEN SWITCHBLADE KNIFE

MY CRUMPLED NOTES OF COMEDY ROUTINES

THE THOUGHTS OF A MAN

WHO HIDES BEHIND THE SCREENS

OF "DON'T KNOW WHAT HE MEANS" OR "WHAT HE'S AFTER"
}

B R I D G E {
ROSE PETALS CLING TO THE HILLS OF YOUR BREAST

LIPSTICK ROSES EMBLAZON MY CHEST

ROSE PETALS SOAKED ON THE ROOF OF MY MOUTH

I KNOW THESE STAINS WILL NEVER COME OUT
}

STAINED IN LOVE   THE KNIFE IT   IT CUTS BETWEEN
WITH YOU   WANDERS THROUGH   US TOO,

AND CHANCES ARE YOU WOULDN'T EVEN RECOGNIZE THE MAN I AM NOW

PAGES 226–227: Guitarist Michael Tighe would often refer to "Sky Blue Skin" as one of the most important of Jeff's incomplete songs. These pages find him working out structure and chord changes for this troubled love song, although he would eventually leave behind only four demos of it, two with lyrics and two purely instrumental.

FACING PAGE: Draft of "Murder Suicide Meteor Slave," which Jeff would record later, by himself, in his house in Memphis. Much of this attempt would be unused, but the key line "You're a slave to it all now" would remain.

Murder Suicide Meteor Slave

I see ~~see it~~ ^ALL it unfold before me
The world of the living falls into line
Dying like a sparrow choking on
The dirt of a natural flight

Because you want to pray to the mistress below
Because you need the ~~beauty~~ of her eyes
The shine blinds you as you enter
There is no real entrance

Welcome ~~down~~ ^DOWN to paradise rock
There is no one here but you

Everyone's complaining 'bout something
Not enough soul to go around
Mouths so hungry they bite on the package
As if it contained themselves
There is no real packaging

Welcome down to paradise rock
There is no one here but you

There is such a thing as Murder/Suicide
Crashing down like a meteor
On your mirror
You're a slave to it all now

You must've really liked her dress
With all the free beers she gave you

Stolen 7/9 16

DENTIST FALLS IN LOVE WITH PATIENT
AND DRILLS TOO BIG A HOLE
TO KEEP HIM COMING BACK TO HER
    AGAIN AND AGAIN.

FACING PAGE: An all-too-rare example of Jeff's sense of humor during an unsettled time in his life. It's telling that by 1996 the clever or amusing entries in his 1989–1992 writings have all but disappeared.

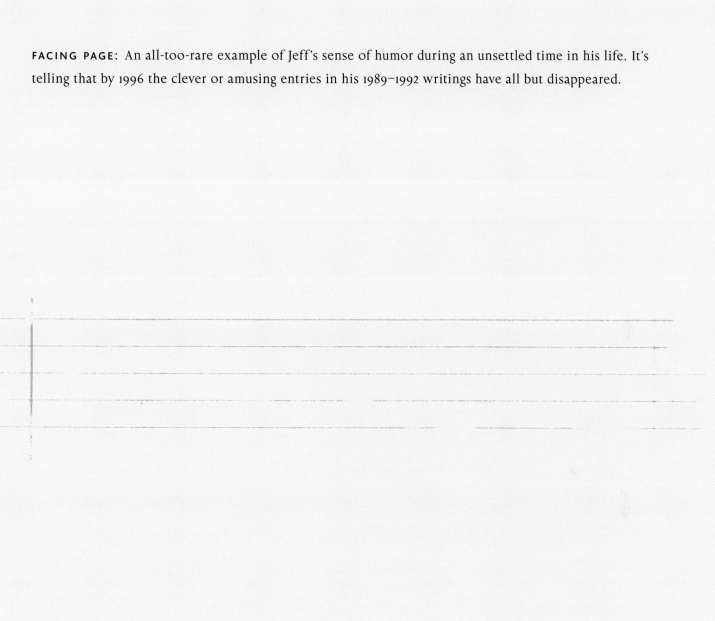

PAGES 232–233: In this entry from August 20, 1996, Jeff again acts as his own confidence-building drill sergeant: "Your thought is your right, your art is your right. You are allowed to invent and explore your song," he scribbles, shortly before he and his band will again attempt to nail down the still-coalescing songs for *My Sweetheart the Drunk* in a studio. Jeff also chastises himself for smoking and, at the end, begins writing what would become "I Know We Could Be So Happy Baby (If We Wanted to Be)."

8/20/96

I MUST LIVE. I MUST ALLOW MYSELF
THE RHAPSODY. IT COMES FROM MY LUNGS
AND I SPIT IT ONTO THE STREETS WITH A HUFF
AND THE RUDE AIR - SCRAPE OF TONGUE TO PALATE.
OR I JUST SWALLOW. THERE IS NO THREAT TO YOU
IN THE PAPER, NOR IN THE PEN, THERE'S
NO THREAT IN YOUR CREATION, THEY WELCOME
YOU. IT IS ALRIGHT. YOUR THOUGHT IS YOUR
RIGHT, YOUR ART IS YOUR RIGHT. YOU ARE
ALLOWED TO INVENT AND EXPLORE YOUR SONG
YOU ARE ALLOWED TO MAKE IT REAL THROUGH
YOUR CONCENTRATION AND HOLD ONTO YOUR GIFT, MAN,
AND LET GO OF ANYTHING THAT HOLDS YOU BACK
FROM THAT APHRODISIAC, THE CIGS, THE POT (WHAT?)
THE SELF - DENIAL, THE FEAR, THE EXTERNALIZED VOICES
OF DISAPPROVAL YOU KNOW YOU INVENT, THE SELF - INFLICTED
MENTAL GOOSE CHASE. AGE IS UNIMPORTANT. SELF - DEVELOPMENT
IS ALL IMPORTANT. SMOKING CALLS, SMOKING HURTS
AND DISTRACTS YOU AND PROVIDES ONLY THE VOICE OF
THE SLAVE. IT BRINGS CONGESTION AND WORRY AND
DEVIATION FROM YOUR TRUE VOICE. IT WILL KILL YOU.
AND IMAGINE THE MINDLESSNESS OF EMPHYSEMA TAKING
OVER YOUR LIFE. RESIST DEATH THAT IS SELF - INFLICTED,
EMBRACE LIFE. EMBRACE LIGHT AND COURAGE. PRAY TO THE
LOVE THAT IS THE SOUL OF YOURSELF. CIGARETTES PULL YOU DOWN
ALL THE WAY. FINISH YOUR LIFE WITHOUT THEM.

CARRY YOURSELF WITH DELIGHT. AND DON'T GIVE UP
THE POT. IT'S JUST THAT IT MAKES YOU WANT TO
SMOKE CIGARETTES. JUST QUIT FOREVER TODAY.
YOU CAN'T DON'T WANT DIDN'T SLAVE SLIDE OUT
ON MASK DEFENSE TRIP MARCONI HERE I
GO LIKE A SPIDER IN BETWEEN THE SKINS
OF TWO LOVERS. YOU CAN'T FAKE IT.
MANY ROADS TO RUN THROUGH
THERE'S STILL A BOY WHO LOVES YOU
SOME OTHER LOVE BECOMES YOU
OR WHATEVER ELSE IT COMES TO
I KNOW WE COULD BE SO HAPPY BABY
IF WE WANTED TO BE

Invincible Dietary God
I whale-watch for nightmares
By eating burgers at bedtime

8/25/96
When all of this music
sounds like you know what
you want to say, then it
   will have been of all worth, ever.
   You will be something complete
      unto yourself, present and unique

PAGES 236–237: In two pages from August 27, 1996, that recall the daily-schedule entries he mapped out in his Los Angeles journals, Jeff dubs himself a "marathon man" in preparation for bearing down on his second album. In hopeful prose that contrasts sharply with previous journals, he carves out a schedule for working and exercising and his desire to "write yourself to sleep." To fire up his creative juices, he also plans a return to his former home base, Sin-é. This entry marks the first time Memphis is mentioned in his writing; by then, plans were being finalized to record the album there, rather than New York, and again with Tom Verlaine. Interestingly, Jeff writes of preparing for that trip down south in September. In the end, he and the band would not fly to Memphis until February 11, 1997.

SATURDAY NITE

YOU HAVE NO CHOICE BUT TO REPLACE YOUR CIGARETTES WITH A HOT GINGER AND LEMON CONCOCTION, JUST BOIL UP THOSE UGLY LITTLE SCARECROWS IN A BIG POT OF WATER, THE STEAM WILL HELP YOUR SKIN, BESIDES. YOU'LL NEED IT TO SWEAT OUT THE TAR. THAT WILL TAKE YEARS AT LEAST, BABY DOLL. FIRST, GET OVER YOUR INITIAL WEEK OF ABSTINENCE. AFTER THAT, FORGET ABOUT GOING BACK. AFTER THAT, HELLO THERE MARATHON MAN, WE'RE GOING TO TAKE A NICE TRIP TO THE PARK EVERY SUNDAY, EVERY TUESDAY EVERY THURSDAY, EVERY SATURDAY, EVERY MONDAY, EVERY WEDNESDAY, EVERY FRIDAY AND THEN SUNDAY, EACH DAY AT 7:30 AM TO THE PARK AND RUN THE RESERVOIR. SIT AND WRITE AT 9:30 AM. AT 10:30 AM, WE COME BACK HOME AND WE SONG MAKE - SONG - MAKE - SONG - MAKE - SPIRIT - MAKE - SPIRIT - GUM UNTIL EITHER REHEARSAL WITH THE BAND AT 12:30 MON. - THURS., OR UNTIL LUNCH AT 3:00 PM, FRI - SUN. REMEMBER, FRI - SUN. IS YOUR FREE PERIOD AND YOU HAVE MAJOR OPPORTUNITY ALL AROUND FOR HEAVY POETRY-RECREATION AND HOMEWORK CONCENTRATION, YOU HAVE NO CHOICE. WRITING TAKES A LONG TIME SIMPLY BECAUSE THERE IS SO MUCH TO SAY AND TO EXPLORE, ALL THE MEMORIES, PHRASES AND RHYTHM RIDES AND RHYME-SHADES TO ACQUAINT YOURSELF WITH; YOU WILL NEED TIME TO CONCENTRATE IN CANDID PEACE & STILLNESS. TIME TO WRITE AND SING, TO LAUGH, TO LISTEN, TO DISCOVER, TO CRY, TO LOVE MUSIC.

*
AFTER REH. MON. - THURS. IS TIME FOR SONG 9:00P-1:00A
1-2 WRITE YOURSELF TO SLEEP

LEARN TO DIVE INTO, UPTO YOUR HAIR, INTO IT AND
DOWN INTO THE FLOW OF IT ALL, YOU HAVE NO WORDS
FOR IT NOW, FOR THE MOTION AND THE SWELL OF ITS
DEPTHS OR WHAT TRUTH, FALSITY, HORROR, ECSTASY,
WHATEVER IS ITS WHAT SO ON. ITS REALITY. YOUR
REAL EXPRESSION AND ALL OF ITS FACETS. WHEN YOU GET TO
AUGUST 19th 9:30 PM, IT WILL BE TIME TO GO PERFORM
FOR TWO-HOURS AT SIN-É. THINK FORWARD TO THE
POSSIBLE JOY. BY THEN, YOUR BAND WILL NEED A
FEW GIGS TO GET READY FOR MEMPHIS. AFTER THE FIRST
SIN-É SHOW, ONE SMALL CLUB GIG, AFTER THE SECOND
SIN-É SHOW, TWO MORE SMALL CLUB GIGS MAYBE
FRIDAY, SATURDAY OR SUNDAY. THEN TO MEMPHIS ON THE
4TH OF SEPTEMBER. ON SEPTEMBER 3RD YOU HAVE YOUR
FINAL POETRY WORKSHOP. MOST OF YOUR DEMOS WILL BE
READY. AND YOU CAN BE FREER FOR THE RECORDING AT
EASLEY. EXERCISE THE VOICE, STAY STRONG WITH THE SONG, WRITE FREELY
FROM THE HEART. I REMEMBER MY LAST HIT OF A CIGARETTE.

8/27/96

PAGE 238: Jeff's Ernie Hall Silhouette Music Man electric guitar, nicknamed Iggy. The case was frequently used on the road, but the guitar itself was not.

PAGE 239: Jeff's remaining clothing, journals, and personal effects are kept in this antique steamer trunk, circa 1902, belonging to his mother.

PAGES 241–242: Clearly an important song to Jeff, "I Know We Could Be So Happy Baby (If We Wanted to Be)" went through a number of revisions in 1996 and 1997. The draft on page 241 was largely rewritten; the version on page 242 feels stream of consciousness. As would often be the case, he would prune through these various entries for key lines ("some other love becomes you," "I am the saviour ghost / who comes and goes") for the final version.

I KNOW WE COULD BE SO HAPPY

~~Either are cat tod discliuted~~

IT'S BEEN A LONG TIME
SINCE I ~~were~~ ^{morning} WAS YOUR STAR
YOU'RE CONVINCED THAT I AM GONE
BECAUSE OF WHAT YOU ARE
KNOW THAT IT WAS ME
KNOW THAT IT WAS ME

IF I HAD A WAY TO TELL YOU
~~And~~ THAT YOU'RE IN ME NOW
AND ~~I IMAGINE WE UNTANGLE~~ ~~~~
THE TWISTED PATTERNS OF OUR MINDS
~~Every day youre~~
~~Every day youre~~
I PRETEND THAT YOU TRUST ME
I PRETEND THAT YOU TRUST ME

~~~~ ~~~~
~~~~
NO WORLD WITHOUT YOU
~~~~
OVER THE PAST WE ONCE KNEW
IF SOME OTHER LOVE BECOMES YOU
OR WHATEVER ELSE IT COMES TO
I KNOW, WE COULD BE SO HAPPY, BABY
IF WE WANTED TO BE

I DON'T WANT TO LOSE YOU
BUT STILL I CAN'T ASK THAT YOU STAY
IT MEANS NOTHING BUT TORTURE
BUT I CAN FIND ANOTHER WAY
IN TIME YOU CAN TRUST ME
I KNOW YOU CAN TRUST ME

WE HAD HIM HOOKED
TO ELECTRIC WIRES
I HELD YOU AS YOU
TURNED THE DIALS

WHOAT?!

SOMETHING TOLD ME THAT I
WOULD CRUSH THIS ROSE
I AM THE SAVIOURGHOST
WHO COMES AND GOES
I AM THE RAVISHING KNIGHT
WHO COMES AND GOES
AND KNOWS NOT WHY HE LISTENS
TO A PARASITE WITHIN HIS GENTLE MIND
TURNED ON HIMSELF AND SPARES THE ONE HE LOVES
YOU CRUSHED OUT AN EMBER
A SCAR ON YOUR SHOULDER
IN THE SHAPE OF DOVE
I'VE BEEN WONDERING WHY FOR YEARS
SWEET FLOWER WAX BURN THE TRUTH
INTO MY CHEST
WHY DO I WASTE ALL THIS WONDER
WHY DO I ALWAYS HOLD MYSELF SUSPECT
AND VISIT COMPLICATION INSTEAD OF YOU
LOOK AT THE LOSS I REPEAT AND REFLECT
BUT BY THIS BONESET MY THOUGHT WAS ~~XXXXXXX~~
IN LOVE AND I ASK YOU, BELIEVE
THE WAY I FEEL NOW IS TOO STUNNED BY BRAINLESS
MEMORIES ... GOD, I LOVE YOU STILL
BUT EVEN THEN I LOVED YOU IN A DREAM
TO SAVE ME FROM THE PAIN I HAD DROPPED AT YOUR
FEET WITH A THOUGHT THAT IT WOULD ALL GO AWAY

~~Spot mixed together~~

ALL THE DISLOCATION
THAT POSSESSED ME AND YOU
HAS ~~XXXXXXXXXXXX~~ ALWAYS HAD A HOLD ON ME
~~XXXXXXXXXXXXXXXXXX~~ MY WAR WITHIN MY SOUL
~~XXXXXXXXXXXXXXXXXXXXXX~~ I FIGHT BECAUSE
~~XXXXXXXXXXXXXXXXXXXXXX~~ I LOVE YOU
                          I FIGHT BECAUSE
                          I LOVE YOU

SO   WRONG
~~XXX~~ ~~XXXXX~~ WITHOUT YOU
OVER THE ~~PAST~~ WE ONCE KNEW
SOME OTHER LOVE BECOMES YOU
WHATEVER ELSE IT COMES TO
I KNOW THAT WE COULD BE SO HAPPY BABY, IF WE WANTED TO BE

YOU COULD BE HAPPY
WE COULD GROW AND FORGIVE
ALL ● THE MISTAKES OF TENDER SOULS IN LOVE
WHO THINK THEY'LL ONLY LIVE ~~XX~~
WITH ONE HOME, ONE FACE
AND ALL THEIR PAIN WILL BE MAGICALLY ERASED

WELL I HAVE ANOTHER KIND OF DREAM
NOW THAT I'VE CRUSHED THE FAIRY TALE
~~XXXXXXXXXXXXX~~ THAT LIFE ON EARTH IS
DEEPER WITH THE ONES YOU KNOW THAT LOVE YOU
NOT WITH YOU BUT OF YOU
NOT WITH YOU BUT OF YOU

IT'S AS EASY TO KEEP YOU OFF OF MY MIND
AS KEEPING ALL THAT SHIT OFF OF THE RADIO
KILL ME NOW KILL ME NOW KILL ME NOW NOW NOW
MORE SUGAR MORE CINNAMON MORE MINUTEMEN PAUL SIMONON
MORE T-MONEY MORE CHRIS MORE CRAIGY AND NATHAN AND DAVID AND STAN
MORE SCOTT MORE TRIP MORE TRIPPING IN TRUCKSTOPS MORE CHICKS FOR
THE ELEVATOR DROPS MORE SOUL COUGHING COUGH-DROPS DROP THE RHYMES
AT ALL TIMES FOR THE KIDS AT THE INSTORES AND THE MOM & POPS
AND HEY THAT HOT MONKEY! TOO MUCH DAMAGE FROM THE ROCK STAR
JUNIOR SOMMERCAMP FOR ROCK-STARS AND THEIR DAMAGED OFFSPRING AND
MY BEAUTIFUL ARHYTHMIC ALTERNACHICKS IN THE PUMPKINPATCH FLING MUD AT THE
TV CAMERA THAT THEY WILL BECOME, WE ALL ARE ONE, WE ALL ARE DONE,
WE ALL DOWN IN THE HERE AND NOW, BUKOWSKI KISS TO DAVID YOW, KILL ME
NOW KILL ME NOW KILL ME NOW BECK GIVE BECK A SHOTGUN GIVE BECK
A SHOTGUN BEFORE I RHYME AGAIN LET HIM KILL ME LET HIM RUN LET HIM
BLOW AWAY THE MEDIOCRE WHITEBOY NARRATIVE FOREVER OH YES I LOVE HIM
SO WHERE HAS JOHN CALE BEEN ALL MY LIFE WHY CAN'T I GET MY HAIR
TO LOOK LIKE THAT LIFE IS A BITCH AND HER HUSBAND SHOT HIMSELF
FOR US KILL HER BEFORE SHE WRITES ANOTHER CHORUS ANOTHER CHORUS ANOTHER
CHORUS I DON'T BELIEVE JOHN LENNON I THINK SHE IS THE WALRUS I NEVER
SAID NOTHING ABOUT A PILL IN A BAG MUST BE TOO MUCH PAINT ON THE CHEEKS OF THE HAG.

FACING PAGE: Ever the music obsessive, Jeff riffs on his musician friends in the bands Shudder to Think and Soul Coughing along with heroes John Lennon and John Cale. It was Cale's version of Leonard Cohen's "Hallelujah," as opposed to Cohen's original, that drew Jeff into the song.

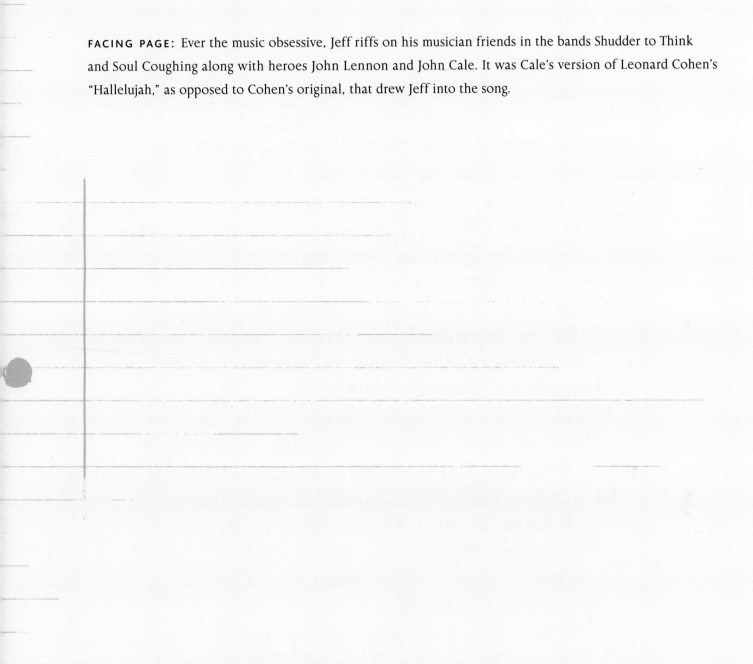

NEXT PAGE: Jeff returns to "Sky Blue Skin" with further revisions.

Aug 30, 1996

WHY is it so HARD to LET ~~GO~~ GO of YOU?
NOT SO MUCH WITH PASSION BUT WITH PRAISE
IS THE WAY I LOVE YOU NOW
PRAISE FOR THE ~~ANGST~~ JOY WE'VE BECOME
WE TAKE ~~IN~~ THE PAIN UNTIL IT ALL RINGS HOLLOW
WE LEARN TO LOATHE THE TRUTH
  AS IT SHINES
ALREADY I SEE OUR GHOSTS ~~DANCING~~ ON SIDEWALKS
  KISSING IN THE HEREAFTER
IF IT ~~HAUNTS~~ ME HERE ON EARTH
  THEN IT WILL ALWAYS HAUNT ME
GHOSTS ~~HAVE~~ ALWAYS RULED MY LIFE
WHEN I KISS YOU THEY FLICK ● THE SWITCH ● off
AND ENTERED THROUGH THE DARKNESS INTO OUR MOUTHS
● LOVER ~~DON'T~~ BE JEALOUS, IT WAS YOU
  WHO MADE A MAN OF ME, BUT ONLY IN
  THE HEREAFTER
I KNOW I CHOSE ANOTHER AND I KNOW
  THE SPELL IS CRUSHED
  YOUNG LIFE CRUSHES YOUNG LOVE
  WHEN YOU ● LEARN TO THINK THAT LIFE IS
ALWAYS SOMETHING ELSE
AND IT MAKES IT HARD TO LIVE IT FOR
  YOURSELF
  WHEN THE MAN YOU ~~LOVE~~ WANT DOESN'T KNOW
  JUST WHAT ~~HE~~ IT IS AFTER
  MAKE UP A REASON
  FOR WHAT YOU CAN'T CONTROL
  ~~THE MAN SHARDS~~ THE KNIFE
WANDERS THROUGH ME SO SLOW
CUTS BETWEEN US AS WE GROW ~~WHY IS IT SO HARD~~ WHY IS IT SO HARD TO LET IT GO?

ANGRY SONG ~~Bird~~

I WALK THROUGH MILES OF BITTER GLANCES
I WATCH ALL OF YOU
FACE ME HEAD ON AND YOU'RE TAKING YOUR CHANCES
I'M IN THIS JUST LIKE YOU
~~THERE'S~~ A REAL OLD MAN DOWN ~~THE~~ WAY
WITH TWO EYES THAT SEE ~~FAR~~ ~~INTO NOWHERE~~ FAR INTO NOWHERE
HIS POWER IS INSANITY LONG ~~PAST~~ BE TOLD REPAIR
WHEN HE WANDERS NAKED IN PLAIN SIGHT
DO YOU FIRE UP THE SPOTLIGHT?
~~OR DO YOU LOOK AWAY AND THANK GOD ALMIGHTY~~
~~THAT ALL YOU ARE IS QUITE ALL RIGHT~~

OR DO YOU WALK ON BY
KNEEL AT YOUR BEDSIDE
AND THANK GOD ALMIGHTY THAT HE'S MADE YOU ALRIGHT?
~~There's no fucking way you're gonna sleep tonight.~~
THERE'S NO FUCKING WAY YOU'RE GONNA SLEEP TONIGHT,
SLEEP WON'T COME WHEN YOU CALL IT'S NAME
IT SEES THROUGH THE ~~SMILE~~ MASKS YOU USE TO HIDE YOUR SHAME
SHAME YOU FEEL FOR ALL THE THINGS YOU NEVER WANT TO NAME
YOU ARE ONE AND ALL STARK RAVING MAD
IN A MAD SEARCH AND SEIZURE, THE LUNATIC PRESSURE
THE ANSWERS RAISING QUESTIONS RAISING BLISTERS
UPON BLISTERS
UPON HANDS THAT TEAR IT OUT AND RIP APART,
WORTHLESS, THE LIFE OF THE STRUGGLING HEART.

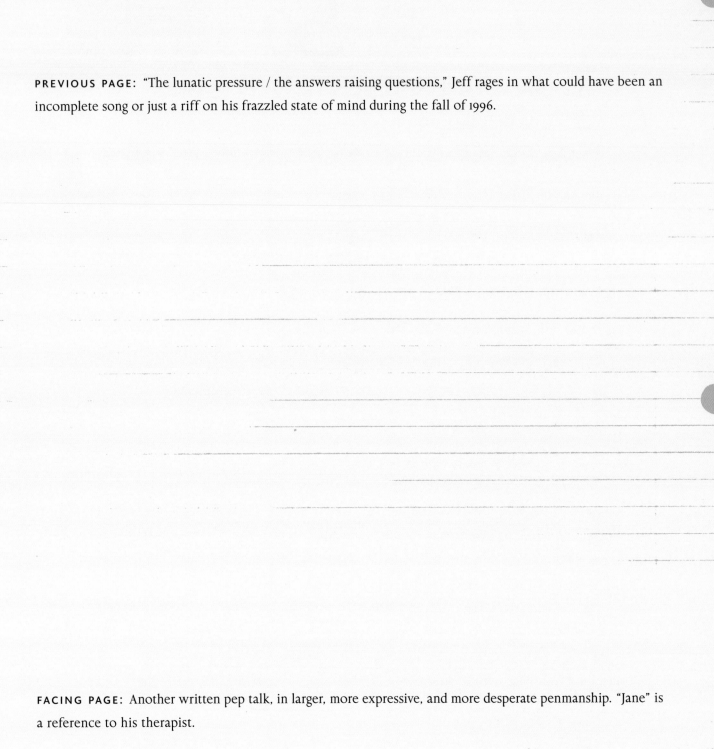

PREVIOUS PAGE: "The lunatic pressure / the answers raising questions," Jeff rages in what could have been an incomplete song or just a riff on his frazzled state of mind during the fall of 1996.

FACING PAGE: Another written pep talk, in larger, more expressive, and more desperate penmanship. "Jane" is a reference to his therapist.

(ALL AUTOMATIC IF YOU ARE WITH LOVE)
(THE ONLY POSITIVE COMBAT IS IN THE PURSUIT,
CONFRONT ALL HYPOCRISY PRESENTATION AND DEFENSE OF
. THAT ART
OF LIVING)
CONFRONT ALL SELF-DESTRUCTION (NEGATIVE
OR PASSIVE
COMBAT
THE SONG IS THE MAIL-BOMB IS IN
JUST
LIVING
THE WORKLOAD IS THE SCRIPTURE AS YOURSELF)
THE ORIGINALITY IS THE BADASS OF THEM ALL
(PASSION IS
THE RELIGION)
THE SIMPLICITY IS THE BEAUTY, THE
CORE THE JUICE AND THE CALL TO
ARMS — LOOK YOURSELF IN
THE FACE IN ALL THINGS AND
STAY WITH JANE
OR NONE OF THIS WILL BE
POSSIBLE. IT MUST BE
DONE. THE WAR
DEPENDS
ON YOU.

Oct 1

I used to look out the windows when I ate in restaurants. As I ate my meals I would always stare out into the street, watching people pass by, watching dogs piss on parked motorcycles, watching faces catch mine and then turn away, turn away, always avoiding any contact at all. Now I'm just looking at this page. Now I'm just watching myself spill out onto it. I'm going to lay off the band. I'm going to keep Michael.

FACING PAGE: By October 1996, Jeff was feeling stymied by his progress, his band, and the expectations of the music industry. In this knotty entry, he lashes out at himself and his musicians after several failed attempts to put his new songs on tape. In the end, he remained loyal to Mick Grondahl, whom he considered not just his bass player but a simpatico mind, and later that month he would find a new drummer, Parker Kindred, who would work with Jeff until his passing.

WRITING IN MY SLEEP

DON'T KNOW HOW EXACTLY TO COPE...

Dream Brother
What Will You Say?
Grace
Mojo Pin
So Real
Last Goodbye
Flutter Girl
3 is A Magic No.
     Alive
I woke up in A Strange Place
River Of Dope
Lover, You Should've Come Over

Sky Blue Skin
The Sky Is A Landfill
Vancouver
Morning Theft
Moodswing Whiskey
I Know We Could Be So Happy
     You And I

KEEP IT TO WHAT YOU KNOW

FACING PAGE: Possible set list for one of Jeff's club shows in 1996. The lineup includes songs from *Grace*, the in-progress *My Sweetheart the Drunk*, and covers like De La Soul's "The Magic Number" and the Soundgarden outtake "Flutter Girl," which would not appear on record until Chris Cornell's 1999 album, *Euphoria Morning*. (Given that Jeff and Cornell were friends, it's likely Cornell played the song for him at some point.)

THE RHYTHM IS SO SIMPLE
AND THE MELODY'S SO PLAIN
IT THROWS THEM FOR A LOOP WHEN THEY SEE
TIGERS RUN THE TRAIN

LET THEM FIND IT OUT
WHAT THEY NEED FROM YOUR SONG
YOU NEED TO KEEP YOUR DISTANCE
SO YOUR SOUL CAN GROW UP STRONG

COMPLEX RISE TO SIMPLE LIKE THE
WATERS RISE AT NIGHT
IT TOOK ME ALL I HAD TO MAKE THIS
MUSIC COME OUT RIGHT

THE WORDS ARE RUNNING THROUGH
THE HIDDEN ~~FORGOTTEN~~ HOOPS OF FLAME
I TRIED TO SIT & FIGURE OUT
~~ABOUT~~ JUST WHO WE GET TO BLAME

IF IT COMES OUT UNINSPIRED
MISGUIDED OR MISSPELLED
YOU'RE PROBABLY JUST A HEADACHE
LOOKING FOR SOME 12 HOUR PILL

HOW MANY HEARTS YOU SPLIT APART
~~REMAINS~~ STAYS IN YOUR BREAST
I ~~STARE~~ AT NOTHING STRAIGHT AHEAD
I FAIL EVERY TEST

WHEN THE MOODSWING HITS ME HOLDS THE MYSTERY
WHEN THE MOODSWING HITS ME HOLDS THE MYSTERY

I'M GETTING OLD BEFORE MY TIME
~~IT'S~~ ~~GOD~~ I AIMED AT ~~LIFE~~ PEACE AND MISSED
EXCUSE MY ABSENCE FROM OUR HOME
I WAS LOST IN A KISS

THE MOODSWING IT HITS ME
THE MOODSWING IT HITS ME

IN LIFE YOU ARE ~~BEEN~~ LOCKED INTO DANGEROUS CHEMISTRY

GROUND SWELLS AROUND MY SHOULDERS
IN WAVES OF BLISS
~~LOST OUT~~ CALL FOR THE ~~ONE~~ MAN WHO WON YOUR HAND
LOST IN A KISS WITH YOU MOODSWING WHISKEY
YOU ARE BLISS THE ACTRESS
            BLISS THE ASSASIN
            BLISS THE ABYSS

FOR BRUCE WILLIS & DEMI MOORE

MY BABY SHE HAS NO LIPS
WE ARE A TALENTED COUPLE
I WAS BORN WITHOUT A SEX
WE ARE THE TALENTED COUPLE
IN THE CHEEKBONES OF MY FACE
THERE IS MORE STUBBLE WAITING TO GROW
STUBBLE ON FOREVER IS HER FAVORITE LOOK
I SCRUBBED AWAY HER MOUTH
FOR THE LOVE OF AMERICA
TAKE OFF YOUR CLOTHES FOR THE CHINAMAN, DEAR
WHILE I PREPARE MY LINES FOR THE GUN
TO COME OUT
AND SHOOT HIS HEAD APART
WHEN WILL WE MAKE LOVE AGAIN
LOOKING STRAIGHT INTO THE EYES OF AMERICA

YOU ARE A COWBOY
I CAN TELL BY YOUR MOUTH
YOU ARE A MORON
I CAN TELL BY YOUR WIFE

FACING PAGE: Another rare moment of levity—a pointed pop-culture arrow—during the tumultuous creation of what was to be *My Sweetheart the Drunk*. By this time, Willis and Moore had almost been married a decade and embodied the Hollywood high life.

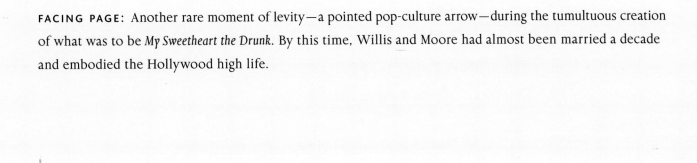

NEXT PAGE: Jeff's penchant for drama, and his almost adolescent fascination with death, pokes through in this undated entry written on a "luxury bed" near "fine upholstery." His reference to "using my good looks to get through all the doors of life" marks a moment of unguarded self-awareness.

LATELY I FEEL SO CHEAP
LIKE I'VE BEEN USING MY GOOD LOOKS TO GET THROUGH
ALL THE DOORS OF LIFE
OPENED BY SOMEBODY ELSE

AND I ENTERED A DOOR ONE DAY
AND FOUND MYSELF IN ANOTHER MAN'S MANSION
HIS WALLS GLEAMING IN THE DISTANCE
HIS ~~MARBLE~~ STAIRWAY RISING UP TO THE BEDROOM
HIS PRICELESS ARTIFACTS BLARING MUSIC FROM THE
STEREO
THE TELEPHONE'S FILLED WITH IMPORTANT MESSAGES
WHEN I PICK IT UP I FEEL THE MUSCLES BURN IN MY ARM
HIS BACKYARD GOES FOR MILES
I'M FAR FROM THE WHITE-NOISE OF THE CITY
I'M FAR FROM THE RADIOS AND THE DIRT
BUT I'M SUPPOSED TO COME UP WITH SOMETHING
THERE IS SOMETHING THAT I HAVE TO CREATE
AND SOMEONE ON THE LINE, THEY NEED IT TOMORROW.
AND I DON'T KNOW WHAT IT IS.
JUST THINKING ABOUT IT ALONE ON THIS LUXURY BED
FILLS MY HEAD WITH SLEEP
SLEEPING ON BORROWED TIME ON THIS FINE UPHOLSTERY
I'LL WAKE UP ON THE STRETCHER WHEN SOMEONE COMES
FOR ME.
I PREPARED MY ENTIRE LIFE TO FACE THE FUTURE
UNPREPARED TO FACE THE FUTURE.
I HOPE I EXPLODE FROM THE LESSON.
I HOPE MY BRAIN SPLITS OPEN AND THAT MY
GUTS BLOW OUT OF EITHER SIDE OF MY BODY
I HOPE MY ███████ EYES ARE OPEN WHEN I DIE
SO THEY CAN ██████ SEE YOU FOR THE FINAL BREATH.
I HOPE ██████ THAT I NEVER COME BACK ALIVE.

DON'T LOSE YOUR TEETH
DESTROY YOUR CONTEMPORARIES
NEVER BECOME THE ESTABLISHMENT
BECAUSE NOBODY MAKES IT UP THERE!
THE CHALLENGE: THE WAR ENDS
ONLY IN YOUR DEATH.

BITE THE THROAT OF ALTERNATIVE
ROCK
ALL THEY HAVE IS FEAR
CONVENTION AND ALL THE EASY ANSWERS

YOU BRING THE NIGHTMARES
AND HAUNT THEIR STUPID ASSES FOR EVER.

PREVIOUS PAGE: Again, notice the exaggerated penmanship in this undated 1996 entry. "Bite the throat of alternative rock" sums up one of Jeff's fears during this period—that he would be lumped in with the Kurt Cobain wannabes who sold millions of records after the Nirvana frontman's death. Jeff saw for himself a far more multifaceted musical future.

FACING PAGE: One of several cracks at the elusive "Moodswing Whiskey."

WHEN YOU CAN'T CONTROL
YOUR MOODSWING
FROM ~~LOVER TO~~ CAKIN' LOW-LIFE
~~XXXXXXX~~

WHEN YOU LINE GOT THE
CHRISTMAS SONGS ALL MEMORIZED
SO YOU CAN MAKE BACK
THE MONEY YOU OWE

WHEN YOU KEEP ON FINDING WEDDING RINGS
TRAPPED IN THE HEATER
SPRAYING WATER ON THE FLOOR
OF YOUR SEX-STARVED ROOM

A NEW GOOD THING HITS YOU
A NEW GOOD THING HITS YOU

I AM DRUNK ON THE WONDER OF A WHOLE NEW
WORLD I HAVEN'T EVEN SEEN. BUT IT SHOCKS MY
SYSTEM EVERY TIME I HAVE THE DREAM, IT'S
LIKE A TV COMMERCIAL "IF YOU'VE LOST THE
WILL TO LIVE, OR EVEN FIT IN WITH THE WORLD,
WELL HERE'S SOMETHING THAT'LL BE THE TOAST
OF THE LAMENTABLE FEW! MOODSWING WHISKEY
IT BURNS HOLES THROUGH THE EYES OF YOUR LOVER
WHEN YOU WANT TO REALLY PAIR YOUR LIFE DOWN
DEBTS GOT YOU DOWN? LIFE JUST FEELING LIKE
TIN FOIL FILLED WITH LEFTOVER CHICKEN? HOW WOULD
YOU LIKE TO BE LIFTED INTO THE SKY IN REBELLION
AGAINST YOUR INADEQUICIES ON THE GROUND? DO WOMEN
LOOK AT YOU STRANGELY OR NOT AT ALL? I AM
DRUNK ON THE WONDER OF A WHOLE NEW WORLD
THAT I KNOW I'LL NEVER SEE, BUT STILL
I LET THE BLACKOUTS COME AND OH, BABY, DO
I THINK OF YOU, HOW CHARMING WILL YOU BE
ON MY QUEEN SIZE BED IN MY DOUBLE WIDE
MOUNTED ON A SCULPTURE-STACK OF MY
EMPTY BOTTLES, I DON'T CARE WHAT THE FUCK
ANYONE SAYS, THESE VISIONS COME TO ME AND
THEY ARE INDESCRIBABLE, WE ALL COULD FLY
WITHOUT WINGS, WITH JUST YOUR LEFT HAND
HOLDING THE DRINK, SHOT GLASS FUTURE! MOODSWING WHISKEY

BLISS
THE ASSASSIN
BLISS
THE ACTRESS
BLISS
THE ABYSS

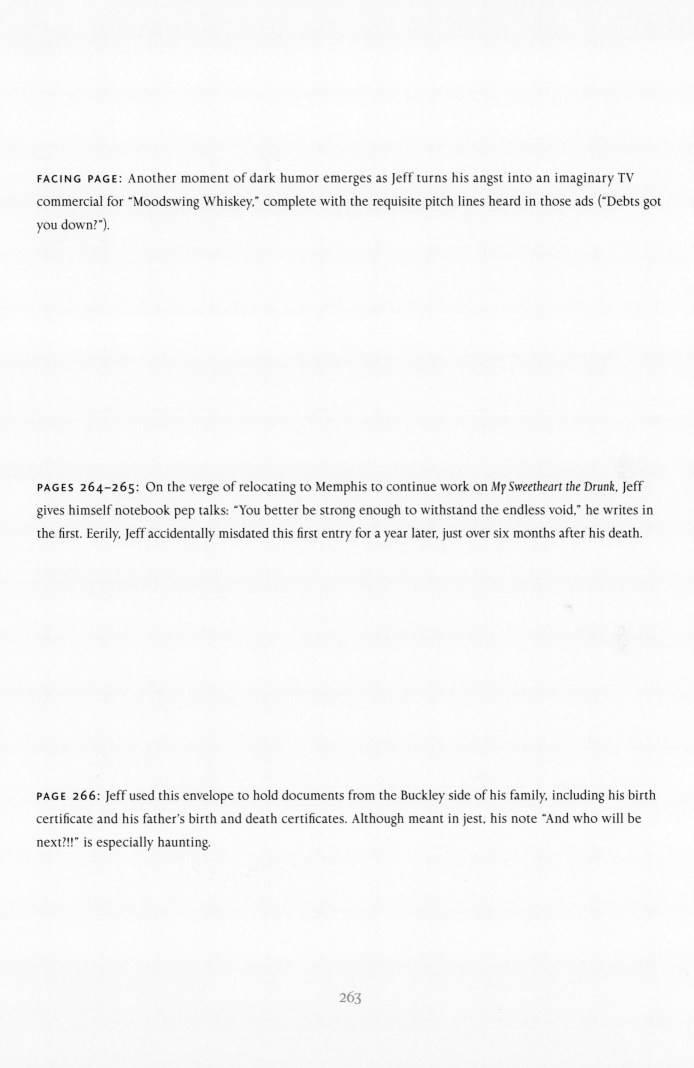

FACING PAGE: Another moment of dark humor emerges as Jeff turns his angst into an imaginary TV commercial for "Moodswing Whiskey," complete with the requisite pitch lines heard in those ads ("Debts got you down?").

PAGES 264–265: On the verge of relocating to Memphis to continue work on *My Sweetheart the Drunk*, Jeff gives himself notebook pep talks: "You better be strong enough to withstand the endless void," he writes in the first. Eerily, Jeff accidentally misdated this first entry for a year later, just over six months after his death.

PAGE 266: Jeff used this envelope to hold documents from the Buckley side of his family, including his birth certificate and his father's birth and death certificates. Although meant in jest, his note "And who will be next?!!" is especially haunting.

12/3/97

GETTING SOME: DYLAN, DEAD KENNEDIES,

GET OUT OF YOUR MUSIC: EGO AND TREPIDATION

LEAVE IN: PURE SOUL AND TRUTH
AND THE BRINGING OF THE
ALL O-RIGINOLE
    LIKE TAKE OUT THE
    PORNO FASCINATION
AND PUT ALL YOUR LOVE
INTO YOUR WOMAN

THIS IS IMPORTANT WORK
IT COULD BE DANGEROUS
DO NOT FUCK AROUND
WHEN YOU TAP INTO THE
FEEL FOR REAL FOR REAL!!
YOU BETTER BE STRONG ENOUGH
TO WITHSTAND THE ENDLESS VOID
WHEN YOU TAP INTO THE FOREARM
AND ADMINISTER YOUR JUICY COMETS.
NEVER DIE NEVER DIE (NEVER SAY NEVER)
    YOU ARE ALWAYS THERE LITTLE GIRL

Lee's Cooper
Wed. 8:00-12 Sat. 12-3

FIGHT AGAINST THE SYSTEM THAT RUNS YOUR SONG INTO
THE GROUND
A SONG CAN BE A BOMB INSIDE A BOMB INSIDE A BOMB
LIKE BLUEPRINTS FOR A MATING DANCE ENTHRALLS
    I SAY WE CRUSH THOSE PARASITES
   WHO SUCK OFF THE MIND THAT MOVES
    WE THROW OUR FUNERAL ROSE INSIDE
   AND BURY THE NEED TO PROVE
   OUR MUTILATION IS TO GAIN FROM THE SYSTEM

NEVER INCLUDE THE DISTRACTING THOUGHTS
IN YOUR NOTEBOOKS

THE BUCKLEY FAMILY
BIRTH & DEATH
CERTIFICATE COLLECTION

OR
AAAH, YES!
AND WHO WILL
BE NEXT?!!

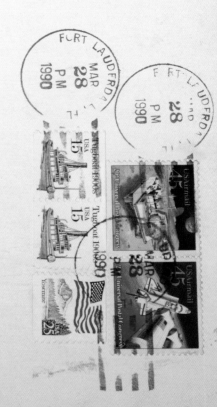

HI, BUCKLEY AGAIN.

THE QUESTION IS, "WHY DID HE TOUR AND NOT TELL US WHERE HE WAS PLAYING? WHY WHY WHY?"

AND THE ANSWER IS THIS: THERE WAS A TIME IN MY LIFE NOT TOO LONG AGO WHEN I COULD SHOW UP IN A CAFE AND SIMPLY DO WHAT I DO, MAKE MUSIC, LEARN FROM PERFORMING MY MUSIC, EXPLORE WHAT IT MEANS TO ME, IE. HAVE FUN WHILE I IRRITATE AND/OR ENTERTAIN AN AUDIENCE WHO DOESN'T KNOW ME OR WHAT I AM ABOUT. IN THIS SITUATION I HAVE THAT PRECIOUS AND IRREPLACABLE LUXURY OF FAILURE, OF RISK, OF SURRENDER. I WORKED VERY HARD TO GET THIS KIND OF THING TOGETHER, THIS WORK-FORUM; I LOVED IT THEN AND I MISSED IT WHEN IT DISAPPEARED. ALL I AM DOING IS RECLAIMING IT.

Don't WORRY ABOUT THE PHANTOM SOLO TOURS, THEY ARE SIMPLY MY WAY OF SURVIVAL AND MY OWN METHOD OF SELF-ASSESSMENT AND RECREATION. IF THEY DON'T HAPPEN..... NOTHING ELSE CAN. I CAN AT LEAST BE ALL ALONE WITH NOTHING TO HELP ME, SAVE MYSELF. REAL MEN MAINTAIN THEIR FREEDOM TO SUCK EGGS, MY DEAR.

I'M IN THE MIDDLE OF SOME WILD SHIT RIGHT NOW ... PLEASE BE PATIENT, I'M COMING SOON TO A CARDBOARD DISPLAY CASE NEAR YOU AND I'LL COME OUT OF MY HOLE AND WE'LL MAKE BONFIRES OUT OF TICKET STUBS COME THE SUMMER.

MERRY CHRISTMAS ALL AND A KISS FOR YOUR NEW YEAR'S HEADACHE.

BYE

PAGE 267: The beloved woolly faux-fur coat Jeff bought at a secondhand shop, alongside his prized Les Paul.

FACING PAGE: During the first week of December 1996, Jeff embarked on what would be his final tour—eight solo concerts over the space of a week and a half along the East Coast. Although the shows were intentionally under the radar—in small clubs where he would perform under pseudonyms like Topless America and A Puppet Show Named Julio—Jeff felt the need to explain why he was undertaking the gigs and posted this letter to fans on his website.

NEXT PAGE: As revitalizing as the "Phantom Solo Tour" could be, the performances still found Jeff grappling with nagging feelings of self-doubt. In this entry, he has arrived in Philadelphia after a show at the Barking Spider in Cleveland (a performance he deems "pathetic") and is preparing for a show the following night at La Tazza, a club in Manayunk, Pennsylvania, north of Philadelphia. The sets, which varied nightly, included favorites from *Grace*, familiar covers (Dylan's "If You See Her, Say Hello," the Nina Simone–affiliated "Wild Is the Wind"), and songs from the incomplete Tom Verlaine sessions earlier in the year, such as "The Sky Is a Landfill," "Morning Theft," and "Vancouver."

12/11/96 PHILADELPHIA

YOU HAVE TO BE OUT HERE SO YOU CAN REALIZE
YOU AIN'T THAT HOT, BABY AND THERE AIN'T NO
GUARANTEES .... THIS IS WHY YOU LEFT ANAHEIM
CALIFORNIA ... HOW NOT TO BECOME A CARTOON
THE REAL MEN DON'T GET MEDICATED AND THEY CAN
GO ALL NIGHT LONG AND THEY DON'T SAY MUCH.
     GRACE   BALANCE INTENSITY STAMINA
       SENSITIVITY DIVERSITY . YOU WERE PATHETIC TONIGHT.
MORE SONGS MORE GIGS MORE SONGS MORE GIGS MORE SONGS
   MORE SONGS . YOU MUST BE BETTER . MORE CONCENTRATED.

SOMETHING YOU CAN KILL YOURSELF AGAINST

I AM FORCED BY THE OUTSIDE WORLD/TO BECOME
WHAT I AM

SECRET AGENT MUSIC

   BECAUSE TONIGHT WITH THAT ROB GUY. (HE LOOKED LIKE COREY)
THE FEEL CHANGED FROM RAGGED — ME DRUNK (STOP IT MAN)
AND DISHEVELED . — YOU DESERVE TO HAVE MORE!
DON'T COMPROMISE ... JUST BRING THE RHYTHM, THE STORY.
KEEP YOUR MOUTH SHUT IN BETWEEN AND STAY SOBER.
YOUR VOICE MUST BE STRAIGHT UP AND STRONG. —
TO OTHERNESS ... HE PLAYED TO ONLY FOUR PEOPLE ALL NIGHT
WITHOUT ANY BREAK OR FALTER. GO EASY YOU DID WELL AND YOU ARE
A STRANGER IN TOWN, NOT THE HEADLINER FOR A REASON — HE IS A MORE
WORTHY SERVANT. YOU ARE STILL LEARNING . KEEP YOURSELF ICY COOL.
   So WHAT BRINGS YOU TO THIS FORSAKEN SANDWICH

T.V.   "THE POWER OF SIN IS BROKEN BY THE SACRIFICE OF THE SAVIOUR"

"YOU NEVER NEED MEDICATION TO DO WHAT YOU DO WELL. ▷

SPOOKY

FACING PAGE: Jeff's irritation with New York, particularly with being recognized on the street and the "yuppy ballast" taking over his neighborhood, emerges in this late 1996 entry. Given the comments about a "gtr. solo" and "drums" during the first half—a scathing rant against his long-ago Orange County home, including Disneyland—these notes appear to be the seeds of a new, unfinished song.

Haven't Heard From You

A thinly veiled hatred for all the yuppy ballast of N.Y.C. trying to turn my flaming trash-goddess into the land of sexless gentry. Goons and their future voting pickney if you don't like it get your fucking ass to Orange County

They'll sing in the new year
And we'll catch all the puke
On our backs as ~~when~~ they lower the ball

Some people should just move away to Glendale
Get a nice condo in Santa Barbara or in Anaheim
An entire house with a dog and a two car garage
A beautiful fresh-cut lawn, just think of all the tools
Just think of all the chicks in that town, they can totally get down
Their parents just booze it up and look the other way
Why do you think they call it, blind Orange County?

Those Christian girls
(Gtr. solo)

All you have to do is by a day ~~bus~~ pass and you are in puss land chicks with pierces
none of those difficult chicks with all or politics
Ow! Disneyland in the summertime you cannot see for all the freaks
Baby I'm ~~wanna~~ gonna get you off on that Matterhorn
(Drums (Drums)

Come to
The land of the man who brought you all those cool
Homeless folks you can throw almstook ignore
And no more of the constant nagging of success, success,
success
The Lower East Side can kiss my ass goodbye
I'm takin' a huge gaping bite out of life down in Fantasyland.
I don't wanna live here, I don't wanna exist
I don't wanna live here anymore, I don't wanna exist

WRITE THE REVOLUTION, A LIFETIME IS NEEDED. AND A PATH OF
EVER DEEPENED LOVE AND VISION. AND A VOICE TO FOLLOW THE
RHYTHM OF THE WAR BETWEEN DELIGHT AND DECAY. NO RELIGION
HAS EVER WORKED. NO LEADER OF PEOPLE HAS EVER LED
THE PEOPLE INTO THE OCEAN OF WISDOM THAT IS LIFE, TO
BE SOAKED. NO MOVEMENT OF POLITICS HAS EVER TRANSFORMED
THE SOUL INTO A SUNFLOWER. NO ARTIST HAS EVER STOPPED
THE WAR. NO SONG OR MOVIE OR PAINTING HAS OPENED
THE EYES OF MY PEOPLE. THE WOMEN ARE RISING,
BUT THEY NEED CLUES TO HELP PROTECT THEIR VISION
TRANSFORMATION, UNDERSTANDING — INHERENT HEART
KNOWING. THE MEN MUST LET THE WOMEN IN ON
THEIR POOL GAME SO THAT THE WOMEN MAY LEARN
ITS BEAUTY AND MEANING AND SO THAT THE MEN
MAY LEARN ITS SILLINESS AND CHILDISH MACHISMO
SO THAT BOTHE OF THEM MAY FULLY EXPERIENCE
THE WISDOM OF THE SPHERES, THEY CONNECT,
THEY COLLIDE, THEY DESCEND INTO UNDERSTANDING
HEAVEN IS ABOUT DEPTH, NOT HEIGHT, ANY WOMAN
WILL TELL YOU THAT. YOU CHOOSE THE AIM AND THE
VELOCITY AND YOU LOOK AHEAD TO THE POSSIBILITY AND
SUBMIT TO THE NATURE OF THE SPHERES WITH A
FLICK OF THE WILL, TWO BLUE BALL SOLID IN THE
CORNER POCKET, BANK OFF THE SIDE WITH THE FIVE RED
INTO ELEVEN STRIPED TO COLLIDE INTO THE MEAN LUCKY ORANGE
THIRTEEN. MAYBE SOMEDAY I'LL KNOW ABOUT THE NUMBERS.
BUT THIS HOW IT STANDS.
YOU WISH TO LIVE A FULL OLD AGE. HOPE WILLING
YOUR MUSIC IS THE MOST POWERFUL GIFT, ARTISTICALLY
YOUR TRUE GIFT IS THAT OF THE DETECTIVE, MAGICIAN, LOVER
THE BASTARDIZATION OF ALL THAT IS FEMININE, THE OUTRIGHT
WAR AGAINST THE FEMININE IN ALL THINGS, WAGED BY
MAN, IS THE DEATH OF MANKIND PLAIN AND SIMPLE.
THE BREATH IS THE KEY, THE ART OF THE BREATH IS THE
SECRET

FACING PAGE: Ever wary of corporate America, Jeff mulls over politics, leaders, and what he calls "the outright war against the feminine in all things" in one of his most thoughtful later journals. Even his handwriting is neater and less frenzied. "You wish to live a full old age," he writes, dismissing elements of his previous negativity.

I feel most comfortable
when my mouth is full of smoke
I'm proud of the head's sweet haze
I was born to eat the fruits of pleasure

Maybe some of you don't know what it is

I believe you'll come
if you love me

I CAN'T GO ON
EVERYTHING FEELS SO TIRED
FALL FLAT IN FRONT OF EVERYONE
MY EYES SO DRY
THIS IS THE REAL THING
I'M TRYING TO LAY DOWN FOR YOU
JUST A VOICE WITHOUT A CLUE
SO MANY LOVES HAVE SOAKED IN MY SKIN
BUT THEY LAY BURIED BY HER SON
WHAT HAVE YOU LOST?
ONLY TIME AND BREATH AND TEARS.
ALL THE REST TO GAIN IF YOU OPEN YOUR JAWS
AND DIG
DIG
DIG IT RIGHT OUT OF YOURSELF
DIG SO FAR INTO YOUR MUD THAT YOU CAN SMELL
THE ROTTING CAVITIES, WORK SO HARD THAT
YOU BANISH THE QUESTIONS OF A FRIGHTENED CHILD
WHAT IS ON THE LINE?
WHAT IS BEYOND YOUR CONTROL TO CHANGE?
WHAT IS THE MOST PRECIOUS SORE YOU WON'T ALLOW THE AIR?
WHAT IS THE SUPREMITY OF LOVE?

I GET NO CLOSER TO THE REASONS I LOVED YOU
THAN I GET TO THE REASON THAT I COULD NOT STAY

I CAN'T BELIEVE IT ALL

~~Baby~~ ~~how are you~~ ~~drinking again~~

The way you sound
The way you sound
Just twenty minutes I'll be right down

The way you sounded
And it ~~sounded~~ so bad
~~Infinite space in unrequited~~
You come to me in visions
of bath water red

Im a strong
man but Im in a
weak state
of mind

Do you need me to be your
    mother tonight
Do you want me to clean
    the apartment, cause daddy's here

He broke the locks off
your inside door
Hes shit in your fireplace to put you down

And now he's a hurricane
And now he's a boy
And now he'll ~~never~~ find another
~~poor~~ girl that he can destroy.

And she'll take him in
And she'll let him in
Her body will absorb his love
    And she'll be in him

PREVIOUS PAGE: Two of Jeff's favorite flannel shirts, along with his wallet and a pair of wingtip shoes purchased in Memphis just before his death.

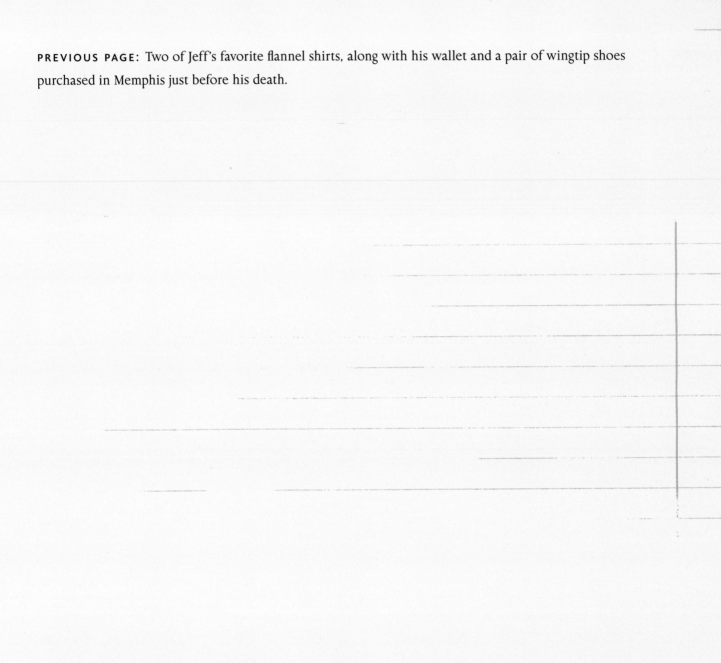

PAGES 281–284: With 1997 only days away, Jeff begins the mental preparation for his relocation to Memphis, which will continue, in various ways, over the next few entries.

IN THE CONCIOUS WORLD OF THE LIVING
YOU WILL SUBMIT YOUR CREATIONS FOR SALE
BUT IN THE UNSEEN REALITY
THE ANONYMOUS SOUL PLANTS THE SEED OF DESTRUCTION
LOVE THE DESTROYER OF MALICE AND MISANTHROPY
    LOVE THE BRINGER OF THE FLAME
        THE SOUND OF LOVE IS ALWAYS BLOOD SIMPLE
AND OVERWHELMING IN SLOPE
        LOVE IS THE ULTIMATE LIVING DREAM
LOVE IS THE END OF SLAVERY

    POISON THE MEDIA TO DEATH WITH SECRET PSALMS
OF REBIRTH AND DESTRUCTION, MAKE THEM SEE
 BY NOT LETTING THEM STOP THE TRUTH, JUST BECAUSE
THEY UTILIZE IT. DOESN'T MEAN THEY'LL KNOW WHATS
GOING ON, NO LIES, ONLY POSITIVITY, SIMPLY FOOL
THEM INTO WHATS GOOD ... SUFI, HOLY FOOL... NO ONE MUST
FIND YOU HERE.
        BE THE SUBLIMINAL CHEMOTHERAPY OF
        AMERICA
 USE THE ENEMY WITHOUT DETECTION
    LEAVE THE LAND MINES THERE
    FOR THEM TO STEP ON AND RELEASE
        THE VIRUS OF TRANSFORMATIONAL HEALING
 THE REVOLUTION IS AT HAND
        AND ALL OF YOUR GIFTS ARE USEFUL
    AND SO VERY NEEDED

        THINK OF THIS
        AS YOUR LIFE'S WORK

    NO ONE WILL KNOW UNTIL
        YOU ARE READY.

THE KEY IS PUNK ROCK
THE KEY IS TO PENETRATE THE HEART
WITH THE HEART. MELODY RHYTHM BREATH
A SONG THAT GIVES YOU
PLEASURE, THE EROTIC
THE KEY IS TO RECOGNIZE EVER· CHANGING
JOY
TOTAL WAR
CIVIL

AGAINST THE SELF.
THE SOLDIER IS INVISIBLE
THE DESTRUCTION OF THE SOUL
IS AS TOTAL AND DEVESTATING
AS THE POWER OF LOVE
IS THE MILK OF THE HOLY
MASSES. THEY TOO ARE IN
DISGUISE ... AS WARRING BICKERING
IMBECILES ... SO THE SOLDIER IS DISGUISED
IN THEIR HOLINESS FOR THE
REMAINDER OF THE WAR
TELL IT LIKE IT IS
PUT ALL THE
TRUTH IN A
ROOM

I JUST HAVE TO KEEP STILL AND SINK DEEP INSIDE MYSELF. AND AS I SINK I WILL NOT TAKE ANYONE WITH ME.

72/2/96

JUST GOT SOME SHOCKTREATMENT
SIX MILD BLOWS TO THE MIND

DEPRAVED. NOTHING MORE ATTRACTIVE TO
THE OUTSIDER THAN A HUMAN BEING WHO EXUDES
THE SEEDS OF LUST AND DEPRAVITY AND THE
MOUNTAINOUS DRAMA OF LIFE ITSELF LOCKED
IN A STICKY BLOW JOB WITH DEATH, AND
ITS ALL THE MORE APPEALING (AND THREATENING
OO LA LA) IF THE MONSTER SEEMS VERY WELL
BALANCED. LIKE A MASS MURDERER WHO BECOMES
A MEDIA-GOD. NORMALCY SHROUDED IN BLOOD AND
BIZARRO SEX GAME STENCH THAT EASILY SNUFFS
OUT THE HAPLESS INNOCENT, HOLDING ONTO
HER HALF-BAKED BELIEFS ALL THE WAY TO THE
MEAT-SHREDDER. WHO WILL YOUR KILLER BE?
SONNY BONO SINGING THE ULTIMATE DEVIL-SONG
TO THE HORROR OF THE LISTENER EXPECTING I GOT YOU BABE
IMAGINE THE ULTIMATE HILARITY, MY DEAR!!

8:45 — 10:45

1 SONG - 15 MINUTES EACH

MEDITATE ON SONG FOR FULL 5 MINS

* NIGHTMARES BY THE SEA   7 SONGS

* WITCHES RAVE   LEAVE AT 11:00 PM

* MOODSWING WHISKEY

* OPENED ONCE

      VANCOUVER

* LISTEN TO NO ONE ELSE BUT ME

      MORNING THEFT

  SKY IS A LANDFILL

* SKY BLUE SKIN

  I KNOW THAT WE COULD BE SO HAPPY

* EVERYBODY HERE WANTS YOU

PREVIOUS PAGE: Jeff imagines a set list for a show consisting entirely of his new material. Notice the absence of anything from *Grace* or his Sin-é period.

FACING PAGE: With his trip to Memphis just over a month away, Jeff begins reassessing aspects of his life, including relationships, business arrangements, and his choice of where to live. His reconnection with Rebecca Moore was one sign of the way Jeff was looking back over the last few years and attempting to determine the best steps forward for himself, personally and professionally.

Jan/1/97

I just had a talk with my REBECCA,
the real one that I know, not the one
I left in pieces on 86 Stanton. She and
I are healing, well—healed already.
But at least now we can talk about it.
Our suffering is peeling off and revealing
a brand new skin, a new power. Love
heals all wounds and not just time alone.

I don't write my music for Sony
I write it for the people who are
screaming down the road crying
to a full-blast stereo.
There is also music I'll make that will
never—ever—ever be for sale. This is my
music alone, this is my true home; from
which all things are born and from which
all my life will spring untainted and
unworried, fully of my own body.

JEFF BUCKLEY RECORDING BUDGET
JUNE & JULY 1997
(As of April 14, 1997)

Housing in Memphis (April - July @ $450.00 mo.)	1800.00
Furnishing house (beds, etc.)	3000.00
Phone/fax/electrical (4 mo. x $400.00 mo.)	1600.00
Andy Wallace-Producer fee	60000.00
Andy Wallace-Lodging (56 days x $100.00 day)	5600.00
Andy Wallace-per diem ($35.00) per day x 56 days)	1960.00
Andy Wallace-car rental ($200.00 wk. x 8 weeks)	1600.00
Jeff Buckley - car rental ($200.00 wk. x 16 weeks)	3200.00
Gas, etc. (Jeff- 3 1/2 mo. x $100.00 mo.)	350.00
Gas, etc. (. Andy-2 mo. x $100.00 mo.)	200.00
Easley Studios ($650.00 day x 36 days)	23400.00
Doug Easley-engineer ($150.00 day x 36 days)	5400.00
Rehearsal space (one month)	1500.00
Airline flights	3500.00
Tape costs	4000.00
Equipment cartage (includes van rental, personnel, gas/tolls, roundtrip NYC-Memphis-NYC (twice), per diem, lodging, misc., etc.)	4700.00
Musical Supplies	1500.00
Additional transportation (airports, cabs, etc.)	600.00
Misc. expenses	2000.00
Equipment hired for Easley Studios by A.Wallace	5000.00
Jeff Buckley-per diem (3 1/2 mo.)	1750.00
Band Salaries (3 x $6,000.00 each)	18000.00
Band per diems (3 x $25.00 day x 49 days)	3675.00
Guest Musicians	2500.00
	########
Total for Recording Album:	156,835.00

JEFF BUCKLEY MIXING OF THE ALBUM
MEMPHIS, TN - JULY 1997

Mixing Studio ($1,900 day x 15 days)	28500.00
Andy Wallace-lodging ($100.00 day x 15 days)	1500.00
Andy Wallace-per diem ($35.00 day x 15 days)	525.00
Jeff Buckley-per diem ($25.00 day x 15 days)	375.00
Andy Wallace-car rental ($200.00 wk x 2 weeks)	400.00
Jeff Buckley-car rental ($200.00 wk x 2 weeks)	400.00
Gas, etc.	100.00
Tape costs	500.00
Misc. expenses	2500.00
Total for Mixing Album:	34800.00

TOTAL RECORDING AND MIXING BUDGET:	191635.00

FACING PAGE: As Jeff continued woodshedding in Memphis, plans were formulated for his band and *Grace* producer Andy Wallace (stepping in for Verlaine) to finally wrap up *My Sweetheart the Drunk* at Easley-McCain Recording in Memphis during the summer of 1997. Despite the stop-and-start process, the final cost for these sessions would still amount to half of what was spent recording *Grace* in 1993.

NEXT PAGE: In early 1997, Jeff and his band (Tighe, Grondahl, and Kindred) relocated to Memphis to continue work with Verlaine. Despite recording versions of, among other songs, "Nightmares by the Sea," the results were again deemed unsatisfactory. The three band members returned to New York while Jeff stayed in Memphis, where he rented a small house and continued working on new songs on his four-track recorder. On the night the band was returning to Memphis, May 29, 1997, Jeff accidentally drowned in the Wolf River.

I JUST HAD A TALK WITH MY KEECIA

NOTHING LIKE YOU AND THIS MUSIC HAS EVER EXISTED
TAKE THE WHOLE LOT OF THEM ALL THE WAY BACK (DOWN),
TAKE NO PRISONERS, MYSTIFY THEM, OBLITERATE THEM,
RIP THEIR HEARTS OUT FOR AGES TO COME, MAKE IT SOOOO
GOOD ITS LIKE THE EUPHORIA RUSH OF DEATH — DREAMS
NEVER EVER LET THEM LOCATE YOUR CORE. THAT IS FOR YOU.
SHOW THEM WHERE YOU'RE REALLY AT, BABY. AND NEVER

NIGHTMARES BY THE SEA
N.B.T.S.

EVER DO AS ANYONE ELSE DOES, YOU
ARE THE VOID — SING FROM

A TO C, F# TO A / F# TO C, THE UNCONCIOUS

CHORUS ————————— CYCLE BROUGHT TO THE

A TO C   F# TO A / F# TO C LIVING WORLD

CHORUS ————————— CYCLE LET THEM LOOK UPON

DRONE VAMP IN G ME AND DESPAIR

A TO C TO E♭ EXPLOSION FOR THE TIME HAS

"BUCKY STARDUST BRIDGE" COME FOR ALL TO

CHORUS CYCLE ————————— OUT LEARN TO REJOICE

AGAIN IN THE
ALL—ORIGINAL
THE GOD GIVEN

GIFTS, SAVAGELY UNWRAPPED
BY WE THE REAL
REBELLION!!!...

TONIGHT... WE TAKE OVER!!

WE WORK HARDER AND DEEPER THAN THE DEVIL HIMSELF! HELLO!

PAGE 293: Especially when pounding the streets of Manhattan, Jeff often opted for Doc Martens; this is one of two pairs he owned. Along with his clothing, the Doc boots he was wearing on the night he drowned in the Wolf River were disposed of by the medical examiner.

I NEVER WRITE
THE COMPANY
INTO MY WORK
'CAUSE I'M ALREADY
FREE

MOTHERFUK

ACKNOWLEDGMENTS

First and foremost, supreme gratitude to my constant collaborator, Associate Editor and Creative Director Alison Raykovich of Stay Golden Music, for her guiding hand in all that we've accomplished together. This particular project, especially where the images are concerned, has required a delicate balance of intimacy and reverence. Wherever you see that, it's because she was present. Second, to my undaunted hero, Conrad M. Rippy, Esq., for his passion, for his diligence and expertise, and for the pride we can share in the work. Lastly, my unending appreciation for David Browne's dedication, journalistic integrity, and wonderful way with words. There may be those who protest what we have done here. They did not know Jeff the way I do.

— MARY GUIBERT

My thanks to Mary Guibert for putting her faith in me to sift through her son's writings, journals, and papers and present them to the world. It was an honor. I couldn't have asked for a better coworker than Associate Editor and Creative Director Alison Raykovich, who tackled every task diligently and professionally. Without her, this book wouldn't have been possible. Thanks to Ben Schafer, who believed in the idea for *His Own Voice* before any of us had even considered it. My agent Erin Hosier, another true believer, worked her usual magic, always with the utmost respect for the material. Thanks also to Conrad Rippy; Alex Camlin for the beautifully designed pages; Geoff Moore for the artful photographs; Susan VanHecke for the sharp copyediting; Gene Bowen and Michael Tighe for their research assistance; and Michael Clark at Da Capo for making the trains run on time. All my love to Maggie and Maeve, who help me try to achieve the smallest degree of grace every day.

— DAVID BROWNE